SAY IT N

Verbal Strategies for Authentic Communication

SAY IT NATURALLY
Verbal Strategies for Authentic Communication

ALLIE PATRICIA WALL

University of North Carolina at Charlotte

Harcourt Brace & Company

Orlando   San Diego   New York
Toronto   London   Sydney   Tokyo

Library of Congress Cataloging-in-Publication Data

Wall, Allie Patricia.
  Say it naturally.

  Includes index.
  1. English language—Text-books for foreign speakers.
2. English language—Spoken English—United States.
3. English language—United States. 4. English
language—Conversation and phrase books. 5.
Oral communications—United States. I. Title.
PE1128.W29   1987   428.3'4   86-14289

ISBN 0-03-002873-6

6 7 8 9 0 1 2 3 4 5 049 18 17 16 15 14 13 12 11 10 9

Printed in the United States of America

PREFACE

Say It Naturally: Verbal Strategies for Authentic Communication is based on a functional/notional approach to language learning. It deals with communicative strategies that are designed to help the newcomer adapt to American social situations, in which a certain amount of verbal knowhow, tact, and polite phrasing is often required and expected. Certain fundamental notions (like thanking and complaining)—that many native speakers take for granted because they are almost intuitive—may cause great difficulty to a person trying to understand a new language and a new culture. For example, how can one tactfully decline an invitation or offer criticism? How does one express sympathy and respond when sympathy is offered? *Say It Naturally* deals with these communicative strategies and others that are a basic part of every American's daily life: greeting and introducing people, making excuses, agreeing and disagreeing, complimenting and acknowledging compliments, and other more sophisticated and delicate verbal skills and strategies.

Say It Naturally is intended for nonnative speakers of English at the intermediate to advanced levels. The text covers concerns that are universal to people—regardless of nationality, language or culture. The text is designed to be used as part of a conversation class, since it focuses on ways to express various notions *verbally,* but it could be used in other parts of an intensive English program. Because the material is action-oriented (with dialogs, role plays, and community-involvement activities), the motivational level is high. Even sluggish or reluctant students can be drawn into the conversations and role plays. And because the exercises are structured from very controlled to free, the instructor can use the material with students of varying verbal proficiencies.

ORGANIZATION   The chapters are arranged from the most frequently used and the least difficult notions, such as greeting people and saying goodbye, to the more sophisticated and difficult notions that require greater tact and command of the language. The chapters build on each other; for example, thanking people and responding are introduced before making, accepting, and declining invitations because knowing how to offer thanks is a vital part of receiving invitations.

An important aspect of the text is the use of American idioms that are a natural, vital part of everyday English. Important vocabulary items and idioms that appear in boldface in the text are glossed and then defined at the bottom of the pages on which they first appear, and many of them reappear in later chapters. Another major focus of the book is cross-cultural. The text covers many aspects of American society that newcomers encounter quite regularly, such as attending social functions; handling day-to-day problems of living in a house, apartment, or dorm; and interacting with salespeople, doctors, repair people, and others in business and service capacities. The discussions of this new lifestyle invite—and indeed generate—comparisons between American culture and the students' native cultures. The result is a deeper understanding of American culture as well as of language.

Each of the book's eighteen chapters is organized as follows:

Introduction

Each starts with an introduction to the notion being presented, as well as a discussion of the social situations or contexts in which the language strategies are likely to occur. The first chapter, "Using the Telephone," is the only exception, since it does not deal with one particular notion; instead, the chapter focuses on important aspects of making and receiving calls, such as answering the phone, taking messages, and dealing with wrong numbers. "Using the Telephone" is placed first because many of the notions that follow require the students to use the telephone when practicing their new language.

Verbal Strategies

Verbal strategies are common set phrases used in expressing the various notions. Students learn, for example, that there are some set expressions used to express sympathy or to apologize. They are also invited to think of others that might be acceptable under certain conditions. These set expressions or verbal strategies are generaly arranged from *formal* to *informal* and are indicated as such where it is possible to make these distinctions. Considerations for using *formal* and *informal* tags—with regard to setting, audience, speakers, and gender—are also discussed at this point.

Practices

Interspersed throughout the introduction and verbal strategies are the practice sections, exercises that reinforce a particular part of the new material. These short exercises give students a chance to put into practice what has just been presented, and they can use the new language immediately. The practices are designed so that teachers can call on students individually or invite voluntary responses from the class.

Situational Dialogs

These examples of typical dialogs use the new verbal strategies in natural, true-to-life situations. Teachers can ask students to take roles and read parts in ordinary dialogs and conversations that focus on the particular theme of the chapter. These dialogs occur after all the new language, explanation, and practice exercises have been presented. Students can see how the new language occurs in normal, everyday situations.

What Do You Think?

"What Do You Think?" is a set of three thought-provoking questions and/or tasks that follow each situational dialog. Generating discussion, they are concerned with the language and cultural aspects of the situational dialogs. They promote cross-cultural awareness as the students compare and contrast the language and the social and work environments in their native country with those in their new culture.

Students can form small groups or work in pairs to read the sample dialogs and answer the questions or do the tasks that follow. Or the teacher can lead discussions of the exercises, and have everyone in the class participate.

Dialog Completions

As each chapter evolves, the exercises become progressively harder and freer. In this section, students choose partners and complete the dialogs as they see fit. Parts of the dialogs and cues are provided, so the students must read through the dialogs first to pick up important signals that will help them respond appropriately. They can then be asked to reverse roles and complete the dialogs again—this time using different words and expressions. Thus, they can begin to understand that very often there are many acceptable ways to convey a notion and to respond, depending on the situation, the speakers, and the environment.

An alternative method is to have the students work in pairs or small groups (depending on the number of characters in each dialog) and present the completed dialogs as short skits in front of the class. Afterward, the audience can discuss and critique the quality of the dialogs, the appropriateness and the authenticity or naturalness of the language and gestures used.

Role Plays

These exercises allow almost total freedom with the language. The situation is set for the students, and a minimum amount of background information is supplied to help them discern the relationships between speakers and the amount of formality needed. A lot of information is purposefully *not* given to allow the students maximum creativity and independent thought about the appropriate language needed. Role plays can be performed before the entire class or in small groups and then be discussed and evaluated.

Real **People,** Real **Situations,** Real **Language**

These are community-involvement tasks, which ask the students to go out into their work, social, or school communities and observe and record the language as it is used by *real* people in *real* situations. Students are asked to record their observations and interactions in a small notebook. These activities immerse the students in their new culture and environment and allow them to put their new language skills to real, functional uses.

Say It Naturally totally involves the students. They cannot simply sit back passively and absorb. They must take an active part in the conversations and role plays, and they must use their minds and imaginations. This kind of natural, functional language learning is vital if students are to be accepted by native English speakers and to feel comfortable and confident in social situations that require newcomers to speak and respond in accepted, expected ways.

ACKNOWLEDGMENTS   I wish to thank my first ESL students, the company members of Fancy Tsuda, Ltd., in Nagoya, Japan, for allowing me to introduce them to American culture and language. They were the inspiration for this book. I also wish to thank the faculty and staff of the English Language Training Institute at the University of North Carolina at Charlotte for their constant support and encouragement. I would like to thank Jean Zukowski/Faust for the time and thought she put into reading my manuscript and helping make the necessary changes. My deepest gratitude goes to David Yarborough, my sounding board, my motivator, my loyal fan.

Thanks are also due the following reviewers for their helpful comments: Joyce Hutchings, Georgetown University; Ann Johns, San Diego State University; James Kenkel, Bowling Green State University;; Anne Merkel, English Language and Multicultural Institute of Ohio; Margaret Ann Ramker, University of Illinois at Chicago; and Katharine Schneider and Scott G. Stevens, both of the University of Delaware.

A.P.W.

TO THE STUDENT

Have you ever been in situations where you knew you had to say something, but you just didn't know what that *something* was? Perhaps someone complimented you on a shirt you were wearing, or maybe you did something wrong but didn't know what to say to apologize. At one time or another, we all face difficult social situations that make us uncomfortable or confused. *Say It Naturally* deals with common, everyday English language communication to help you become more accustomed to your new social life in your new country.

The book will teach you how to be polite and tactful (doing or saying the right thing at the right time) or how to be strong and direct, depending on the situation. You will learn how you can vary the degree of formality (from very formal to very casual) of your language. You will learn how to use and interpret body language, the nonverbal communication that often accompanies or substitutes for spoken language. You will learn what to say (and what *not* to say) in "sticky" or difficult situations. You will learn some new customs and ways of behaving in your new culture, and you will come away with a better understanding of the people, your new community, and life in this new country.

Say It Naturally was written to help make you more comfortable, confident, and knowledgeable in your home away from home. It was written especially to explain the parts of language and culture that we Americans take for granted but that newcomers have had to struggle with by themselves until now. So relax and get ready to have fun as you learn how to speak more naturally and say what you *want* to say.

CONTENTS

CHAPTER 1

USING THE TELEPHONE

Using the telephone is an essential part of our everyday lives. We use the phone to call people to find out how they're doing, to ask for information, to complain, to apologize, to relay messages, to request favors, to ask for and give directions, and for any number of other reasons. Many people who speak English as their second language find using the telephone a frightening, or at least an uncomfortable, experience. But it doesn't need to be that way at all. Telephone etiquette (the social rules of making and receiving phone calls) involves common sense and politeness.

Indeed, when we are speaking on the phone to someone, politeness and clear speaking are probably the two most important guidelines to follow.

Because you cannot rely on gestures and facial expressions to help carry your messages (as you can when you are speaking with someone face to face), you must be as clear and as exact as possible to avoid any misunderstanding or confusion. At the same time, you must be certain to listen carefully and understand what is being said to or asked of you. In simple terms, if you are a caller, it is polite to offer a greeting, identify yourself, and state your business or reason for calling. Don't leave the person on the other end of the line guessing your reason for telephoning. If you want to speak to someone in particular, ask for that person by name. If you are calling a friend at home, you might say, "Hello. This is Michael Deering. Could I speak to Tom, please?" But if you're calling someone at a large company, you might want to ask for the person's department first and then, when you're connected with someone in that department, ask for the person by name.

You'll notice that most places of business answer with the name of the company and "May I help you?" or "How can we help you?" Individuals (at home) often answer with a simple *hello* or occasionally the name of their residence, as in "Greyson residence." Sometimes people at work or home may answer the phone with their names, as in "David Bailey speaking" or "Pat McCall here."

Some general ways of asking to speak to someone are as follows:

> **May**°
> ✣ Could } I speak to John Toomy, please? This is Tad Andrews
> Can   } calling.
>
> ✣ I'd like to speak to John Toomy, please. This is Tad Andrews. (*Formal*)
> ✣ This is Tad Andrews from Union National Bank. Is John Toomy in, please?
> ✣ Is John Toomy there? (*Informal*)
> ✣ John Toomy, please. (*Informal*)
> ✣ _____
> ✣ _____

Can you think of any other ways? Notice that these openings are arranged from *formal* to *informal* and that in most of the examples (all but the last two), the caller identifies himself. Although it is polite and appreciated by the person on the other line, we don't always remember to do this, and the other person sometimes must ask who we are.

May is more polite than *could* or *can*.

PRACTICE 1

Choose partners and practice both parts: answering the phone and asking to speak to the person indicated.

> **EXAMPLE:**   *You're calling the law office of McDermitte and White, and you want to speak to your lawyer, Marvin Linville.*
>
> **Secretary:**   *Good morning. McDermitte and White. May I help you?*
> **You:**   *Yes, this is Peter Li, and I'd like to speak with Mr. Linville, please.*

1. You're calling your friend Sarah, and her roommate answers.

2. You're calling your professor, and her secretary answers.

3. You're calling your older sister, and her husband answers.

4. You're calling your doctor at the hospital. She's with a patient.

5. You're calling your friend José at work, and the receptionist answers. José works in the finance department.

If a secretary or receptionist greets you first, you may be required to state your business with the person to whom you'd like to speak—especially if that person is in an executive position or is very busy. Don't be offended by this procedure. It is the secretary's job to **screen**° calls for his or her employer, and this is standard procedure for most American companies.

Screen means "ask questions of a person to find out whether the reason he or she is calling is serious enough to interrupt what the boss is doing."

A conversation with a secretary might go something like this:

Secretary: Good morning. Jones Construction Company. May I help you?

You: Hello. This is Ali El-Hussein. May I speak with Mr. Jones, please?

Secretary: May I ask the nature of your business, please?

You: I'm with Duke Power, and I need to talk with Mr. Jones about his building project on Woodlawn Road.

Secretary: Thank you. Just a moment.

Notice that the secretary finds out the caller's name and reason for calling so he or she can decide if the call is important or is worth disturbing the employer. In addition, this screening information can be relayed to Mr. Jones first—as a way of preparing him for the call: "Mr. Jones, Mr. El-Hussein from Duke Power is calling about the Woodlawn Road project."

PRACTICE 2

Using the same dialogs you created in Practice 1, add to them so that the secretary (or whoever answers the phone) makes inquiries into the caller's business or reason for calling. The caller must then respond accordingly.

EXAMPLE: (from the example in Practice 1) *You're calling your lawyer, and his secretary answers.*

Secretary: *Whom do you represent, Mr. Li?*

You: *My company is Li and Associates Engineering.*

1. You're calling Sarah, and her roommate answers.

2. You're calling your professor, and her secretary answers.

3. You're calling your older sister, and her husband answers.

4. You're calling your doctor, and the hospital receptionist or operator answers.

5.   You're calling José, and the finance department receptionist answers.

If the person you are asking for is not immediately available, the person you are talking to might ask you to wait a moment. Here are some common expressions used:

* ✤ Would you mind holding a minute while I try to find her? (*Formal*)
* ✤ Could you hold, please?
* ✤ Please hold a moment.
* ✤ One / Just a / Wait a } moment, please.
* ✤ Hang on. I'll get him. (*Informal*)
* ✤ Just a **sec.**° (*Informal*)
* ✤ _____
* ✤ _____

What happens if the person you are calling is not there or is too busy to come to the phone? The person who answers the telephone will relay this information and then usually ask if you'd like to leave a message for that person, if you'd like to have the person return your call, or if you'd like to call back later. Here are several ways the person might express this information. Try to think of others.

* ✤ I'm sorry, but Mr. Jones is not here right now. May I take a message, or would you like to call back later?

* ✤ Ms. Lee is { **tied up**° / busy / occupied } now. Would you like to { leave a message? / call back later? / have her return your call? }

* ✤ I'm afraid Dr. King can't { come to the phone / speak to you / take the call } at this time. Could you call back { in a few minutes? / in a little while? / later? }

Sec is a reduction (shortening) of *second*, often used in informal conversations.
Tied up is an idiomatic expression for "busy" or "occupied."

✦ I'm sorry, but Margarita is not in at the moment. Would you like to leave a message or call back later?

♣ _____

♣ _____

PRACTICE 3

Choose partners and create a short telephone conversation for each situation. The person you are calling is not in. Follow the cues and (A) leave a message, (B) ask to have your call returned, or (C) tell the person you'll call back later.

EXAMPLE: *You call your eye doctor, and he's with a patient. (B)*

Receptionist: *Dr. Spivey's office.*

You: *Hello, this is Janice Winfield. May I speak to Dr. Spivey?*

Receptionist: *I'm sorry. She's with a patient. May I help you?*

You: *I really need to talk to her. Could you have her call me soon?*

Receptionist: *All right, Ms. Winfield. What's your number, please?*

You: *It's 334-0988. Thank you.*

Receptionist: *You're welcome. Goodbye.*

1. You call your friend Mohammed, and he's sleeping. (A)

2. You call your brother, and he's out of town. (B)

3. You call the roof repairman, and he's not there. (C)

4. You call your insurance agent, and she's talking to someone else on the phone. (B)

5. You call a co-worker, and he's out to lunch. (A)

If you call the wrong number, don't be embarrassed or upset. Everyone makes mistakes. Here are some simple things to say if you reach the wrong number:

* Oh, I'm sorry. I $\begin{Bmatrix} \text{have} \\ \text{guess I have} \\ \text{must have} \end{Bmatrix}$ the wrong number.
* Oh, I was trying to reach _____ (*give name*).
* Is this _____ (*give telephone number you dialed*)?
  (*Then, after negative response, such as "No, it isn't"*):
* Oh, I'm sorry. I dialed the wrong number.
  (*After positive response, such as "Yes, it is"*):
* I'm trying to reach _____ (*give name*). Is he/she there?
* _____
* _____

If you answer the phone, and the person has obviously called the wrong number, simply say

✤ I'm sorry. You have the wrong number.

or

✤ I'm sorry. There's no one here by that name. I think you dialed the wrong number.

The Telephone Directory   One of the handiest, most information-packed books around is the telephone directory. Besides being able to find telephone numbers and addresses of people, shops, restaurants, doctors, florists, taxi companies, plumbers—and thousands of other people, professionals, businesses, and services—you can also use the telephone book to find other valuable information that doesn't even require picking up a telephone. For example:

• Long-distance rates and time charts
• Instructions for credit card calling, paying phone bills, international calling, installing a phone, and other services the phone company offers
• Consumer and safety information
• Area codes and time zones
• Postal zip codes of your city and surrounding areas
• City transportation information
• Facts and information on your city: climate, population, government, history, libraries, education, recreation and sports, medical facilities, arts and entertainment, points of interest, and much more

Finally, the directory is usually divided into two sections: the White Pages include individuals' and companies' names, addresses, and phone numbers and are arranged in alphabetical order (*Abrams, Richard J.; Arnold Trucking Company; Atkinson, R. H.,* for example). The Yellow Pages include businesses, organizations, stores, professionals, and services arranged by subject (*Banks, Beauty Salons, Bicycle Dealers,* for example) in alphabetical order. Advertisements in this section often provide a lot more information than just addresses and phone numbers. They often give hours of operation, credit cards accepted, location, and other specific information. In many large cities (New York, for example), the information is so extensive that the White Pages and Yellow Pages are published in separate volumes.

PRACTICE 4

This exercise has two parts. First, use your directory to find the appropriate phone number and/or person to call. Then make the call, ask the questions or get the information asked for, and record your conversation as accurately as you can.

1. What is the time-of-day service number? What other information, if any, is provided when you call this number?

2. Find the area code of Pickens, South Carolina. How would you get the telephone number for Edmund A. Simons in Pickens?

3. Call to find out what the garbage pick-up schedule is in your neighborhood—during normal weeks and during weeks with holidays.

4. What number would you call to get weather information? What kind of information is given? Is it a recorded message or not?

5. Call to find out all the information you can about having your electricity connected and disconnected to a home or an apartment in your city.

SITUATIONAL DIALOGS
Choose partners, take roles, and read the following telephone conversations. Discuss the language used to ask to speak to someone and to respond. When you have finished, answer the questions or do the tasks asked of you.

A. *Jim Davis is calling his friend Luis at work.*

Receptionist: Smith, Martin, and Colson Attorneys.
Jim: This is Jim Davis. May I speak with Luis, please?
Receptionist: What company are you with, sir?
Jim: I'm not calling on business. Luis is a friend of mine.
Receptionist: Thank you. Just a minute. I'll connect you.

What Do You Think?

1. *Why does the receptionist ask Jim what company he's with? What other expressions could she have used?*
2. *What else could Jim have replied when the receptionist asked about his company?*
3. *How common is it in your country to make a personal call to someone who's at work? Are you allowed to accept personal calls at most workplaces in your native country? What about in the United States?*

B. *Carol answers the phone.*

Carol: Hello?
Joel: Hi. It's Joel.
Carol: Joel?
Joel: Joel Franklin.
Carol: I'm sorry. You must have the wrong number.
Joel: This isn't Margaret?
Carol: No, it isn't.
Joel: Well, may I please speak to her?
Carol: There is no one here by that name.

Joel: I'm sorry to disturb you. I guess I dialed the wrong number.
Carol: That's okay.

What Do You Think?

1. *Why does Joel start the conversation the way he does—and continue it? What mistake does he make, and why do you think he makes it?*
2. *Does Carol handle the wrong number in an acceptable way? Why or why not? Are there any other ways she could have replied?*
3. *Change the dialog so that Margaret is Carol's roommate, who is out for the evening.*

C. *Nadia needs to talk with her lawyer very urgently.*

Secretary: Peebles and Baker Law Firm. Mr. Baker's office.
Nadia: May I speak with Mr. Baker, please?
Secretary: Who shall I say is calling?
Nadia: Nadia Encino.
Secretary: One moment, please. I'll see if he's in.
(A few seconds later)
Secretary: I'm sorry, Ms. Encino. Mr. Baker isn't answering. Perhaps he stepped out for a moment. May I have him return your call?
Nadia: Yes, thank you. I'm at 376-0945. Please tell him it's *very* important.
Secretary: I'll give him the message.

What Do You Think?

1. *What is another way the secretary could have asked, "Who shall I say is calling?"*
2. *What does the secretary mean by "Perhaps he stepped out for a moment"? (How else do we use this idiom,* step out*?)*
3. *Change the conversation slightly so that Nadia does not leave a message or a phone number.*

D. *Pablo is calling his friend David, and David's roommate answers.*

Carl: Hello.
Pablo: May I please speak to David? This is Pablo Gomez.
Carl: I'm sorry, but he's not in at this time. Would you like to leave a message?
Pablo: Yes. Ask him to call me, please. It's about our camping trip this weekend.
Carl: Okay, Pablo. Does he have your phone number?

> **Pablo:** Probably, but let me give it to you just in case. It's 276-9462.
> **Carl:** All right. I'll tell him.
> **Pablo:** Thanks.
> **Carl:** You're welcome.

What Do You Think?

1. *If Pablo couldn't be reached by phone and therefore didn't want David to call him back, what other kind of message could he have left?*
2. *Pablo uses a command, "Ask . . . . " when he leaves his message, but he softens it a little. How does he do this? With what more polite words could he have begun this request?*
3. *Change the situation. This time Helen's roommate Patricia answers the phone.*

E. *Peter Cummings wants to speak with Steve Adams, so he calls him at his office.*

> **Secretary:** Adams, Smith, and Associates. Good morning.
> **Peter:** Hello. This is Peter Cummings. May I speak with Mr. Adams?
> **Secretary:** May I ask the nature of your business, Mr. Cummings?
> **Peter:** I'm with the Cleveland Arts Council, and I'd like to talk with Mr. Adams about making a corporate contribution to the Museum Fund.
> **Secretary:** I'm sorry, Mr. Cummings, but Mr. Adams is quite busy at the moment. May I take your number and have him return your call?
> **Peter:** Yes, thank you. I can be reached at 689-0034 until 6:00 P.M.
> **Secretary:** I'll see that he gets the message, Mr. Cummings.
> **Peter:** Thank you very much, ma'am.

What Do You Think?

1. *Why does the secretary ask Peter about the nature of his business with Mr. Adams? Does Peter's answer in any way determine how the secretary replies to his request to speak with Mr. Adams? If you think it does, how?*
2. *Change the conversation in the following ways: Peter Cummings is a client of Mr. Adams with a business reason for calling. The secretary checks to see if Mr. Adams is in and then responds positively.*
3. *Change the conversation again. This time Peter Cummings is an insur-*

ance salesman, speaking to Mr. Adams himself, who is definitely not interested.

DIALOG COMPLETIONS
All these incomplete dialogs involve using the telephone in some way. Pay attention to the information and clues given and complete the dialogs appropriately. When you have finished, change roles and complete the dialogs by using different words and expressions.

1. *Susan is calling her travel agent, Georgia Miller.*

Receptionist: Travel Unlimited. May I help you?
Susan: Georgia Miller, please. This is Susan Greene.
Receptionist:
Susan: Do you have any idea when she'll be back?
Receptionist:
Susan: I'm sorry. I didn't hear you.
Receptionist:
Susan: Oh, I understand.
Receptionist:
Susan: Yes, please. My number is 378-3734.
Receptionist:
Susan: Thank you very much.

2. *Daryl is calling Marilyn Wilson, a friend, at her office. She works in the engineering department.*

Receptionist: Cummings and Associates.
Daryl:
Receptionist: Just a moment, please. I'll connect you.
(Pause)
Secretary: Engineering.
Daryl:
Secretary:
Daryl: This is Daryl Rogers. I'm a friend of Marilyn's.
Secretary:
Daryl: Yes, I will. Thanks.
(Pause)
Secretary:
Daryl: No, that's okay. I'll try again later.

3. *Carol is at a restaurant and needs to use a phone to call a friend.*

Carol:
Waiter: Yes, there's a pay phone in the hall near the restrooms.
(Carol places her call.)

Luis:
Carol: May I speak to Mohammed?
Luis:
Carol: Carol Tompkins.
Luis:
Carol: He's not? Well, could you take a message for him, please?
Luis:
Carol: Please tell him I'll meet him at the theater at 9:15.
Luis:
Carol: No, I can't be reached by phone. There's no way he can call me.
Luis:
Carol: Thanks very much. Bye.

4. *Yoko needs to change her dentist appointment, so she calls the dentist's office.*

Receptionist: Good morning. Dr. Patterson's office.
Yoko:
Receptionist: Excuse me, what did you say your name was?
Yoko:
Receptionist: Oh, yes. Miss Kamitake.
Yoko:
Receptionist: I'm sorry, but there are no more appointments available this week. What about next Tuesday at 3:00?
Yoko:
Receptionist: Well, we have an opening at 4:30 on Friday.
Yoko:
Receptionist: Fine. We'll see you at 4:30 on June 18.
Yoko:
Receptionist: You're welcome.

5. *Marilyn calls Tom to get some information about a homework assignment. Ameed, someone she doesn't know, answers the phone.*

Ameed: Hello.
Marilyn:
Ameed: Just a sec. I'll see if he can come to the phone. Who did you say you were?
Marilyn:
Ameed: Okay. Hang on.
(A minute later)

Ameed:
Marilyn: No, that's okay. Tell him I'll talk to him tonight at the meeting.
Ameed:

6. *Mr. Nelson wants to speak with Mr. Matthews about a house Mr. Matthews is interested in buying.*

Mrs. Matthews: Hello. Matthews residence.
Mr. Nelson:
Mrs. Matthews: I'm sorry. He's not in. This is Mrs. Matthews. May I help you?
Mr. Nelson:
Mrs. Matthews: Certainly, I'll tell him. Pardon me, what real estate agency did you say you're with?
Mr. Nelson:
Mrs. Matthews: Okay, Mr. Nelson. I'll give him the message as soon as he comes home from work.
Mr. Nelson:

7. *David is calling Ed Nichols, a friend from work. A person whose voice he doesn't recognize answers.*

Person: Hello?
David:
Person: Who?
David: Ed Nichols.
Person:
David: Oh? Is this 649-0933?
Person:
David: I'm sorry. I must have the wrong number.
Person:

8. *Henry is calling a number in a newspaper advertisement about a couch for sale.*

Person:
Henry: Hello. I'm calling about the ad in today's paper for a couch for sale. Could you tell me about it?
Person:
Henry: Oh, well, when will she be back?
Person:
Henry: Yes, please. My name is Henry Wearing, and my number is 918-6473.

Person:
Henry: Yes, I will—until about 7:30 this evening.
Person:
Henry: Thanks. I appreciate it.

9. *Bob answers the phone. It's for his roommate Saeed, who's in the middle of cooking dinner.*

Bob:
Susan: May I please speak to Saeed?
Bob:
Susan: Susan Tanner.
Bob:
(Pause)
Bob:
Susan: Sure. When should I call back?
Bob:
Susan: Okay. Thanks.

10. *Samuel and Chen are talking when the phone rings. Samuel answers, and it's Noriko.*

Samuel:
Noriko: May I please speak to Chen?
Samuel:
Samuel (to Chen):
(Pause)
Chen: Hello?
Noriko:
Chen: Oh, hi, Noriko. How are you?
Noriko:
Chen: Sure. That sounds fine. What time?
Noriko:

ROLE PLAYS   Here are ten situations that require proper phone etiquette. Read each situation, and then create a short dialog with a partner to show how you would handle the call. When you finish, change roles and create a different role play.

1. Laura Mason calls Tom Edward, who has advertised in the newspaper

that he sells cut firewood. Laura speaks to his wife, who tells her that he's not home.

2. Joe calls a friend to give him information about the beach trip he has organized for next weekend. The roommate tells Joe that the friend is sick and can't talk.

3. Pedro calls a friend, Marcia Jacobs, to ask if she'd like to have lunch today. Her secretary tells Pedro that Marcia has already gone to lunch.

4. Laura calls Ken Thomas at the bank where he works. He works in the trust department. Maria speaks to two receptionists before she learns that he's with a client.

5. George calls his neighbor, Mary Stanley, to thank her for the cake she brought him last night, and her seven-year-old daughter answers. Mary isn't there.

6. Craig Fox calls Tom Barston, president of Barston Trucking and Moving Company, to complain about the poor job the movers did when Craig hired them two days ago. He speaks with Mr. Barston's secretary, who tells him that Mr. Barston is very busy.

7. Matilda calls the telephone company to ask a question about her bill. She speaks to a phone company representative first and the department manager after that.

8. It's 11:00 P.M. Chen calls his English teacher at home to tell her why he can't give his speech tomorrow. Her husband answers and tells Chen that she's already gone to bed.

9. Lee calls his sister to tell her about a change in plans concerning a party he's giving next week. Her roommate answers and can't understand him very well.

10. Sam calls the bank and asks to speak to someone who can help him with his checking account. The person he needs to talk to is at lunch.

REAL **PEOPLE,** REAL **SITUATIONS,** REAL **LANGUAGE**

A. Call each of the following people or places and do what is described. Use your notebook to record the conversation as accurately as you can, paying special attention to the words and phrases used in telephone etiquette.

1. Call a friend you know is out and leave a message with his or her roommate.
2. Call a friend at work and ask to speak with him or her.
3. Call a supermarket and ask what kinds of apples they sell.
4. Call the post office and request some information about pick-up times for mail.
5. Call a friend just to say "hello."

B. Call the following stores and ask for the information described. In your notebook, try to record as much of the converation as you can.

1. Supermarket—ask the price of a gallon of low-fat milk.
2. Video rental store—ask the price of a membership and a movie rental.

3. Restaurant—ask if they take reservations and what kinds of credit cards they accept.
4. **Sporting goods store°**—ask if they sell exercise mats and the prices if they do.
5. Shoe store—ask their operating hours and what kinds of basketball shoes they sell.

A **sporting goods store** is one that sells sports-related equipment, such as basketballs, swimming fins, tennis rackets, and running shoes.

CHAPTER 2

GREETING PEOPLE AND RESPONDING

American greetings and responses to them are not the most exciting, refreshing parts of the English language. In fact, greetings are almost "formulas"; there are correct ways to use greetings and to answer them. Often when someone says, "Hi! How are you doing?" the greeting sounds expected or mechanical. It doesn't convey a genuine interest in knowing the person's state of health or being. And just as the greeting may seem rather automatic, often so is the response. "Fine" (with a quick "And how are you?" added) is perhaps the most common (and dullest!) response to a greeting. Of course, there are many variations to these greetings and replies. Sometimes we don't want to get into a long discussion of the true state of our health or feelings, so we give a noncommittal or neutral reply, such as "Okay," and stop there.

In less mechanical greetings, we show concern for a person by asking about something specific, and we usually have some prior knowledge to help us form these questions:

+ Hello, Jack. How's your jogging coming these days?
+ Hi, Margot. How's your new job working out?
+ Good morning, Mrs. Lowell. I heard about your husband's operation. How's he doing?

In these three examples some genuine interest or concern is shown. We give a greeting and then ask about something we know is important to that person.

PRACTICE 1

Greet each person that follows and ask a question by using the information provided after each name.

> **EXAMPLE:** *Mr. Garfield—your 70-year-old neighbor who just returned from visiting his grandchildren in Florida.*
>
> **Greeting:** *Hello, Mr. Garfield. How was your trip to Florida?*

NOTE: Be sure to use the appropriate degree of formality that the situation calls for. For example, if you are talking to someone much older than you or someone with a high rank or position, you need to be more formal than if you are talking to your best friend or your brother.

1. Valerie—your next-door neighbor in the dorm, whom you haven't seen since she **broke up with**° her boyfriend.
    Greeting:

2. Ken—your friend who scored the winning goal in last night's soccer game.
    Greeting:

Broke up with means "came to an end." We use this expression informally to talk about relationships between men and women that end. We sometimes say, "Their marriage *broke up* two months ago" or "John and Laura *broke up* last week."

3. Mr. Jackson—an elderly neighbor who has just returned from a stay in the hospital after he broke his hip.
    Greeting:

4. Mr. Williams—your mail carrier who just bought a new house.
    Greeting:

5. Cindy—an acquaintance in your psychology class who just announced her **engagement**.°
    Greeting:

   The reply given to your greetings may depend on how much the person wants to reveal. A short, vague reply of "Fine" to "How's your jogging coming these days?" can be a way of ending the discussion before it ever gets started. But more often, *fine* is just the first word we think of. We say it automatically.

   Tone of voice (the way our voice goes up and down to show different meanings or feelings) sometimes reveals more than words do. Suppose Bob is asked how his new job is going, and he says "All right" with a fall in tone on *right* and a sigh (a heavy breath) at the end: "All right" (sigh). We might conclude that his new job is not "all right" at all. He just doesn't want to talk about it, and he probably doesn't want to be asked any questions about it. His words say one thing, but his tone and perhaps even his facial expression and gestures (such as a frown and **a shrug of the shoulders**°) say another.

   Here are some common ways of greeting people and responding to the greetings. Those that are considered more formal (for business and some social situations, for example) are so indicated, as are those that are more informal (for casual or everyday situations with close friends, for example). Those that are not marked can be considered normal usage in almost any situation. The list is by no means complete, and many variations of the expressions are possible. In fact, you may think of others you would like to add.

An **engagement** is an agreement to marry. A couple announces their engagement to make the news public.

A shrug of the shoulders is a raising of the shoulders in an expression of doubt, lack of interest, or other feeling.

Greetings

+ **Good day**,° Dr. Olson. How are you? (*Formal*)
+ **Good evening**,° Mr. Polinski. How are you tonight? (*Formal*)
+ Good afternoon, **ma'am**.° You're looking well today. (*Formal*)
+ Good morning, **sir**.° (*Formal*)
+ Hello, Jihad. How're you doing?
+ Hello. It's a nice evening, isn't it?
+ Hi, Paula. What are you **up to**° these days?
+ **'Morning**,° Li. Are you doing okay?
+ Hey, Mashan! What have you been doing these days?
+ Hey, Jack. How's it going?
+ Hi, Jay. **What's happening?**° (*Informal*)

+ _____
+ _____

Responses   (to "How are you?" and other variations)

+ I'm doing very well, thank you. **And you?**° (*Formal*)
+ I'm fine, thank you.
+ Fine. How are you?
+ Great, thanks. What about you?

Good day and **Good evening** can be used as a greeting *and* as a closing (for saying goodbye). **Good afternoon** and **good morning** are usually used only as greetings, and **good night** is used only as a closing—never for a greeting.

Ma'am is often used in formal settings when a woman is being addressed. It means *madame* and is used with both single and married women to show respect; however, some young women do not like to be called *ma'am*.

Sir is used the same way as *ma'am* but with men.

Up to is an informal expression that means "doing."

'Morning is an informal reduction of *good morning*. We often omit the *good* in *good morning*, *good afternoon*, *good evening*, and *good night* in casual conversation.

What's happening? (or *What's up?*) are expressions often used by young people. Slang (very informal language) changes constantly, so what is popular one year may not be in style the next. "What's happening?" for example, was often heard among young people several years ago, but it seems to have become less popular in recent times.

And you? or *You?* means "And how are you doing?" It's polite to ask about the other person after we have given our replies.

✤ **Couldn't be better!°** Yourself?
✤ Not bad. You?
✤ Okay, I guess. **You doing all right?°**
✤ **Can't complain.°** How about you?
✤ Lousy! (*Informal*)
✤ Fantastic! (*Informal*)

♣ _____

♣ _____

Range of Responses   The following diagram illustrates the range of responses you might hear to the question "How are your doing?" These answers vary from the very positive (+) to the vague or ambiguous (when a reply can be interpreted in several different ways) (0) to the very negative (−). It is interesting to note that often the very positive or the very negative replies are followed by some sort of explanation or reason. For instance, a person replying "Fantastic!" usually has a good reason for being so happy and using such a strong response, and often the person wants to let the asker know what it is. So the speaker offers an explanation: "I just got promoted to supervisor at work!" or "I finished my accounting course with an A!" A reply of "Awful!" might be followed by "My wallet was stolen on the bus this morning!" or "I have a terrible cold, and I think I'm getting the flu!"

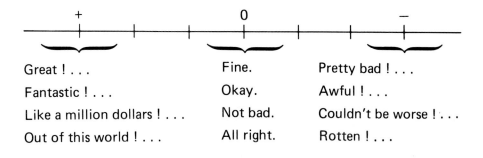

+	0	−
Great ! . . .	Fine.	Pretty bad ! . . .
Fantastic ! . . .	Okay.	Awful ! . . .
Like a million dollars ! . . .	Not bad.	Couldn't be worse ! . . .
Out of this world ! . . .	All right.	Rotten ! . . .

Couldn't be better means "*I* couldn't be better" or "Things in my life couldn't be better."
You doing all right? means "*Are* you doing all right?"
Can't complain means "*I* can't complain."

    These last three responses are examples of reductions. Reducing or shortening statements or questions by leaving out a word or phrase is common in casual speech.

PRACTICE 2

In each of the following situations, a greeting is being made and a *How are you doing?*-type question is asked. Using the cues (+, 0, and −) based on the diagram, give an answer and then a short explanation if one is appropriate.

EXAMPLE: *Jack: Hey, Larry! Good to see you! How's it going?*

Larry(−): *Terrible! I just found out I failed my grammar test — and I studied all night for it, too!*

1. **Michael:** Hi, Abdulla. How are you doing?
    Abdulla(+):

2. **Kathy:** Greetings, José! How's everything?
    José(−):

3. **Barry:** Hello, Mrs. Johnson. How are you today?
    Mrs. Johnson(+):

4. **Professor Tanner:** It's good to see you, Margarita. Are you doing all right?
    Margarita(0):

5. **Sue:** Hi, Juan. **It's been a long time.**° How're things with you?
    Juan(−):

After greetings have been exchanged and the conversation is starting to close, one person sometimes mentions getting together with the other person at a later date. It is important to realize that these little added suggestions of "getting together later," "having lunch sometime," or **"having a drink**° together after work" often do not materialize (happen or occur).

It's been a long time means "It's been a long time since I've seen you."
Having a drink does not always involve alcohol. Although with many people it often does mean having a beer or perhaps a glass of wine, it can also mean having a soft drink or a cup of coffee, so you don't need to be afraid of, put off by, or discouraged by the word *drink.* Alcohol is not necessary to "have a drink," especially today when health and fitness are so important to most people. If you are offered a drink of alcohol, and you don't want it (for personal or religious reasons), just say, "No, thank you." You can also ask for something else: "No, thank you, but I will take a Coke, please."

They may be wishful thinking or simply polite endings to brief conversations (see Chapter 4, "Saying Goodbye," for more details). So if your friend says, "Let's get together for lunch soon," don't keep all your lunch times open or sit around, waiting for her to call. She may just have been making the suggestion out of politeness, without meaning or intending to call you for lunch.

It would *not* be wrong, however, for you to follow up your friend's suggestion if you want to. It would be fine for you to call your friend in a few days and say, "Well, why don't we have lunch on Thursday, Sherry? Are you busy?" Don't be afraid to take the first step in setting up a meeting place and time. You'll be able to tell if the person was being sincere in her suggestion or if she was just making it out of politeness.

SITUATIONAL DIALOGS

The following dialogs show some typical ways people greet each other and respond to greetings. Choose a partner, take a role, and act out the dialogs, putting in any gestures or facial expressions you think would be appropriate. At the end of each dialog, talk about the situation, and answer the questions or do the tasks. In the first two, the scene is set for you, and a little explanation is provided. But in the next three, you must try to discover the degree of formality, the relationship between the speakers, and other important facts.

A. *A polite, rather formal greeting between two adults who know each other only casually:*

Mr. Mason: Good morning, Juanita.
Ms. Castillo: Hello, Frank. It's good to see you. How are you?
Mr. Mason: Just fine, thanks. And you?
Ms. Castillo: I'm doing very well, thank you.
Mr. Mason: That's good. See you later.
Ms. Castillo: All right. 'Bye now.

What Do You Think?

1. *Can you tell that these two people don't know each other very well? What lets you know?*
2. *Mr. Mason is a city engineer who just got a promotion. Ms. Castillo is a lawyer who just won an important case. Assume that they know this information about each other, and change this dialog to make it a little more personal and less formal.*
3. *Change* And you? *into a complete question.*

B.   A very informal exchange between friends:

Paul: Hey, Kelly! What's up?
Kelly: Nothing new. Same old thing.
Paul: Yeah. Same here. See **ya**° around.
Kelly: Okay. **Later.**°

What Do You Think?

1.   *What is another—more formal—way of saying* same old thing?
2.   *What does Paul mean by* same here? *Change his reply into a complete sentence.*
3.   *In what situations and under what circumstances would it* not *be acceptable to use words or reductions such as* ya *and* later? *Can you think of a few where it would be perfectly acceptable?*

C.   **Melanie:**   Good morning, Professor. How are you today?
Prof. Lane: Very well, thank you, Melanie. It's a beautiful day, isn't it?
Melanie: Yes, it certainly is.

What Do You Think?

1.   *Do you think a younger person—perhaps a classmate of Melanie— would have answered in the same way? Why or why not?*
2.   *Suppose it were raining and cold. How might Professor Lane have replied to Melanie's question?*
3.   *If Melanie had been speaking to a friend her own age, she might not have said, "Yes, it certainly is." Based on your own observations of young people around you, what other way(s) could Melanie have agreed with the speaker?*

Ya is the unstressed, informal use of "you." Many Americans, especially young people, let the very relaxed *ya* slip into their everyday colloquial speech. In certain situations that require more formality and seriousness, however, *you* should be used. For example, "Where ya going?" is often heard in the dorm rooms and at parties or other informal gatherings, but "Where are you going?" is definitely more acceptable with people we respect and in formal settings.

Later is a reduced form of "I'll see you later" and is often used by young people in casual situations.

D. **Helmi:** 'Afternoon, Yoko. How's it going?

   Yoko: Oh, so-so.

   Helmi: Why do you say that? What's wrong?

   Yoko: Nothing really. I just have **the blahs**.° How are you?

   Helmi: I don't feel so great, either. I'm ready for some sunshine and warm weather!

What Do You Think?

1. *What does Yoko mean when she says* so-so? *What are some other ways she could have expressed her feelings?*

2. *Do you know some other expressions like* have the blahs? *Give one or two others. Do you have any expressions like this in your native language? How are they translated into English?*

3. *How should Yoko's voice sound when she says* so-so? *Does it go up or down at the end? What kind of facial expressions or gestures might go with her speech? Ask your classmates and teacher for their ideas on these questions.*

E. **Paul:** Hi, Ina. I hear your ski trip was out of this world!

   Ina: It was wonderful! I didn't want to come back to the real world! How have you been? I haven't seen you in a while.

   Paul: I've been burying myself in the books. I can't believe how much studying I've got to do—just to keep up!

   Ina: Well, we should get together some time.

   Paul: Sure. Just let me finish this semester, and I'll be ready to come out of hiding!

What Do You Think?

1. *Paul uses several expressions or idioms to describe the condition he's been in:* burying myself in the books *and* come out of hiding. *What do these mean and how is he using them?*

2. *What does* out of this world *mean and what are several other idiomatic expressions you can think of that have a similar meaning?*

3. *What does Ina mean when she talks about coming back to* the real world? *Can you use this phrase in a few more examples? Do you have any expression similar to this one in your native language?*

The blahs is a feeling of boredom, lack of interest, or general feeling of dissatisfaction with life.

DIALOG COMPLETIONS   Choose a partner and take roles. Then complete each dialog, either by greeting the person or by responding to the greetings. Then switch roles and complete the dialog again, this time using different lines. Pay special attention to the information given, so you will know how formal your language needs to be.

1. **Michael:** Hey! Mario! How's it going?
    Mario:
    Michael: I could be better. I think I'm **coming down with**° a cold, and that's the last thing I need—right before the big game on Saturday!
    Mario:

2. **José:**
    Dave: Not bad. How about you? Playing any tennis lately?
    José:
    Dave: Yeah. That would be good. Call me sometime.
    José:

3. **Mr. Hager:** Good afternoon, Karen. How are you today?
    Karen:
    Mr. Hager: I'm glad to hear that. As usual, I'm **up to my ears**° in **paperwork.**° But I'll survive, I guess.
    Karen:
    Mr. Hager: I don't have time right now. I've got a class in ten minutes. What about at 3:00? I'll be in my office then.
    Karen:

4. **Sam:** Hello, Ali! What've you been up to? I haven't seen you **in ages!**°
    Ali:
    Sam: Really? Sounds interesting. Let's get together sometime.

Coming down with means "starting to get (sick)." We use this expression with the name of an illness or the word *something*.
Up to my ears is an idiom that means "very busy" or "deeply involved." It is similar to "burying myself in" (see *E.* in Situational Dialogs).
Paperwork is the daily or routine work of keeping records or filling out forms, which must be done with many jobs.
In ages is a colloquial expression that means "in a long time."

Ali:
Sam:

5. **Mr. Lowery:** Good day, Ms. Kami. I was very sorry to hear about your father's illness. How is he doing now?

    Ms. Kami:
    Mr. Lowery:
    Ms. Kami: Thank you. I appreciate your concern. How are you doing? I hope you're enjoying your new house.

    Mr. Lowery:

6. **Beatrice:** Good morning, Ms. Cobb. You haven't had any calls. Do you need me to do anything before your 9:00 o'clock meeting?

    Ms. Cobb:
    Beatrice: Oh, he's much better today, thanks. I think he just had a very bad cold, but he went to school today, so I know he's feeling better.

    Ms. Cobb:

7. **Jorge:**
    Lynne: Hello, Jorge. No, I was just waiting for the bus.
    Jorge:
    Lynne: Sure. That would be **super!**° I'd love **a lift.**°

8. **Patty:** Hi, Sal. How've you been lately?
    Sal:
    Patty: Really? I'm sorry to hear it. Is there anything I can do?
    Sal:
    Patty: Well, I hope you feel better.
    Sal:

9. **Christina:**
    Nancy: Hello, Chris. I didn't see you at first. How have you been?

Super! is very informal for "wonderful."
A lift is informal for "a ride."

        Christina:
          Nancy:
        Christina:

10. **Mr. Nichols:** Hello, Mr. Sanchez. How have you been doing? I haven't seen you in several weeks.
     Mr. Sanchez:
     Mr. Nichols:
     Mr. Sanchez:

ROLE PLAYS

Choose partners and take a role that is described in the situation. Create an exchange of greeting and a short introductory conversation between the people. Be careful to use the appropriate level of formality when you choose your greetings and phrases. You can then reverse roles and change the conversation.

1. Sue is walking her dog one evening, and she sees her employer and his wife taking a walk. She greets them first.

2. Martin is washing his car on Saturday morning, and a friend from the university walks by, carrying her tennis racket. Martin greets her first.

3. As Barry is putting his ticket into a subway machine, he sees an American friend of his grandmother (an elderly gentleman whom Barry has met several times). The man is going into the subway near Barry. Barry speaks first.

4. Joe is standing in line to enter a movie theater, and a neighbor walks by, carrying a shopping bag filled with groceries. He sees Joe first.

5. Paula is sitting at her desk in the office, and a fellow employee, who has just returned from a business trip to Switzerland, walks in. Paula greets her first.

6. As Samar is shopping in the supermarket, he turns a corner suddenly and almost runs into his hair stylist. Samar speaks first.

7. Tom walks into the elevator in his office building and sees his doctor and her husband. Tom greets them first.

8. Pedro is running to catch his bus and sees a girl from his English class, walking toward him and carrying a suitcase. She calls out to him first.

9. Margot is sitting in a restaurant, having a cup of coffee by herself, and the elderly gentleman who lives alone in the apartment above her comes in by himself. She hasn't seen him for a long time; Margot speaks first.

10. Sandy is in the university bookstore, looking for a birthday card for a friend, when her English instructor comes in and begins looking at cards, too. Sandy speaks first.

REAL **PEOPLE,** REAL **SITUATIONS,** REAL **LANGUAGE**

Now it's your turn to open your eyes and ears to the world around you. As you do your everyday activities at school, at work, or in town, pay special attention to those around you. Listen carefully to the ways people greet each other and respond to those greetings. Record at least five observations of the ways you greet people and respond and the ways others greet you and respond. Some situations might include the following:

- Seeing your ex-roommate in the cafeteria
- Being greeted by the person who cuts the grass at your apartment complex
- Greeting the girl who sits behind you in math class
- Seeing a co-worker at a restaurant on Saturday night
- Being greeted by a salesclerk at the supermarket when you **check out**°

Use your notebook to record the conversations as accurately as you can, but don't worry about remembering every single word. Try to write down the phrases and expressions of the greetings and responses. Use the journal entry format:

> **EXAMPLE:** *April 2—7:30* A.M.—*At a coffee shop having breakfast alone. The waitress walks over to take my order.*

Waitress: *Good morning, sir. How are you today?*
Me: *Pretty good, I guess. It's still a little too early to tell.*
Waitress: *I know what you mean. What can I get you?*

Your teacher may want you to bring your observations to class to discuss and compare them with other members of the class.

Check out means to "have the items totalled and to pay for them."

CHAPTER 3

MAKING AND RESPONDING TO INTRODUC- TIONS

Years ago there were many social rules and etiquette procedures involving introductions. Some formal introductions between two people were made by letter by a third party. A person had to be very careful to weigh the importance of social class or status, age, and gender (male/female) when deciding which person should be presented or introduced to the other person first. The matter could be made very difficult if the two people were equal in most respects because the person making the introductions could risk offending one of them if the wrong person were introduced first.

However, times have changed, and most of the social rules about introducing older people *to* younger ones, women *to* men, and those in higher positions *to* those in lower positions have changed, too. Many people now feel much more relaxed about making introductions. Now when we introduce one person to another, we don't usually consider all those details. There are basically two kinds of introductions: third-party introductions and self-introductions. This chapter will discuss them separately because different words and phrases are used with each type.

Third-Party Introductions

In this type of introduction, a third person, C, who knows A and B, introduces A to B or B to A. For example, suppose Paul and his roommate Christos are at a soccer game. Paul sees Bob, an old friend from high school, and invites him to join them. Paul knows both Christos and Bob, but Christos and Bob don't know each other, so Paul makes the introductions:

> **Paul:** Bob, I'd like you to meet my roommate, Christos. Christos is from Greece and is studying English as a second language before he starts undergraduate school in architecture. I think you've heard me talk about Bob, Christos. He's a good friend from high school, and we played basketball together.
>
> **Christos:** Oh, yes. Nice to meet you, Bob.
>
> **Bob:** Nice meeting you, Christos.

Notice that Paul offers more than just "Bob, I'd like you to meet Christos. Christos, this is Bob." Paul gives a little background information on and his relationship to each, so the two new people will have some basis on which to begin a conversation.

In informal introductions, if there isn't much difference in the two people's position, status, or age, formal **titles**° and last names are not usually used. The person doing the introducing might use first and last names at first (for identification), but when the two begin talking, they often just naturally use their first names. For example,

> **Harriet:** Kerry! Hi! I'd like you to meet my friend, Lee Jones. Lee, this is Kerry Fields, an old friend from college.
>
> **Kerry:** Hi, Lee. It's nice to meet you.
>
> **Lee:** It's nice meeting you, too, Kerry.

Typical **titles** include *Mr., Mrs., Miss, Ms.,* and *Dr. Ms.* (pronounced /miz/) is now in common usage and has replaced *Mrs.* and *Miss* in many places—especially when the marital status of the woman is not known or doesn't need to be emphasized.

In formal introductions if there *is* a difference in the two people's age, status, or position, the third party might want to provide this information (as well as formal titles) in the introduction.

> **Lynne:** Dr. Jackson, I'd like to introduce you to my room-mate, Sharon Harrison. Sharon, this is Dr. Harold Jackson, my chemistry professor.
>
> **Dr. Jackson:** How do you do, Sharon (or "Ms. Harrison," depending on how formal he is). It's a pleasure to meet you.
>
> **Sharon:** It's nice to meet you, too, Dr. Jackson. (She wouldn't use his first name because of his position and title—unless he asked her to.)

In most situations, handshaking is optional, but these days it is more often done than not—especially in formal social or business settings. It's very common for one person (or both) to extend a hand when meeting someone. If you are in this situation, and you are offered a hand to shake, you should grasp it firmly and shake it briefly. Americans often tend to make some judgments about people according to their handshakes, so make sure yours is not too weak or limp, not too hard, and not too long-lasting. It should be firm and brief.

Here are some typical ways to begin third-party introductions. Of course, background information, some details about the people's relationship to you, and things they may have in common may follow these openings. They are arranged from formal to informal:

> ♣ A, it's my pleasure to introduce you to B . . . . *(Formal)*
> ♣ A, I'd like to introduce you to B . . . . *(Formal)*
> ♣ A, let me introduce you to B . . . .
> ♣ A, I'd like you to meet B . . . .
> ♣ A, I don't believe you've ever met B . . . .
> ♣ A, have you met B? . . .
> ♣ A, $\left\{ \begin{array}{l} \text{meet} \\ \text{this is} \\ \text{\_\_\_\_} \end{array} \right\}$ B. B, A . . . . *(Informal)*
>
> ♣ _____
> ♣ _____

PRACTICE 1

Make introductions in the following formal and informal situations. Give appropriate background information, your relationship to the two people, and something they may have in common, according to the clues provided. You don't have to use all the information given; just use what you think would be appropriate.

> **EXAMPLE:**   *You're at the library with Sam, and you see Maria.*
>
> > *Sam Watson—your cousin / visiting from New York for a week / studying economics / likes swimming and running*
> > *Maria Gomez—classmate / excellent swimmer / from Venezuela / working on a research paper*

> **You:**   *Hi, Maria. I don't think you've ever met my cousin Sam. Sam, this is a friend from school, Maria Gomez. Maria's from Venezuela. Sam's just visiting from New York for a week or so. Sam, Maria is the great swimmer I was telling you about last night at the pool.*

1.   You're at lunch with Mark, a co-worker. An acquaintance of yours asks to join you.
     Mark Pratt—has worked with the company for five years/moved here from Texas
     Rita James—from Austin, Texas/just got married/lives very near you

2.   You're at a party with José, a friend. You see your dentist.
     José Ricardo—from Panama/studying biology/leaving for Spain on vacation soon
     Dr. Richard Welk—loves to travel/knows Luis, José's cousin/from Chicago

3. You're at a conference with Janice, a colleague. You see a business acquaintance.

    Janice Ruppersburg—graduated from Georgetown University in Washington, D.C./new to company/likes horseback riding and tennis

    Mel Brandon—from Washington, D.C./works for a competitor in Atlanta

4. You're with your boyfriend or girlfriend at a play. You see your boss, Ms. Middleton.

    Ms. Middleton—used to live in Los Angeles/has three children/enjoys the theater

    Chris Massy—from Los Angeles/studying acting/works part time at a bank

5. You're sitting out at your apartment pool with Bassim, and George joins you.

    Bassim Khatib—friend from school/good runner/enjoys sailing and surfing

    George Smelter—your brother's roommate/jogs every day/from Indiana/good cook

Responding to Introductions

Responses to introductions don't have to be very complicated or elaborate; they are usually quite simple because there are only a few set expressions we use in responding. So, after C has introduced A and B, the responses might be as follows (from formal to informal):

♣
    A: **How do you do,**° B?
    B: It's a pleasure to meet you. (*Formal*)

♣
    A: Hello, B. I'm pleased to meet you.
    B: Yes, it's nice to meet you, too.

♣
    A: Hello. Good to meet you.
    B: Nice meeting you, too.

♣
    A: Hi, B. Nice to meet you.
    B: Same here. (*Informal*)

Self-Introductions

What happens when there's no one around to do the introducing for you? Suppose you're at a party and see an interesting-looking person you want to meet. The introduction might go like this:

    You: Hi there. Are you enjoying the party?
    Girl: It's okay. I don't know many people here.
    You: Well, let me introduce myself, and you'll know one more person. I'm Pat Bordon. Who are you?
    Girl: Natasha Wolinski. I just moved in next door. Do you live in the building?
    You: No, but I have some good friends who do. I'll be glad to introduce you to them tonight.
    Girl: Thanks. That would be nice.

Or what if you're supposed to pick up a business client at the airport, and you've never met him, but you know what he looks like? Here's another dialog to illustrate how the self-introduction works:

    You: Mr. Franks? I'm Jerry Kominami. It's nice to meet you finally—after all these months of corresponding.

How do you do? is not a real question and doesn't need an answer (it is *not* the same as "How are you doing?"); it is used mostly in formal introductions.

Client: It's good to meet you, too. (They shake hands.) Please call me George.

You: Thanks. Call me Jerry.

Here are some ways to begin self-introductions. Remember that the same "rules" about background or some personal information that apply to third-party introductions apply to self-introductions. After you have introduced yourself, give the person some information about yourself or ask the person a question about himself or herself to have a basis for beginning a light conversation.

- ♣ May I introduce myself? I'm . . . . *(Formal)*
- ♣ How do you do? My name is . . . . *(Formal)*
- ♣ Please let me introduce myself. I'm . . . . *(Formal)*
- ♣ Hello. My name is . . . .
- ♣ Hi, I'm . . . . *(Informal)*
- ♣ _____
- ♣ _____

It's not usually necessary for you to ask, "And who are you?" after you have introduced yourself because most people will naturally follow with something like

- ♣ It's a pleasure to make your acquaintance. My name is . . . . *(Formal)*
- ♣ Hello. It's nice to meet you. I'm . . . .
- ♣ Hi, I'm . . . . Nice meeting you, too.
- ♣ Good to meet you. I'm . . . .
- ♣ _____
- ♣ _____

PRACTICE 2

Choose a partner and introduce yourself to that person. Create a short dialog between the two of you, and then change roles and make the introductions and responses again. Be sure to consider shaking hands and using titles and/or first and last names if you think it is appropriate. Then switch roles and change the introductions slightly.

EXAMPLE: *Introduce yourself to your new next-door neighbor.*

You: *Hi. I'm your neighbor in 405—next door. My name's Yumi Kaneko.*

Neighbor: *Hello. (They shake hands.) It's nice to meet you. I'm Jill Kingston. Have you lived here long?*

You: *About two years. I think you'll really like it here. There're a lot of young people here, and everyone's very friendly. Where did you move from?*

Neighbor: *Tennessee. I was finishing law school at Vanderbilt University, and now I'm joining a law firm here in the city.*

1. Introduce yourself to the new student who has just entered your math class.

2. You have an appointment to meet the director of admissions to talk about admission requirements to the university. Introduce yourself first.

3. You've just moved into a new house. Introduce yourself to the mail carrier, a man about 55 years old.

4. Your sister's new boyfriend comes over to see her, but she's not home. You've never met him before, so introduce yourself to him.

5. As you are taking your dog for a walk, you notice a moving truck nearby. An elderly lady is instructing the movers where to put the furniture inside the house. Introduce yourself to the woman.

SITUATIONAL DIALOGS   Look at these examples of typical introductions. With a partner or partners, act out the roles, and then answer the questions that follow.

A. *Jason is with Belinda at a disco. He sees a friend from work standing by himself.*

Jason: There's Stan. Come on. I'd like you to meet him.
(A few seconds later)
Jason: Hi, Stan. I'd like you to meet my girlfriend, Belinda Berstein. Belinda, this is Stan Maxwell, who's been working with me on the new assignment.

Stan: (extends hand) Hi, Belinda. It's nice to meet you finally. Jason talks about you all the time.

Belinda: Nice to meet you, too. I hope you hear only the good things and not the bad. You're new at Powell, aren't you?

Stan: Yeah. I just started three months ago, but I really like it, and I love the city!

What Do You Think?

1. *Why do you think Stan and Belinda use each other's first names immediately?*
2. *Jason doesn't tell very much about either one of their backgrounds when he introduces them. Do you think there's a reason?*
3. *Change the dialog slightly so that Jason gives some personal information about both of them. Then, Belinda and Stan make different small talk (light conversation).*

B. *Paula and Tim work for an advertising agency and are at a business meeting in Atlanta. Their appointment is with a client Paula knows but Tim does not.*

Paula: Good morning, Mr. Barnes. It's good to see you again. (They shake hands.)

Mr. Barnes: Hello, Paula. Nice to see you again, too. Did you have a good flight?

Paula: Fine. I thought we'd circle Atlanta forever, but I've come to expect that at this airport. Mr. Barnes, I'd like you to meet Tim Myers, my associate. Tim is going to be helping me on the advertising campaign.

Tim: (offers his hand) How do you do, Mr. Barnes? It's nice to meet you.

Mr. Barnes: My pleasure, Tim. Let's have some lunch, so we can start talking.

What Do You Think?

1. *What clues from the conversation let you know the status and/or age differences between the speakers?*
2. *Paula does not begin immediately with the introduction of Mr. Barnes and Tim. What does she do first, and do you have any ideas why?*
3. *Why do you think Paula doesn't give more background information on both men when she introduces them? What kinds of responses do the men make after being introduced?*

C. *It's raining hard, and Zena is standing under an umbrella outside her office building, trying to get a taxi. An older man who works for the company but whom Zena doesn't know is waiting also.*

Man: Hello. It's an awful day, isn't it?

Zena: It certainly is. I've been trying to get a cab for 15 minutes, but I've had no luck.

Man: Excuse me, but I know I've seen you before. Don't you work in the legal department?

Zena: Yes, I do. I'm Zena Vernon.

Man: Glad to make your acquaintance. I'm James Carlson, head of accounting.

Zena: How do you do, Mr. Carlson?

Man: Please—call me Jim.

Zena: Thank you. It's nice to meet you, Jim. You looked familiar to me, too.

What Do You Think?

1. *Is it considered acceptable or polite in your country for two strangers to begin a conversation like this—before they are introduced?*

2. *What reasons might Zena have for using* Mr. Carlson *instead of* James *or* Jim *when she first meets him? Change the dialog so that Jim calls Zena* Ms. Vernon, *and then Zena asks to be called by her first name.*

3. *Change the situation slightly so that Zena's co-worker introduces Zena and Jim.*

D. *Tom Postell has recently moved into the neighborhood and has been buying gas at the neighborhood station for the last several weeks. The service station owner greets and welcomes Tom to the neighborhood.*

Owner: Hello there. I believe you moved into the old Jackson house, didn't you?

Tom: Yes, I did. I'm Tom Postell. (He extends his hand to the man.)

Owner: Well, it's a real pleasure to meet you. I'm Randall McEntire. I've noticed you buying gas here a few times, and I thought you might be the one who moved in on Ashe Avenue.

Tom: You got it right. Well, it's nice meeting you, Mr. McEntire. It's great having a service station so close to home.

Owner: Well, Mr. Postell, if you ever have a problem with your car, just call me. I'll be happy to take a look.

Tom: Thanks, Mr. McEntire. That's good to know. I'm glad I got to meet you. See you again.

What Do You Think?

1. *Why do you think Tom and Randall use* Mr. *and their last names with each other even though they give their first names in the introductions? What might this tell you about them and their relationship?*

2. *How might two people in this situation or a similar one (a customer and a restaurant owner, for example) introduce and address each other in your native country? Are there any social rules governing customer-owner relationships in your country? What about here in the United States?*

3. *Change the dialog so that Tom, his wife, and his daughter are at the gas station when Mr. McEntire introduces himself to them.*

E. *Johan has just moved into the downstairs apartment. He meets his new neighbor at the mailboxes in the hall.*

Johan: Hello. My name's Johan Gutenburg. I've just moved into 1-A. You live above me, don't you?

Carol: Yes, I do. I'm Carol Swanson. How do you do? (They shake hands.)

Johan: It's nice to meet you, Carol. You play the piano, don't you? I've heard music coming from your apartment a few times.

Carol: Oh, I hope I'm not disturbing you. I try to play during the day when most people are working.

Johan: You're not bothering me at all. I enjoy listening to you play.

What Do you Think?

1. *Is it common in your country for men and women to shake hands? If not, do they use any other gestures when they meet each other?*

2. *Change the dialog: Carol goes to Johan's apartment and introduces herself to him first.*

3. *Expand the dialog between them: Carol offers to help Johan in some way and then closes the conversation.*

DIALOG COMPLETIONS   Choose partners and complete these dialogs, making appropriate introductions and responses. Include handshaking where you feel it is called for. When you finish, change roles and complete the dialogs differently.

1. *Joe is at a party and introduces himself to a woman he would like to meet.*

Joe:

Woman: Nice to meet you, too. I'm Ellen Franklin.

Joe:

Woman: No, I'm friends with Marsha Robinson. She's over there by the mirror. Do you know her?

Joe:

Woman: Well, it was nice meeting you, too. Enjoy the party.

Joe:

2. *Ameed is moving in with Ricardo. Ricardo introduces him to Mrs. Ketterly, the manager of the apartment building.*

Ricardo:

Mrs. Ketterly:

Ameed: Hello, Mrs. Ketterly. It's a pleasure to meet you, also. I really like the apartment.

Mrs. Ketterly:

Ameed: Yes, I'll be a graduate student in computer science.

Mrs. Ketterly:

Ameed: Thank you. I'm sure I will. It was very good to meet you, too.

3. *Teruo is a new student and has an appointment to talk with the foreign student advisor, whom he has never met.*

Ms. Bailey: Hello. You must be Teruo.

Teruo:

Ms. Bailey: Yes, I'm Ms. Bailey, the foreign student advisor. Now, I believe you wanted some information on housing, didn't you?

Teruo:

Ms. Bailey: Would you be interested in an apartment near Southpark Shopping Center and on the bus route?

Teruo:

4. *Juan's father is visiting for a few days and has never met his American roommate.*

Juan: Dad, I'd like you to meet Tim Jenkins, my roommate. Tim's from Ft. Worth, Texas, but has lived all over the world. Tim, this is my father, Colonel Luis Valdez.

Tim:

Father:

Tim: Yes, sir. Very much. It's a fine school.

Father:

Tim: That's good. I hope you enjoy your stay. I need to run because a friend's waiting.

Father:
  Tim:

5. *Patty Garrison is on a plane to Hawaii for a vacation. The man beside her introduces himself first.*

Man:
Patty:
Man: No, I've been to Hawaii several times, but it's such a wonderful place, I keep coming back. How about you? Is this your first trip?
Patty:
Man: Well, I'm sure you're going to love it—especially Maui. It's my favorite island.
Patty:
Man:

6. *Gail is in line at the checkout counter at the supermarket, and behind her is a man who looks very familiar.*

Gail: Excuse me, but you look extremely familiar. Do you have a child at Spring Valley Elementary?
Ted:
Gail: I thought that was where I'd seen you. My name's Gail Yadkins. My son David is in the fourth grade.
Ted:
Gail: It's nice to meet you, too. How does your daughter like her teacher?
Ted:
Gail: David has the same complaint. I guess I need to talk with the teacher to see if his complaint is valid.
Ted:
Gail: Yes, it was good to meet you, too. I'm sure we'll see each other again at various school functions this year.

7. *Beverly is at a Nursing Society meeting and introduces herself to a new member.*

Beverly:
  Paul: How do you do? I'm Paul Olson. I work at Davidson Memorial.
Beverly:
  Paul: No, I haven't met her. What floor does she work on?

Beverly:
Paul: Yes, I'd like to talk some more, too. Can we get together after the meeting?
Beverly:
Paul: Good. I'll talk to you then.

8.   *Liza is waiting to see the dentist. An elderly man is sitting beside her.*

Man: 'Morning, young lady. My name's Arthur Ringwald. I believe I've seen you in here before, haven't I?
Liza:
Man: Yes, ma'am, I'm sure. I never forget a face. What's your name?
Liza:
Man: Well, it's a pleasure to meet you, Miss Matthews.
Liza:

9.   *Cindy and Delores are walking downtown. Yasser, an acquaintance of Delores from the language lab, is walking toward them.*

Delores: Hello, Yasser. What's happening?
Yasser:
Delores: Oh—Yasser, meet Cindy. Cindy, Yasser. I met Yasser last summer at the foreign languages lab.
Yasser:
Cindy: It's nice to meet you, Yasser. Where are you from?
Yasser:
Cindy: No, I've never been there. I haven't done much traveling at all.
Delores:
Cindy: Oh, you're right, Delores. We do need to be going. It was a pleasure meeting you, Yasser. I hope to see you again soon.
Yasser:

10.   *Khalid is walking down the hall with a colleague when he sees the vice-president of finance, whom he has never met, getting a cup of coffee. Khalid asks his friend to introduce them.*

Khalid: Charles, isn't that Mr. Beane, the V-P of finance?
Charles:
Khalid: No, I haven't. Would you introduce me, please?
Charles: Sure, come on.

(A few seconds later)
    Charles:
Mr. Beane: Oh, how do you do? I'm sorry I haven't come by to meet you sooner. I've been on a business trip for the past two weeks.
    Khalid:
Mr. Beane: Well, I'm glad to hear that. If you have any questions, please feel free to call on me. It was a pleasure to meet you.
    Khalid:

ROLE PLAYS

Here are some common, everyday situations involving various kinds of introductions. Take roles and create short role plays with introductions, responses, and light conversation. Use appropriate gestures (handshaking, for instance) where necessary. When you have finished, change roles and create new role plays.

1. Chris Bassett is on a plane going to Japan on business. She introduces herself to the elderly man beside her and starts a conversation.

2. Chen and a friend are sitting in a theater, waiting for the movie to begin. Someone Chen knows comes up and asks to join them. Chris introduces the two people to each other.

3. Hector and his girlfriend are in an elevator. Hector's 55-year-old accountant, whom he has just hired, gets in. Hector begins the introductions.

4. Ali's father is visiting him for a few days and has come with Ali to the university. Ali introduces him to several classmates and to his English teacher.

5. Sue Jones is at a job interview. She introduces herself to the department manager.

6. Carla is seated at a dinner party between Mrs. Barnes, a 65-year-old author, and Peter Simon, a 22-year-old salesperson. She introduces them to each other.

7. Jimmy is doing his laundry at a self-service laundromat near his house. A young woman whom he's seen several times is there, too. He introduces himself to her.

8. Martin is alone at lunch in the company cafeteria. He takes his tray to a table where an unfamiliar man is sitting. Martin asks to join the other man and introduces himself.

9. Margaret is in New York at a business meeting. At a coffee break, she introduces her boss to a high-level employee from another company.

10. Greg Lane is having dinner with Jean Wong at her house when the doorbell rings. It's Linda Blakeman, a friend of Jean's, who has come to return some cookbooks she borrowed last week. Jean introduces Greg and Linda.

REAL **PEOPLE,** REAL **SITUATIONS,** REAL **LANGUAGE**

A. Go out into your community and introduce yourself to five new people. Here are some possibilities, but you may choose whomever you wish:

- A person you don't know at work
- Someone sitting near you in the cafeteria or a lunch place
- Your mail carrier
- Your apartment manager
- Someone you speak to often but have never met
- The cashier at the supermarket or drugstore where you usually shop
- A person by him- or herself at a party
- A new neighbor

Record the conversations in your notebook, using the journal entry format.

> **EXAMPLE:** *June 16—a new person at work*
>
> **Me:** *Um...excuse me, but aren't you new here?*
> **Woman:** *Yes, I am. I'm Lynn Wallace. I work in the accounting department.*
> **Me:** *It's a pleasure to meet you, Lynne. I'm Ray Finlay. I'm in marketing. (We shake hands.)*
> **Me:** *How do you like your job so far?*
> **Woman:** *Oh, I really like it. It's quite challenging.*

B. Now listen to other people introduce themselves to others (or to you) at work, at parties, at school, or in the community. Use your notebook to record your observations, paying special attention to the words and expressions people use. Record any kind of nonverbal communication used, too.

> **EXAMPLE:** *Thursday, April 2—in a theater waiting for the movie to begin. The two people in front of me are approached by a young girl.*
>
> **Girl:** *Hello, Dr. Linwood. I thought that was you. How are you?*
> **Man:** *Well, hi there, Pam. I'm fine. What about you?*
> **Girl:** *Great! I can't wait to see the movie!*

Man: *Yes, me, too. Pam, I don't think you've ever met my wife, Jane. Honey, this is Pam King. She's one of my best patients— especially when it comes to <u>measles</u>!°*

Woman: *Hi, Pam. It's nice to meet you. You're not sick now, are you?*

Girl: *No, ma'am. That was last month. I'm fine now. Well, I'd better go back to my seat. It was nice seeing you, Dr. Linwood, and nice meeting you, Mrs. Linwood.*

Man: *Bye, Pam.*

After you have finished collecting your samples, your teacher may want you to bring them to class to discuss and to compare them with other class members' examples.

Measles is a disease (usually childhood) whose symptoms are a high fever and red spots all over the body.

CHAPTER 4

SAYING GOODBYE

There are many ways to tell someone goodbye, and most of them depend on the situation at hand. However, there is one rule that all situations observe: We seldom say goodbye abruptly. In English it is necessary to prepare a person for our departure. We lead into the farewell by saying something pleasant and thoughtful like "I've really enjoyed talking to you," or we might say something relating to the time like "Gosh, I can't believe how late it is! I really must be going!" The following are examples of these two types of lead-ins (openings) for goodbyes:

Pleasantries°

+ I've enjoyed $\left\{ \begin{array}{l} \textbf{meeting}° \\ \textbf{talking to}° \\ \text{seeing} \end{array} \right\}$ you.

+ It's been good seeing you again.
+ It was nice talking to you.
+ I'm glad I **ran into**° you.
♣ _____
♣ _____

Time-Related Expressions

+ I'd better be going. It's almost . . . (give time).
+ Well, it's getting late. I've got to $\left\{ \begin{array}{l} \text{run.} \\ \text{go.} \\ \text{hurry.} \end{array} \right.$

+ Look at the time! I've really got to go!
+ I should be going. It's getting late, and I have a lot to do.
+ Where has the time gone? I guess I'd better be running along.
♣ _____
♣ _____

Pleasantries are light, pleasant expressions used in openings and closings of conversations, greetings, and partings.

Notice that there's a big difference between saying **meeting** and **talking to.** We say "I've enjoyed meeting you" after we have been introduced to someone the first time. To someone we know already, we say, "I've enjoyed talking to (or seeing) you."

Ran into (in this case) is an idiom that means "met by accident."

PRACTICE 1

Before actually using the word *goodbye*, say something pleasant or something having to do with the time to lead into the farewell.

> **EXAMPLE:** Susan: *Well, it's getting pretty late. I'd better be going. See you later.*

1. **Karl:** _____
   Goodbye **for now.°**

2. **Mrs. Fredrickson:** _____
   See you next week.

3. **Kim:** _____
   So long.

4. **Samir:** _____
   Bye.

5. **Lisa:** _____
   Good night.

   Before parting, one of the speakers sometimes adds a wish of staying in touch. For example, if Helen were leaving for two months in New York, her roommate might say, "Don't forget to write!" or "Let's call each other once a week!" When the goodbyes are between people who live in the same town or see each other fairly often, one person might add, "Let's keep in touch" or "Call me sometime." As we discussed briefly in Chapter 2, "Greeting People and Responding," the person issuing the "call me sometime" request may just be doing it out of politeness, since many Americans have the habit of ending a conversation with a pleasant, optimistic (but not always genuine) mention of "getting together soon" or "having lunch sometime." Some other expressions you may hear and use are listed. Can you think of others?

For now means "until we meet again."

Wishes to Keep in Touch

✤ Let's get together (again) soon.
✤ Give me a call/ring sometime.
✤ Keep in touch!
✤ Let's have $\left\{ \begin{array}{l} \text{lunch} \\ \text{dinner} \\ \text{coffee} \end{array} \right\}$ soon.
✤ **I hope we meet again.°**
✤ **Drop me a line.°**
✤ Stop by and see me sometime!
✤ _____
✤ _____

PRACTICE 2

After each farewell, add a wishful phrase about keeping in touch.

> **EXAMPLE:** **Tom:** *It's been great seeing you.*
>
> **You:** *It certainly has. Let's not wait so long next time to get together again.*

1. **Karen:** I've really had a wonderful afternoon.
   You:
2. **Jihad:** I'm really going to miss you.
   You:
3. **Chen:** It was nice meeting you. I'd heard so many great things about you!
   You:
4. **Mari:** What a super party! I had a fantastic time!
   You:
5. **Terri:** It's been wonderful seeing you again after all these years!
   You:

Finally the actual goodbye arrives (or sometimes the order can be reversed, and the wish to stay in touch can be last). The word *goodbye* is not the only word that can be used; in fact, *goodbye* sometimes has such a *final*

I hope we meet again is used after two people have met for the first time.
Drop me a line means "Write me a note or letter."

feeling about it that other words and expressions are often substituted for it. Here are some other expressions of farewell. Notice the informal ones at the end.

Goodbyes

+ **Farewell!**°
+ Take care.
+ Have a good/nice $\left\{ \begin{array}{l} \text{afternoon.} \\ \text{day.} \\ \text{week.} \end{array} \right.$
+ So long!
+ Take it easy.
+ Later. (*Informal*)
+ **See you around/later.**° (*Informal*)
+ _____
+ _____

"Sticky" Situations
The different parts of saying goodbye that have been discussed are fairly standard for most situations. But sometimes we find ourselves in "sticky" (difficult, sensitive, or "hard to get out of") situations; perhaps the person is talking endlessly, or the party or meeting we're attending is terribly boring, and we want to leave. The key to getting out of one of these sticky situations is politeness. It is not polite just to jump up, grab our bag or coat, and announce, "I'm leaving now. Goodbye!" Instead, we sometimes think of a reason for having to leave. For instance, "I need to be leaving, **I'm afraid.**° I have a lot of work to do at home." If we feel we have been imposing too long on someone (taking up too much of the person's time), we might say, "Well, I've taken up too much of your time already. I'd better go" or "Let me leave so you can get back to work." By showing some thoughtfulness and consideration and by stressing the value

---

Farewell is seldom used, but it is sometimes said by someone exaggerating the seriousness of the situation—and trying to be funny.

See you around and **see you later** should not be used with people whom you probably will *not* see again.

I'm afraid is a polite way of preparing the listener for a response that is going to be negative, and the person replying is expressing his or her regret or concern.

of the other person's time, we can ease ourselves out the door and make our goodbyes less awkward for both people.

PRACTICE 3

Read each situation and begin your goodbye with a polite excuse.

> **EXAMPLE:** *You're at a dull party, and it's past midnight.*
>
> **You:** *Well, I need to be going. I've got an early meeting in the morning.*

1. You've just finished lunch with a talkative friend, and it's almost time for you to be back at work.
   You:

2. You've been talking on the phone for 40 minutes to a classmate.
   You:

3. You've been sitting outside your apartment in your friend's car, after having been to the movies.
   You:

4. You're at a soccer club meeting, and it's getting very late.
   You:

5. The elderly man who lives next door has stopped you on the sidewalk and has been **talking** your **ear off**° for twenty minutes.
   You:

SITUATIONAL DIALOGS
The following dialogs are examples of various ways of ending conversations and saying goodbye in different settings. Choose partners, take roles, and act out the dialogs. Every verbal exchange is accompanied by body language, such as facial expressions (smiles, frowns, the lifting of eyebrows) and gestures (a wave of the hand, a handshake). Ask your teacher for more explanation of body language that would be appropriate in the situations. Then discuss the questions at the end of each situational dialog.

Talking (someone's) **ear off** is an idiom that means "talking continuously for a very long time."

A.   *Sara and Lisa have just been to the movies together, and Lisa is **dropping** Sara **off**° at her house.*

Sara: Thanks for driving tonight, Lisa. I had a great time.
Lisa: Me, too. Let's plan to go together and see the new James Bond movie when it starts.
Sara: Sure thing! You know I wouldn't miss it. See you later!
Lisa: Okay. 'Night.

What Do You Think?

1.   *What pleasantries do the two women use to start the process of saying goodbye?*
2.   *Is there any wish to keep in touch? If so, does it seem genuine to you?*
3.   *Suppose Sara had continued talking about the movie and Lisa needed to go home. What could Lisa have said to end the conversation?*

B.   *Irvin and Jorge have been talking outside the post office, where they met by accident. Irvin glances at his watch and realizes that he's late.*

Irvin: My gosh! I'm going to miss the subway if I don't hurry! Nice talking to you, Jorge.
Jorge: Same here. Take it easy.
Irvin: Yeah. You, too. Catch you later!

What Do You Think?

1.   *Catch you later is a slang expression that means "I'll see you later." Have you heard any other similar expressions from your American friends or on television or in the movies?*
2.   *What does Jorge mean by* same here?
3.   *How does Irvin use the time in his excuse to leave?*

C.   *Pam sees Donald at the bus stop. They haven't seen each other in a long time.*

Pam: Hi, Don. Long time, no see.
Donald: Pam! Where have you been for the last three months? I never see you anymore.
Pam: Oh, I've been working strange hours these days. I don't see much of anyone anymore.
Donald: Well, I understand. I wish I could stay and talk, but here comes my bus. Why don't we **go out**° sometime?

Dropping (someone) **off** means "letting a rider out of a vehicle at a destination."
Go out means "on a date" or just "get together somewhere for a nice time."

Pam: I'd like that. Call me soon.
Donald: For sure! So long!
Pam: Bye, Don. Take care.

What Do You Think?

1.   *What is another way of saying* long time, no see?
2.   *Can you think of two or three other informal expressions for* for sure?
3.   *How is Pam using* take care? *Take care* of what?

D.   *Henry has been talking and talking to Maria about his vacation in the Bahamas. Maria is getting bored, and she has to go to class.*

Henry: . . . and the next day we went surfing around the other side of the island. The water was perfect! And then. . . .
Maria   (interrupting and looking at her watch): Gosh, Henry, that sounds wonderful, but I'm afraid I have to go. My next class starts in a few minutes.
Henry: Oh, is it that late? Sorry. I didn't mean to **hold** you **up.**°
Maria: Well, have a nice day, and I'll see you around.
Henry: Likewise. So long.

What Do You Think?

1.   *How does Maria tactfully end the conversation?*
2.   *Change* likewise *into a complete sentence. Are there any other short expressions similar to this one?*
3.   *In your native country, is it considered polite to interrupt someone who is talking? How would you go about it?*

E.   *Carol and Wayne, two casual acquaintances, have been standing in line at the bank's 24-hour teller machine. Wayne has finished his business and is leaving.*

Wayne: Nice running into you, Carol.
Carol: Same here. By the way, have you seen Diane lately?
Wayne: Not since Joe's party. I heard she went to Mexico for a vacation.
Carol: Really? No wonder I haven't seen her at exercise class lately.

Hold (someone) **up** means "delay or detain."

Wayne: Well, let me run. Stop by and see me sometime.
Carol: I might do that. Are you still living in the same apartment?
Wayne: On Walker Avenue.
Carol: Okay. Take care.
Wayne: I will. You do the same.

What Do You Think?

1. *Why does Carol begin her question about Diane with* by the way? *What function does the phrase serve? Have you ever heard the expression before? If so, how was it used?*
2. *Wayne's remark,* let me run, *is not a command to Carol. How is it used? Can you think of other expressions that are structured like commands but are not meant as such? (One such example—that you probably hear quite often—is "Have a good day!")*
3. *Does Carol commit herself to stopping by and seeing Wayne? Why or why not? How do you know?*

DIALOG COMPLETIONS   Choose partners and take roles. Then complete the conversations, using the given parts of the dialogs as clues. You may need to use some or all of the various parts of a goodbye (a pleasantry, a time-related expression, a wish to keep in touch, an excuse to leave). Then reverse the roles and complete the dialogs differently.

1. *Patty and Glenda have just taken their children for a walk to the playground. They are going their separate ways, so it's time to say goodbye.*

Patty:
Glenda: I did, too. I need to get out in the fresh air more often.
Patty:
Glenda: That sounds good. What about next Friday?
Patty:
Glenda: You, too. See you then.
Patty:

2. *Napoleon and his boss, Ms. Lynch, have been having dinner together and discussing business. They are in the parking lot next to their cars.*

Napoleon: I'm very glad we had this opportunity to discuss that issue, Ms. Lynch. I appreciate your taking the time from your busy schedule.
Ms. Lynch:

Napoleon: I hope your trip to Seattle goes well. I guess I'll see you sometime next week.
Ms. Lynch:
Napoleon: Thank you. The same to you. Drive carefully.
Ms. Lynch:

3. *Pedro and Rana have been sitting on the steps of their apartment building and talking.*

Rana (looking at her watch):
Pedro: Is it that late? I need to go, too. Give me a call next week about the party, okay?
Rana:
Pedro: Great! I look forward to it! See you later!
Rana:

4. *Alan and Carla have been to Carla's office party. Alan has taken her home and is ready to leave, but Carla keeps talking.*

Carla: I had a wonderful time, Alan. Thank you for **escorting°** me.
Alan:
Carla: Would you like to come in and have a cup of coffee or **a nightcap°**?
Alan:
Carla: Oh, do you really? I'd love for you to come in and tell me a little more about your trip. It sounds fascinating!
Alan:
Carla: Well, all right. If you really must. Thanks again for the evening.
Alan:
Carla: Good night, Alan.
Alan:

5. *David and Theresa have been walking across campus together. They arrive at the building where Theresa has her exam.*

Theresa:
David: Good luck! I'm sure you'll do well.
Theresa:
David: I don't have any definite plans, but I'm not sure. I'll call you tomorrow, and we can talk about it.

Escorting means "going with someone as a companion or date."
A nightcap is a drink (usually alcoholic) taken before bedtime.

Theresa:
  David: Likewise. Catch you later.

6.   *Darlene is preparing to leave a reception and is saying goodbye to the* **hosts,°** *Sharon and Mike Fisher.*

Darlene:
Sharon: I wish you didn't have to leave so soon.
Darlene:
Sharon: Well, thank you for coming. It was nice meeting you—
          after hearing Mike speak so highly of you.
  Mike:
Darlene: Oh, I did. I met some very interesting people tonight.
          It's so hard to get to know people when you move to a
          new place.

7.   *Luis and Greg pass each other in the hall at school.*

Luis:
Greg: Hey, Luis! **You've been making yourself pretty scarce°**
          lately. What're you up to these days?
Luis:
Greg:
Luis: You know, I've been thinking. We really ought to go on
          that canoe trip we talked about last month. Are you still
          interested?
Greg:
Luis:
Greg: That sounds good to me. I'll call you next week, and we can
          discuss it.
Luis:
Greg:

8.   *Celina and Jill are talking in Jill's office. Celina looks at the wall clock and remembers an important meeting in five minutes.*

Celina:
  Jill: It was no trouble. See you at lunch.
Celina:
  Jill: Thanks. You, too.

Hosts are people who give a party or receive (welcome) guests at a party. A female host is usually called a *hostess*.
You've been making yourself pretty scarce means that Luis has not been seen very much lately.

9. *Don's sister Pat, who lives 500 miles away, has been visiting him for a few days, and it's time for her to leave.*

Pat: I really hate to leave. It seems like I just got here. But I had a wonderful time.

Don:

Pat: Of course, I will. I'll call you every week. And you could drop me a line every now and then, too, you know.

Don:

Pat: All right. Take care of yourself. I love you!

Don:

10. *Juan and Ellen have just returned from attending a rock concert. Juan has driven Ellen home, and they are parked outside her apartment.*

Ellen: That was a super concert, Juan! Thanks for inviting me!

Juan:

Ellen: Why don't we have lunch next week?

Juan:

Ellen: Great! I'll call you early next week.

Juan:

Ellen: Take it easy. Bye-bye.

ROLE PLAYS Choose partners and take a role that is described in the situation. Using the information provided, create a short dialog that involves saying goodbye. When you have finished, exchange roles and redo the role plays, using different dialogs.

1. Mohammed and José have been sitting in José's dorm room, talking about life in the United States. José suddenly glances at his watch and realizes that he's supposed to pick up his sister at a friend's house in a few minutes.

2. Marta and Sam are talking while walking toward Marta's office. Sam keeps talking and doesn't seem to notice that Marta is becoming a little impatient about getting back to work.

3. Bob is being interviewed for a very important job. The interviewer finally stands up, and Bob understands that the interview is over.

4. Margaret and Ali have been jogging side by side for about a mile. They are approaching the street where Ali needs to turn to go home.

5. Nancy and Jim have been talking on the phone for a long time. Nancy is bored and wants to say goodbye, but she doesn't want to appear rude.

6. Samar has just spent a nice evening with Linda and Rolf Miller, his new neighbors. It's late and he has to leave.

7. Gina and Elizabeth, friends who haven't seen each other in a long time, ran into each other in a women's clothing store and have been talking. They both want to see each other again, but they must go.

8. Mr. Johnson, an elderly neighbor, has been in the park talking with Mrs. Franks, a young mother with two small children. The children are pulling on her and wanting to go home. Mr. Johnson doesn't seem to notice, as he talks on and on.

9. Luis has been meeting with his teacher for about 45 minutes. He still has some questions to ask, but he sees her look at the clock a few times.

10. Marvin and Pam have been on their first date together and are now standing outside Pam's apartment, talking. Marvin obviously doesn't want the date to end yet, but Pam is very tired and wants to go in.

REAL **PEOPLE,** REAL **SITUATIONS,** REAL **LANGUAGE**

This is your chance to go out into your community and observe *real* people using the language in *real* situations. Use your ears and eyes to observe the way other people say goodbye (to you and/or others). Using your notebook, record what you hear from

1. The checkout cashier at the supermarket where you shop
2. Your landlady or landlord
3. The postal clerk at your local post office
4. The salesperson at a department store
5. The clerk at the local dry cleaners

Your teacher may want you to bring in your observations to discuss and compare with your classmates'.

CHAPTER 5

ASKING FOR INFORMATION

Everybody needs information sometimes, and we have to know how to ask for it politely and clearly. Read these two situations and tell how you would handle them:

• You have the address of an apartment for rent that you want to look at, but you don't know what bus will take you there. Whom should you ask, and what should you say?

• You're at the supermarket and want to buy some raisins, but you don't know where to look. Whom should you ask, and what should you say?

In the first situation, you might ask someone like a police officer or a person standing at the bus stop, but the most knowledgeable person would probably be a bus driver. You might say, "What bus goes to this address?" or "Do you know which bus I should take to get to this address?"

In the second situation, a store clerk or a cashier would be the best person to help you, since they both work there and would be familiar with the organization of the store. But you could also ask a shopper if you couldn't find one of the others. You might ask, "Where would I find the raisins?" or "What section are the raisins in?"

When we need to find out information about something, we usually use one of the six question words to begin:

Who . . . . ?	(*Who* is going to pick me up at the airport tomorrow?)
What . . . . ?	(*What* is the name of that new Italian restaurant?)
When . . . . ?	(*When* does the next train to Washington leave?)
Where . . . . ?	(*Where* is the best place to have my suit dry-cleaned?)
Why . . . . ?	(*Why* are the windows closed?)

	_____ . . . . ?	(*How* do you want your steak cooked?)
	long . . . . ?	(*How long* do you plan to travel in Europe?)
	many . . . . ?	(*How many* employees work for Frank?)
How	much . . . . ?	(*How much* does a pint of milk cost?)
	far . . . . ?	(*How far* is Los Angeles from San Francisco?)
	easy . . . . ?	(*How easy* is it to find the subway station?)

And, of course, there are many other questions that *how* can start. What others can you think of?

PRACTICE 1

Practice forming information questions (like the ones just presented) with each of these question words:

1. When _____

2. How much _____

3. Who _____

4. How often _____

5. What _____

The answers that we receive when we ask information questions are specific. For instance, the responses to the first five questions (*Who? What? When? Where? Why?*—used in the first examples) might be these:

José will.
It's called the Italian Isles.
5:30 P.M.
Miller's Cleaners on Oak Street is pretty good.
Because the air conditioner is on.

PRACTICE 2

Now try to answer the five questions that you just wrote in Practice 1.

1. _____

2. _____

3. _____

4. _____

5. _____

We can also ask for information by beginning our questions with an auxiliary verb, but the result is a little different. Instead of replying with specific information, we usually reply with *yes* or *no*—but then we might add some sort of explanation that delivers more information to the asker. For example,

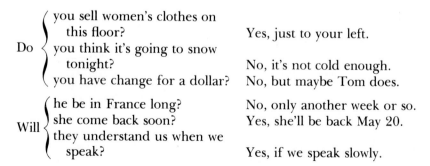

Do
- you sell women's clothes on this floor? — Yes, just to your left.
- you think it's going to snow tonight? — No, it's not cold enough.
- you have change for a dollar? — No, but maybe Tom does.

Will
- he be in France long? — No, only another week or so.
- she come back soon? — Yes, she'll be back May 20.
- they understand us when we speak? — Yes, if we speak slowly.

In each case, the person asking the question receives some information just from the *yes* or *no* reply, but do you see how much more was learned when the person replying offered additional information in the explanation that followed? Notice, too, that *do* and *will* are only two auxiliary verbs, and the English language consists of many more that can be used to begin *yes* or *no* questions.

PRACTICE 3

Now you try it. Respond to these questions with a *yes* or *no* (or even a *maybe*, if it is appropriate) and then explain your answer by giving a little more information.

1. Do you like American food?_____

2. Will your parents be visiting you soon?_____

3. Have you seen a good movie lately?_____

4. Is your roommate going with us to dinner?_____

5. Did you sleep well last night?_____

Courtesy When Asking for Information   In many situations it would be considered almost rude to begin a question without some kind of basic courtesy. We don't just ask a question; we get the person's attention politely in one of these ways first:

+ Excuse me. When . . . ?
+ Pardon me, ma'am, but where . . . ?
+ I hate to bother you, but what . . . ?
+ Sir, could you help me? How many . . . ?
+ Please, Mr. _____. Why . . . ?

These are just a few ways to start a question. Can you think of others?

If you begin a question with certain polite phrases like, "Could you tell me . . . ," "I was wondering . . . ," or "Do you know . . . " (Notice that these opening phrases all contain a subject and verb), in the rest of the sentence, the normal verb-subject order of questions is reversed. Thus,

When <u>does</u> the next <u>plane</u> <u>leave</u>? (auxiliary-subject-main verb)

becomes

Could you tell me when the next <u>plane</u> <u>leaves</u>? (subject-verb)

Here are three more examples:

+ Excuse me, but would you mind telling me where the nearest bank is?

+ Sir, I $\begin{Bmatrix} am \\ was \end{Bmatrix}$ wondering if you $\begin{Bmatrix} know \\ knew \end{Bmatrix}$ when the bank $\begin{Bmatrix} closes. \\ closed. \end{Bmatrix}$

+ Ma'am, would you be so kind as to tell me how often the Dallas flight leaves?

The third example ("Would you be so kind . . .") is very formal and is language that can best be described as *flowery*, meaning it is embarassingly elegant and showy. Sometimes this type of language makes a person appear a little snobbish or haughty (overly proud). You probably would not use this kind of language with your friends, but it's good to be able to recognize it when you hear it.

PRACTICE 4

Try to begin each of these questions with some courteous opening.

> **EXAMPLE:** *To a bus driver:*
>
> <u>Pardon me,</u> but does this bus stop at 5th Avenue and Jackson Street?

1. To a female salesclerk:

    _____, do you know where I can find men's belts and shoes?

2. To a taxi driver:

    _____, about how much is it going to cost to go to the Bank Street Hotel?

3. To your teacher:

    _____ why the past perfect is used instead of the simple past in this sentence?

4. To a bank teller:

_____, what is my checking account
balance°?

5. To your waiter:

_____ how the Chicken Surprise is prepared?

Finally, when you have received the information, you should thank the
person politely. And if you don't hear part of the information or think you
may have heard it incorrectly, don't hesitate to ask the person to repeat it.
If the person realizes you are not a native speaker of English, he or she will
usually try to help you by speaking more slowly or by giving you more
careful, clearer answers.

SITUATIONAL DIALOGS   In the following dialogs you can see how people
ask for certain information and how they respond when it is provided.
Choose partners and take roles. Then, discuss the questions or do the tasks
at the end of the dialogs.

> A. *Yoko is eager to get to New York City to meet a friend for the weekend,
> so she asks the airline clerk at Eastern to give her some information.*

Yoko: Excuse me, but could you tell me when the next plane for
New York leaves?

Clerk: The New York **shuttle°** leaves every hour, so the next one
is in 20 minutes—at 6:00.

Yoko: How much is a second class ticket, please?

Clerk: We have only one class of ticket; it's $65 one way.

Yoko: Okay. I'd like one for the next flight.

Clerk: I'm sorry, but I don't sell shuttle tickets. You can get one
from the machine over there or wait till you **board°** and
buy one from the airline attendant.

Yoko: Oh, I didn't know you could do that. What is the gate
number?

The **balance** is the amount of money in your account at a particular time.
A **shuttle** is a vehicle (airplane, in this case) that goes back and forth on a regular
route at frequent intervals.
Board means "get on a plane" (or train or bus).

Clerk: Five. Down the hall behind you and to the right.
Yoko: Thank you very much.
Clerk: My pleasure. Have a nice trip.

What Do You Think?

1. *What information questions does Yoko ask? Does she receive all the information she needs?*
2. *When Yoko asks the gate number, the clerk tells her, and then gives her more information. What question might she have asked to get this information?*
3. *Think of some questions Yoko might ask the airline attendant when she boards the plane. Write and act out a short dialog between Yoko and the flight attendant in which Yoko asks at least four information questions.*

B. *Ali has never been to a zoo before, so he has a lot of questions to ask his friend David.*

Ali: I've never seen that animal before, David. What is it?
David: It's a reindeer. We have some in North America.
Ali: Where do they live?
David: In cold places like Alaska and Canada.
Ali: How much do you think it weighs?
David: I bet it weighs 400 or 500 pounds. It has some big antlers, too.
Ali: Antlers? You mean those things that look like tree branches?
David: Yeah. Male reindeer have them. They're horns. Haven't you ever seen animals with horns before?
Ali: Only in pictures.

What Do You Think?

1. *David begins his answer about the reindeer's weight with* I bet. *How is he using this expression? What is another meaning of* I bet? *Are they related? If so, how?*
2. *Change the first part of the dialog slightly so that Ali addresses a stranger next to him at the zoo. How might Ali have phrased his first question a little differently?*
3. *Continue the dialog so that Ali asks David a few more information questions about the reindeer or another animal he sees.*

C. *Saleh is baking a cake. His roommate Carl is watching TV.*

Saleh: Sorry to bother you, Carl, but could I ask you a question about this recipe?

Carl: Sure. What is it?

Saleh: It says to use a whisk to mix all the cake ingredients. What's a whisk?

Carl: It's a small wire kitchen utensil used for beating eggs and mixing things. I don't have one.

Saleh: Well, what should I use?

Carl: A fork or a spoon will be fine, I'm sure.

Saleh: Okay. One more thing. Where do you keep the cinnamon?

Carl: It should be in the cabinet to the left of the stove on the second shelf.

Saleh: Thanks. Sorry to disturb you.

What Do You Think?

1. *Saleh doesn't interrupt Carl abruptly with his question. What does he do first? In what other ways could he have done this?*

2. *What does Saleh mean by* Okay. One more thing? *Change this into a complete sentence or question.*

3. *Add a little more to the dialog so that Saleh asks Carl a few more information questions—one beginning with* what *and another with* how.

   D.   *Lillian and Martha are discussing their vacation plans for the beach.*

Lillian: When do you want to leave, Martha?

Martha: I'm not sure yet, but maybe we should leave Friday after work. It's a long drive, but I'd rather get there late Friday than midday Saturday.

Lillian: How long is it?

Martha: Five or six hours.

Lillian: What are you going to take?

Martha: Mostly shorts and T-shirts. I think I'll take a couple of pairs of pants and maybe one dress.

Lillian: You don't think it's going to be cool at night?

Martha: Well, a little chilly maybe. I'm going to take a sweater or a light jacket—just in case.

What Do You Think?

1. *How else could Martha have answered the question "How long is it?"*

2. *By phrasing the question in the negative ("You don't think it's going to be cool at night?"), what is Lillian implying? What's the difference between "Do you think it's . . . ?" and "You don't think it's . . . ?"?*

3. *Add a little more to the dialog so that Lillian asks two more information questions about the trip—one beginning with* how much *and the other with* why.

E. *Brenda and Claudia have just arrived at a party and are looking around.*

Brenda: Do you know many people, Claudia?
Claudia: Only a few. Oh, I see Amin!
Brenda: Where?
Claudia: Over there by the kitchen door. He's talking to a pretty girl.
Brenda: Who is she?
Claudia: I don't know. I'm sure I've seen her before, but I can't place her.
Brenda: She looks familiar to me, too. Maybe she's in the Intensive English Program.
Claudia: Maybe. Let's go over and introduce ourselves.
Brenda: Do you think we should? They seem really involved right now.

What Do You Think?

1. *What does Claudia mean by* I can't place her? *What other way(s) could she have expressed the same idea?*
2. *Why does Brenda hesitate when Claudia suggests they go over to Amin and the girl and introduce themselves? What does Brenda mean when she says, "They seem really involved right now"?*
3. *Add to the dialog so that Brenda asks Claudia some questions about Amin, and then the two girls go over to Amin and his friend and introduce themselves.*

DIALOG COMPLETIONS
Choose partners, take roles, and complete these dialogs. Supply the missing lines that ask for information or provide the necessary responses to the questions. If you don't have real answers to all the questions, just use your imagination and try to think of answers that might be appropriate. When you have finished, switch roles and try to complete the dialogs a little differently.

1. *At a grocery store:*

Joe:
Clerk: Yes, we do. They're in the dairy section next to the cheese and milk.

Joe:
Clerk: No, I'm sorry, we don't. Raspberries aren't **in season**° now.

In season (used with fresh foods) means "ready for eating."

2. At the supermarket:

Frank:
Cashier: Yes, but we require two forms of identification.
Frank:
Cashier: Visa and Mastercard.
Frank:
Cashier: The total is $35.73.

3. At a department store:

Aziz:
Clerk: No, I'm sorry, we don't. Perhaps you can find them at a sporting goods store.
Aziz:
Clerk: There's one on the corner of Millwood Drive and Devine Street, near the high school.
Aziz:
Clerk: My pleasure. Sorry we couldn't help you.

4. At a theater **box office°:**

Samar:
Attendant: At 9:15.
Samar:
Attendant: $4.50 for adults and $2.00 for children twelve and under.
Samar:
Attendant: 115 minutes.
Samar:

5. At a drugstore:

Nora:
Pharmacist: I would suggest you buy this cough medicine: Cough-ease.
Nora:
Pharmacist: It's less expensive than the other brands, and it's just as effective.
Nora:
Pharmacist: You'll find it on the second aisle near the side door.

A **box office** is the small booth outside or just inside a theater or stadium, where tickets are sold.

6. *At a restaurant:*

Waiter: Excuse me, sir. What kind of salad dressing would you like?

Man:

Waiter: No, I'm afraid we don't. We have Italian and French.

Man:

Waiter:

Man: Just water, please. I'll have coffee later.

7. *At a noisy party:*

Abdulla: Excuse me for interrupting, but is there someplace I can go to make a private phone call?

Hostess:

Abdulla:

Hostess: It's up the stairs—the second door on your right.

Abdulla:

8. *In a classroom:*

Marie:

Instructor: Of course, I'll be glad to answer any question.

Marie:

Instructor:

9. *At an art gallery:*

Sara:

Stranger: Yes?

Sara:

Stranger: She's a local artist from a small town near here, I think, but I'm not positive. Perhaps the person at the front desk will know.

Sara:

Stranger: I'm not sure. There's a price list on the front desk.

10. *At a restaurant:*

Chen:

Waiter: No, I'm sorry. We don't **carry**° Shredded Wheat. Would you like another kind?

Chen:

Carry means (in this situation) "sell" or "have in stock."

Waiter: Rice Krispies, Corn Flakes, and Product 19.

Chen:

Waiter: Fine. Would you care for strawberries or bananas with your cereal?

Chen:

ROLE PLAYS   Choose partners, take roles, and create a role play for each situation described. Each one will require you and your partner to ask for specific information and then respond to the questions. When you have finished, exchange roles and create new dialogs for each situation.

1. Claude is downtown, looking for a shoe repair store. He sees a police officer and asks for help.

2. Napoleon is at a post office and wants to mail a package to his brother in Venezuela. He asks a postal clerk for some information.

3. Valerie is in a large department store and needs some help picking out a tie for her father. The clerk offers to assist her.

4. Diego is in a jewelry store and wants to make an expensive purchase, but he doesn't have enough cash. Diego asks the salesclerk about methods of payment.

5. Jamal would like to plan a trip across the United States by car. He asks a travel agent some questions to help him plan his trip.

6. Diana is in a job interview with a large company, and the interviewer asks if she has any questions. She does.

7. Rana is at the Greyhound Bus station and wants to know the time schedule for buses leaving for Miami, the cost, the time it takes to get there, and other important information. She asks the ticket seller.

8. Ina is watching a TV program with her American roommate, Karen, and has some questions about the characters and what's happening in the show.

9. Aziz is in a restaurant and wants to know what special accommodations it has for young children (**high chairs**,° special children's menus, etc.), so he asks the waitress some questions.

10. Yoko is in a large, modern supermarket that is supposed to have a variety of foods from all over the world. She is looking for several specific foods from her country, but she can't find them. She asks one of the clerks to help her.

High chairs are chairs for very young children. Such chairs have long legs and special trays for holding food.

REAL **PEOPLE,** REAL **SITUATIONS,** REAL **LANGUAGE**

A. Go out into your work, school, or social community (or use the telephone) and ask these people information questions based on the following clues. Use the journal entry format to record your questions and the people's responses in your notebook.

1. Ask a theater box office worker

    a. the cost of the early show versus the evening show
    b. the names of movies now playing
    c. the length of time for one of the movies

2. Ask a telephone company worker

    a. how to pay a phone bill (methods of payment)
    b. the cost to rent a push button telephone
    c. the area code for Tacoma, Washington

3. Ask a postal worker

    a. the zip code for Bluefield, West Virginia
    b. the cost to send a postcard in the United States
    c. the differences in cost and time to send a package first class and second class

4. Ask a stranger on the street

    a. the time
    b. the location of the nearest bank
    c. change for a dollar

5. Ask a salesperson in the men's department of a large store

    a. the location of umbrellas
    b. the brands (names or kinds) of jeans sold there
    c. the average cost of athletic socks

B. You are interested in renting an apartment. You see the advertisement at the top of page 86 in the newspaper and want to find out more information about the apartment. You have a dog and want a big backyard. You want to rent the apartment for only six months. You don't want to have to pay a big deposit. You call the number and ask at least five questions about it. Choose a partner to act as the person who has the apartment for rent.

FOR RENT

Beautiful 1 BR apt. near university. Quiet neighborhood. AC. Utilities included.$400/ month Call 334-5987.

1. _____

_____

2. _____

_____

3. _____

_____

4. _____

_____

5. _____

_____

C. You're in a sandwich shop, looking at the menu on page 87. You have several questions to ask the waiter about how the food is prepared, what is served with each item, and other concerns. Choose a partner to play the waiter and act out a short play, using this menu as the basis. Ask at least five questions.

1. _____

_____

2. _____

_____

SAM'S SANDWICH SHOP

All sandwiches served on whole wheat, onion roll, or pita bread. Choice of french fries or potato salad.

- **Chicken Salad**-*tender chicken, seedless grapes, apples, & pecans* $3.95

- **Turkey International**-*sliced turkey w/melted Swiss cheese* $3.50

- **Shrimp Salad**-*tiny bay shrimps, Dijon mustard, celery, & walnuts* 4.95

- **Hot Roast Beef**-*lean roast beef, melted cheese, horseradish dressing* $3.95

Soup of the day $1.25

Cole slaw $1.00

3. _____

_____

4. _____

_____

5. _____

_____

CHAPTER 6

GIVING DIRECTIONS AND INSTRUCTIONS

You learned how to ask for directions and instructions in the last chapter, "Asking for Information," because you begin such requests the same way you begin requests for information. For example,

- ♣ Excuse me. How do you get to the library from here?
- ♣ Pardon me, but could you tell me how to load this camera?
- ♣ Uh, sir, would you mind telling me where the nearest bank is located and how to get there?

But how do you respond when someone comes up to you and asks you for directions or instructions? This chapter will discuss both topics, but we'll start with ways to offer directions first.

Giving Directions

There are many specific expressions we use when directing someone to a particular place. First, we usually use simple commands (the imperative form), as in

- ♣ Walk two blocks west.
- ♣ Turn right.
- ♣ Drive south for three miles, then follow the signs to Lake Wylie.
- ♣ Stop at the third house.
- ♣ Look for a store that sells groceries.

Or sometimes we might add *you*: "You walk two blocks west, and then you turn right."

Many special words and expressions deal with geographical location and position. They have been arranged here according to how they function in a sentence or a simple command. Here are some verbs commonly used when giving directions to a place. Can you think of others?

• go	• turn	• take (a left)	• head for
• walk	• get on/off	• look	• stop
• drive	• continue	• stop	• keep + VERB + ing (going)
• _____	• _____	• _____	

Now let's examine some set spatial expressions we often use when describing a location or position. Notice that many of them *are* prepositions or prepositional phrases or *contain* them:

• near	• on the opposite side of (the street from)
• between	• around the corner from
• next to/beside	• on your left/right (-hand side)
• in front of	• on the corner (of)
• behind	• on (street name)
• across from	• _____
• **adjacent to°**	• _____
• to the left/right	• _____

Adjacent to means "very close; touching or almost touching."

Look at Map 1 and notice how some of the expressions below it are used to show location, position, and relationship.

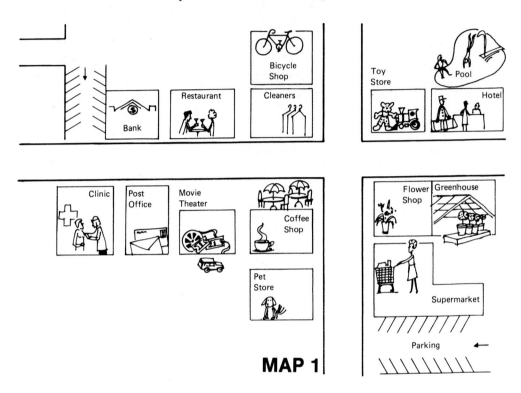

MAP 1

The pet store is *beside/next to* the coffee shop.
The movie theater is *between* the post office and the coffee shop.
The coffee shop is *across from/across the street from* the cleaners.
A parking lot is *adjacent to* the bank.

PRACTICE 1

Now you try it. Using the same map, fill in the blanks with some of the words and expressions previously listed. You may be able to use more than one expression to indicate the location.

1. The pet store is _____ the movie theater.

2. The toy store is _____ the cleaners.

3. The bank is _____ the restaurant.

4. The car is _____the movie theater.

5. The toy store is _____ the flower shop.

PRACTICE 2

Now write a sentence that tells the location or the relationship of one place to another, using the same map.

> **EXAMPLE:** toy store/hotel   *The toy store is next to the hotel.*

1. post office/movie theater _____

2. **greenhouse°**/flower shop _____

3. pool/hotel _____

4. restaurant/bicycle shop _____

5. tables and chairs/coffee shop _____

   When we're giving both directions and instructions, we often want to indicate chronological (time) order; we do this by using certain transitional devices or connectives, such as the following:

- first (second, third, etc.)
- next
- after that
- then
- now
- afterward
- finally
- _____
- _____
- _____

   Some other nouns and miscellaneous words and expressions you might need in directing people to places are as follows:

- intersection ("at the intersection of _____ and _____"—street names)
- crosswalk
- traffic light/signal

A **greenhouse** is a building made of glass, used for growing plants that need special conditions: sunlight, heat, and so on.

- stop sign
- corner
- block ("Walk 3 blocks" or "It's 3 blocks from . . . . ")
- parallel (streets run like ========)
- perpendicular (streets run like ___⊥___)
- dead end (when the street ends and there's no way to get out without turning around; also called "no outlet")
- uptown/downtown (usually no distinction made between them except in a few cities, like New York, that have specific sections: Uptown, Downtown, Midtown)
- north/south/east/west
- _____
- _____

Finally, when you have given the directions, you might say something to indicate you've finished:

- ✤ You can't miss it!
- ✤ You'll run right into it! (You'll drive or walk right up to it.)
- ✤ You'll see it immediately.
- ✤ It's right there.
- ✤ _____
- ✤ _____
- ✤ _____

PRACTICE 3

Look at Map 2 on page 93 and tell a stranger how to get from one place to another, according to the clues.

EXAMPLE: *From Mary's Dress Shop to the Methodist Church*

If you leave Mary's Dress Shop by the 5th Street exit, turn right onto 5th Street and go through the intersection and up one block to Oak Street. Take a right onto Oak and walk one block. Then turn left onto 4th Street, and the Methodist Church is the first building on your right, next to a parking lot. You can't miss it!

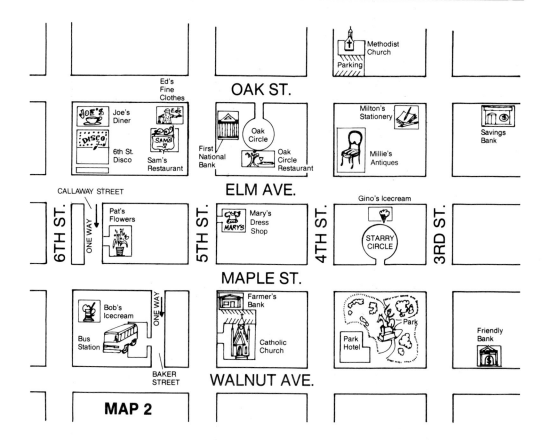

1. From Friendly Bank to Oak Circle Restaurant

2. From Millie's **Antiques**° to the Catholic Church

Antiques   are pieces of furniture, jewelry, and other items that are old and becoming rare and valuable.

3.   From Sam's Restaurant to Gino's Icecream Parlor

4.   From Gino's Icecream Parlor to the 6th Street Disco

5.   From the Savings Bank to Mary's Dress Shop

PRACTICE 4

Choose a partner and use the same map. This time, pretend you are at the Park Hotel on Walnut Avenue and you need directions to the following places. Create a short conversation between yourself and your partner. If you don't understand any part of the directions, ask your partner to repeat it.

1.   Directions to Oak Circle Restaurant

2. Directions to Milton's Stationery Store

3. Directions to Pat's Flower Shop

4. Directions to the First National Bank

5. Directions to the bus station

Giving Instructions

Giving instructions involves using the same basic form (simple commands) as that of giving directions. We also use the same transitional devices or connectives to indicate time order. We give instructions to people when we want to tell them how to do or make something. For example, if Dean were telling a friend how to turn on his stereo, he might say:

> First, plug in the stereo. Then press the "power" button and hold it down firmly until a green light appears. Next, select the equipment you want to play: the radio, the tape player, the record player, or the television. Turn the switch to the proper one. If you want to play a record, put it on the turntable and press "start." If you want to play a cassette, insert the cassette face-up, close the door, and press "start." If you want to play the radio or TV, select the proper channel. After that, adjust the volume and enjoy the entertainment.

Notice the time-order transitions used in the instructions: *first, then, next, after that.* Each of these words helps move the instructions along smoothly.

PRACTICE 5

Here are some simple, everyday situations. Be as detailed as possible and give instructions on how to

1. change a light bulb

2. cook pasta

3. clean a bathroom

4. wash a car

5. make a tossed salad

SITUATIONAL DIALOGS   Choose partners, take roles, and read and act out the following conversations that illustrate giving (and asking for) directions and instructions. Then answer the questions and/or respond to the instructions that follow.

A.   A stranger stops and asks Paula where the nearest drugstore is.

Stranger: Excuse me. Could you give me some directions?
Paula: What are you looking for?
Stranger: A drugstore, and I don't have a car.
Paula: Well, there's one about five blocks away on Elliott Street.

Stranger: How do I get there?

Paula: Walk straight ahead until you come to the second traffic light. Then turn right.

Stranger: Do you know the name of the street?

Paula: I can't remember, but it's the second light. Turn right and the drugstore will be on your left about two blocks down. It's next to a bank. I don't think you'll have any trouble spotting it.

Stranger: Thanks a lot. I appreciate it.

What Do You Think?

1. *Why do you think the stranger adds "and I don't have a car"? What meaning is relayed by that statement?*
2. *What other ways could Paula have asked, "What are you looking for?"?*
3. *Draw a simple map of these directions to show you understand them.*

B. *Mr. and Mrs. Mason are leaving their one-year-old daughter with Belinda, their* **baby-sitter°**.

Belinda: Mrs. Mason, before you go, do you want to give me any special instructions about Jennifer?

Mrs. Mason: Just a few. First, give her her bottle in about an hour. Warm it for three minutes and test it to make sure it's not too hot. Then put her down, and she should sleep till we return. Leave the light on in her room, though.

Belinda: What if she wakes up?

Mrs. Mason: Just pick her up and hold or rock her. She hasn't slept much today, so I don't expect she'll wake up after you put her down.

Belinda: Okay. That doesn't sound too difficult.

What Do You Think?

1. *Underline all the verbs used in simple commands.*
2. *What transitions are used to help establish proper order in the instructions?*
3. Put (someone/something) down *usually means "to place or move (someone/something) to a particular place." But* put a baby down *has a special (but related) meaning. Can you tell what it is by its use in the dialog?*

A **baby-sitter** is a person who takes care of the children while the parents are away (usually for a fee).

C.   *Anton has never used a pay phone before. He needs help in making a local call, so he asks his friend David.*

Anton: David, would you mind showing me how to use a pay phone? I need to call Omar.
David: Sure. It's easy.
Anton: What do I do first?
David: First, **pick up the receiver°** and then put a quarter in the slot at the top. You can use any combination of coins as long as it totals 25 cents—but no pennies.
Anton: Okay. Then what?
David: Next, listen to make sure you have a dial tone. If you do, dial the number—or I guess I should say, push the numbered buttons. Very few phones have rotary dials nowadays. Most are pushbutton—especially pay phones. For a local call, don't dial the area code—just the seven-digit number. Got it?
Anton: That sounds easy enough. Thanks a lot.

What Do You Think?

   1.   List all the imperative verbs used in the instructions. Then list any transitions used by David or Anton to help order or move the instructions along.
   2.   What does David mean by Got it? *What is another way he could have expressed the same thought?*
   3.   What is a dial tone? How does it sound? What does a busy signal sound like?

   D.   *A young boy is standing on a street corner, examining a map and looking confused. Martin walks up to him.*

Martin: You look a little lost. Can I help you?
  Boy: I wish you could. I'm trying to find St. Joseph's Cathedral. I know it's around here someplace.
Martin: It's not too far. Just walk up this street you're on for six blocks or so, and when you come to Henley Avenue, take a right. Go one block, and then turn left. The cathedral will be on your left about halfway down the block.
  Boy: Did you say right or left on Henley?
Martin: Right. Then one block and take a left. It'll be on your left in the middle of the block.

Pick up the receiver means to "take the phone (the piece that you put up to your ear—the receiver) off the hook (the piece that cradles or holds the receiver)."

Boy: I think I can find it. Thanks for your help.
Martin: Don't mention it.

What Do You Think?

1. *Martin uses the expression* or so *in* "*walk . . . six blocks or so.*" *What does it mean? What other ways could he have said the same thing?*
2. *What are other ways the boy could have said,* "I know it's around here somewhere"?
3. *Draw a simple map to illustrate these directions.*

E. *Lauren is walking around the exercise class, making sure everyone is doing the exercises correctly. She notices Diego is having a little trouble.*

Lauren: Here, Diego. Watch me. Sit on your left hip and bend your left leg under you. Extend your right leg.
Diego: Like this?
Lauren: Yeah—but lift your body up and out. Don't lean back. There you go. Now slowly raise your right leg about eight inches off the floor. No! Slowly, Diego. Not so fast. It's not doing as much for your legs and hips if you move your leg too fast.
Diego: Should I be on one arm like this?
Lauren: Yes, that's right. Try to lift your body higher, though. Pull out. Tighten your stomach. Keep your right leg straight.

What Do You Think?

1. *List all the verbs used in simple commands. Are there any you don't know?*
2. *What does the expression* There you go *mean, and how should it be spoken? What times might you use it?*
3. *Write your own set of instructions on how to do a certain exercise that you've done before.*

DIALOG COMPLETIONS   Choose a partner, take roles, and complete the following dialogs, giving (or occasionally asking for) directions or instructions. When you finish, trade roles and try them again, changing the words and phrases you use. Be sure to read the dialogs all the way through before trying to complete them because there may be clues to help you respond.

1. *Barney can't find any place to park his car downtown. All the parking lots and spaces are filled. He sees a police officer and asks for help.*

Barney: Excuse me, but do you know if there are any other public parking lots nearby?

Officer:

Barney: How do I get there?

Officer:

Barney: And what do I do after I turn left at the second intersection?

Officer:

Barney: I'm sorry. I didn't understand you. How many blocks?

Officer:

Barney: Oh, I see. Thanks a lot for the directions.

2. *Gerald has just started working for a large company and has not toured the building yet. He wants to know where the cafeteria is, so he asks his secretary.*

Gerald: Excuse me, Carl, could you direct me to the cafeteria?

Carl:

Gerald: The elevator is on the east or the west side?

Carl:

Gerald: Which floor?

Carl:

Gerald: Okay. Thanks. I'll find it.

3. *Melanie is leaving for a week's vacation. Nora has graciously agreed to take care of Melanie's house for her.*

Melanie: I really appreciate your offering to look after my house while I'm gone, Nora.

Nora:

Melanie: Yes, I do need to tell you a few things.

Nora: Okay. I'll make a list.

Melanie:

Nora: How often should I water them?

Melanie:

Nora: Which lights?

Melanie:

Nora: Okay. No problem. What else should I do?

Melanie:

Nora: How do I lock it?

Melanie:

4. *Margot has asked Ahmed to drive her home from work. He agrees but doesn't know the way, so she must give him directions as they go.*

Ahmed: You'll have to tell me how to get there, Margot. I'm not at all familiar with this side of town. Should I stay on Sanford Drive?

Margot:

Ahmed: Well, how do I get there?

Margot:

(Later)

Ahmed: When do I turn?

Margot:

Ahmed: Keep straight? I thought you said I should turn right?

Margot:

Ahmed: Oh, I see.

Margot:

Ahmed: Where?

Margot:

Ahmed: Next to the yellow house?

Margot:

Ahmed: Well, at least I got you here **safe and sound**°. It would have been a lot easier if it had been daylight.

5. *Ali goes to the doctor, complaining of a sore throat, fever, and headaches. The doctor gives him some instructions on what to do.*

Doctor:

    Ali: Well, what should I do, Doctor?

Doctor:

    Ali: You mean I can't go to work?

Doctor:

    Ali: For how long?

Doctor:

    Ali: What should I eat?

Doctor:

    Ali: Soup? I really don't like soup. Can't I eat something else?

Doctor:

    Ali: What about to drink?

Doctor:

    Ali: Okay. Anything else I should or shouldn't do?

Safe and sound means "completely unharmed." Another idiom with the same meaning is *All in one piece*.

Doctor:
   Ali: How many and how many times a day?
Doctor:
   Ali: Okay, Doctor. I sure hope I can remember all that.

6.   *Bassim is taking the bus to the university from his apartment for the first time. A neighbor gives him instructions.*

Bassim: First, where is the bus stop, Sam?
   Sam:
Bassim: Okay. I have the time schedule. I just need to know how to transfer and where to get off.
   Sam:
Bassim: I have to have exact change? Can't I buy a monthly or weekly ticket?
   Sam:
Bassim: Okay. I understand. Where do I get off first?
   Sam:
Bassim: And which bus should I take next?
   Sam:
Bassim: That's all I have to do? Show the driver my ticket?
   Sam:
Bassim: I'll be fine after that. I just wait till I get to the university. Oh—one more thing. How do I let the driver know when I want to get off?
   Sam:
Bassim: Thanks. That sounds easy.

7.   *John returns home one night to find that his apartment has been robbed. He goes next door to ask David, an American friend, what to do.*

John: So what should I do, David? I know that at least my stereo and computer were taken. Maybe other things, too.
David: First you have to notify the police and file a report.
John: File a report? Is that difficult?
David:
John: Will the police come to my house and inspect it?
David:
John: Okay. I'll do that.
David:
John: The insurance company? Why?
David:

John: All right. Is there anything else I should do?
David:

8.   *Heinz has offered to take care of Mr. Hudson's dog while he is away on vacation. Before he leaves, Mr. Hudson gives Heinz some instructions.*

Mr. Hudson:
    Heinz: Oh, I don't mind at all. Just tell me what to do.
Mr. Hudson:
    Heinz: And where do you keep the dog food?
Mr. Hudson:
    Heinz: Could you explain her feeding schedule again? I didn't quite get it.
Mr. Hudson:
    Heinz: Okay. I see. And how often should I take her out for a walk?
Mr. Hudson:
    Heinz: All right. Anything else I need to know?
Mr. Hudson:
    Heinz: Okay. I can handle it from here.

9.   *Nancy is explaining how to do an exercise to Romulo.*

Romulo:
  Nancy: No, Romulo. Don't bend your legs. Keep them straight—as straight as you can. Tighten your stomach muscles when you lift up. Keep your lower back flat on the floor.
Romulo:
  Nancy: No, don't come up so much. Lift slowly and without straining your lower back. Press it to the floor.
Romulo:
  Nancy: Yes, that's right. Now come up a little higher and reach a little further.
Romulo:
  Nancy: That's exactly right. Good work!

10.   *Ken is trying to learn how to set his new watch. The written instructions are confusing, so he asks Jean, a friend and neighbor, to help.*

Ken: I really need some help, Jean. Can you help me set my watch?

Jean:
Ken: Here they are, but I don't understand them at all.
Jean:
Ken: Push which button? There are four—one in each corner.
Jean:
Ken: Okay. I did that. What next?
Jean:
Ken: All right. How many times do I push it?
Jean:
Ken: For how long?
Jean:
Ken: Okay. I think it's set. Thanks a lot, Jean.

ROLE PLAYS
Here are some situations involving directions and instructions. Choose partners, take roles, and act out these role plays, using some of the words and expressions from the chapter. When you finish, change roles and try to create new dialogs.

1. Paul's roommate doesn't know how to operate the new stereo he just bought. Paul instructs him carefully.

2. Barbara is having a costume part next Saturday. She gives her friends directions to the party and instructions on what to bring and wear.

3. A friend from overseas wants to come to the United States to study. Ali gives him instructions on how to get the proper passport, visa, and necessary papers.

4. Betty is in the library, and a new student asks her how to find the cafeteria. She gives him or her directions.

5. Frank made dinner for Laura and Sam, and they were very impressed with his cooking. They want him to instruct them on how to make a special dish from his country.

6. Elizabeth is away from home for the first time and suddenly finds herself having to do all kinds of things for herself. She asks a neighbor, Paula Harris, how to use coin washers and dryers.

7. Two friends who are coming to visit Dan next week are arriving by plane and renting a car at the airport. Dan gives them directions from the airport to his home.

8. A friend from Pedro's country has just arrived in the United States and needs some instructions on how to open a checking and/or savings account. Pedro helps him.

9. Laura's friend wants to sell his car, but he doesn't know anything about writing and placing an advertisement in the newspaper. She gives him some instructions.

10. Maria's cousin is coming to the United States to visit her for two weeks in August. Maria gives him instructions on what to bring.

REAL **PEOPLE,** REAL **SITUATIONS,** REAL **LANGUAGE**

A. Go out into your school, work, social community and ask people for directions or instructions for the following things. Have your notebook ready to record them as accurately as you can.

1. Ask a bank employee to explain to you how to use the 24-hour banking machine.
2. Ask a classmate or friend to give you directions to his or her house from the university or your workplace.
3. At a supermarket, ask a clerk how to pick out a ripe avocado or cantaloupe.
4. Ask a friend to give you instructions for making one of his or her favorite dishes.
5. At an appliance store, ask a clerk to give you instructions on how to operate an appliance, such as a microwave oven or a food processor.

B. Think about your own neighborhood and city in the United States. Answer the following questions by giving directions as accurately as possible.

1. How do you get from your residence to the university or the place you work?
2. Where is the closest shopping mall to you right now, and how do you get there?
3. How would someone find the nearest mailbox to your home?
4. From your school or workplace, where is the closest bank, and how do you get there?
5. How do you get from your home to your favorite restaurant?

CHAPTER 7

THANKING PEOPLE AND RESPONDING TO THANKS

Thanking people is an important part of every culture. We thank people for many things, including information, invitations, gifts, help or favors, and compliments. We express our gratitude (thanks) in many ways—from a very simple "Thanks" or "Thank you" to more elaborate or formal shows of gratitude like "Thank you ever so much for . . ." or "You have no idea how grateful I am for. . . ." Sincerity and tone of voice are vital parts of thanking someone. That person must realize that you mean what you say. So if you can offer very simple thanks with just a few words, a warm tone of voice, and a genuine smile—that's all it takes.

After you have been thanked for something, probably the simplest and most common response is "You're welcome." But there are many other ways to respond, too. Here are a few replies to "Thank you":

- ✤ It was my pleasure. (*Formal*)
- ✤ You're $\begin{Bmatrix} \text{very} \\ \text{more than} \end{Bmatrix}$ welcome. (*Formal*)
- ✤ Oh, it was the least I could do.
- ✤ Think nothing of it.
- ✤ It was nothing.
- ✤ My pleasure.
- ✤ Don't mention it.
- ✤ Any time. (*Informal*)
- ✤ No big deal. (*Informal*)
- ✤ _____
- ✤ _____

Now let's put the thanks and responses together. Below are five different categories of "thank you's," based on *what* we are thanking the person for. The very formal and informal ones are indicated as usual. Also included are some typical responses to or acknowledgements of the thanks.

Information or Directions

1. **A:** I want to thank you so much for the map and directions. You have no idea what a tremendous help you've been! (*Formal*)
   B: It was my pleasure. (*Formal*)

2. **A:** Thank you for all your help. I think I can find my way now.
   B: You're welcome. Good luck.

3. **A:** Thanks a lot for the information. I really appreciate it.
   B: Oh, you're very welcome. Any time.

4. **A:** Thanks for taking the time to explain it to me. I hope it wasn't too much of a bother.
   B: Not at all. It was the least I could do.

5. **A:** Thanks a million for the **info**!° (*Informal*)
   B: You bet! Any time (*Informal*)

Info is very informal for "information."

PRACTICE 1

Following are the information or directions that have been given by certain persons. Choose a partner, thank the person, and respond to the thanks.

EXAMPLE: *A police officer gave you directions to the driver's license bureau.*

You: *Thank you for your help, officer. I think I can find my way now.*

Officer: *I'm glad I was able to help.*

1. A travel agent gave you information about airfares to, and hotels in, Los Angeles.
   You:
   Travel agent:

2. Your teacher explained the past perfect tense to you after class.
   You:
   Teacher:

3. A bank worker gave you information about applying for a major credit card.
   You:
   Bank worker:

4. Your roommate gave you directions to the new disco.
   You:
   Roommate:

5. A gas station attendant gave you directions to a German restaurant nearby.
   You:
   Gas station attendant:

Invitations   Whether you accept or decline an invitation (for more information, see Chapter 8), you should always thank the person sincerely for inviting you. Notice that the person who has made the invitation doesn't usually respond with a "You're welcome" *unless* the thank you comes at the end of a comment. For example, in 4, the person replies "You're welcome" because the first person ends the comment with "Thanks for the invite." The same is true in 5, where the person ends the comment with "Thank you for the invitation." The next words of the reply are "It's my pleasure."

1. **A:** Many thanks for inviting me to your dinner party, Mrs. Gray, but I'm afraid I won't be able to come because of **a previous commitment**.° (*Formal*)

   B: Oh, I'm sorry to hear that. We certainly will miss you. (*Formal*)

2. **A:** Thanks, Anne! I'd love to go to the beach this Saturday!

   B: Great! I know we'll have fun!

3. **A:** I appreciate the invitation, Tom. Of course I'll come!

   B: Good! The play starts at 8:00, so I'll pick you up at 7:30. Okay?

4. **A:** Sure! I've been wanting to go to a soccer game. Thanks for the **invite**!°

   B: You're welcome. I'm glad you can come.

5. **A:** What a fantastic idea! I've been **dying**° to see them in concert for a long time! Thanks for the invitation.

   B: It's my pleasure!

PRACTICE 2

You've been given invitations by the following people. Reject or accept each invitation as indicated, but also thank the person sincerely. Then have your partner respond.

> **EXAMPLE:** *José, who's in your exercise class, wants you to have dinner with him tomorrow night after class. (Reject)*

You: *Thanks for inviting me, José, but I've already made other plans.*

José: *That's too bad. Maybe another time.*

1. Your roommate wants you to go with him or her to a basketball game tonight. (Reject)

   You:

   Roommate:

A previous (or *prior*) **commitment** is an appointment or obligation made before this one.

Invite is an informal reduction of "invitation."

Dying is very informal for "very eager."

2. An acquaintance from work asks you to have a drink together after work. (Accept)
   You:
   Acquaintance:

3. An American family you know well wants you to go with them on a picnic Sunday. (Accept)
   You:
   Mr. Oliver:

4. A friend from the university invites you to dinner at his home tonight. (Reject)
   You:
   Friend:

5. Your boyfriend/girlfriend asks you to go to the Billy Joel concert in two weeks. (Accept)
   You:
   Friend:

Gifts

Here are some examples of showing gratitude for gifts received and responses to the thanks.

1. **A:** Thank you very much for the beautiful book, Mr. Kincaid. It was very nice of you to remember my birthday. (*Formal*)
   B: It was the least I could do. I hope you enjoy it.

2. **A:** The flowers are gorgeous! Thanks a lot, Bob!
   B: Don't mention it. Happy **anniversary**!°

3. **A:** That was nice of you to bring us the **coffee cake**,° Sarah. We'll really enjoy it for breakfast in the morning!
   B: Oh, it was nothing! I hope you like it.

4. **A:** Wally, the bracelet is beautiful, but really, **you shouldn't have**!°
   B: You're welcome. I think it looks beautiful on you.

An **anniversary** is a day that is the exact number of years after something has happened (for example, a wedding anniversary).

Coffee cake is a sweet pastry with nuts and spices, sometimes eaten for breakfast.

You shouldn't have is an informal reduction for "You shouldn't have done it (bought me this bracelet)."

5. **A:** Doris, these vegetables look fantastic! And you know what a salad eater I am. Thanks **a zillion!**°

   B: Any time! There are a lot more in my garden, so I'll bring you more later.

PRACTICE 3

You just received a gift from a person for the reason mentioned. Thank each one appropriately and have your partner respond.

> **EXAMPLE:** *A sports watch from your roommate for your birthday*
>
> **You:** *Oh, it's just what I wanted, Marie! Thanks a million!*
>
> **Marie:** *You're welcome. I hope you enjoy it.*

1. A cake from your next-door neighbor to welcome you to the neighborhood (you've just moved in)
   You:
   Neighbor:

2. A magazine subscription to *Newsweek* from your uncle as a graduation gift
   You:
   Uncle:

3. A plant from your friend as a **"get-well" gift**°
   You:
   Friend:

4. A T-shirt from your friend as a congratulations gift for losing ten pounds
   You:
   Friend:

5. A book of love poems from your girlfriend or boyfriend for **Valentine's Day**°
   You:
   Friend:

A zillion is a very large number (imaginary); it means "a lot."
A get-well gift is a small present (flowers or a book, for example) given to a sick person.
Valentine's Day (February 14) honors Saint Valentine and is a day for sending valentines (hearts), candy, flowers, and gifts to the ones we love.

Help or Favors

Saying "thanks" is a common and expected courtesy after receiving help or favors.

1. **A:** Janice, you're a lifesaver! I don't know what I would have done if you hadn't helped me make the decorations for the party! Thanks so much!
   B: Oh, it was nothing. I'm glad I could help out.

2. **A:** Thanks for working with me on the computer, Bob. I'd been struggling with it for over an hour before you came along.
   B: Don't worry about it. I enjoyed helping you.

3. **A:** Thanks for helping with the dinner, Joe. I really appreciate it.
   B: It was the least I could do! Thanks for inviting me over.

4. **A:** Thanks a million for lending me your car, Ted. That was a big help!
   B: I'm glad I could help. Let me know if you need to borrow it again.

5. **A:** You're so nice to help with the broken lamp, Don. I'm no good at mechanical things.
   B: You're welcome. I'm glad I was able to fix it.

PRACTICE 4

You have received the following help or favor from a person. Thank each one sincerely, and then let your partner respond politely to the thanks.

EXAMPLE: *Your American roommate has helped you with your homework.*

You: *Kerry, I can't thank you enough for the help you've given me. I understand the journal article a lot better now.*

Roommate: *I'm glad to hear that. Let me know if you have any more questions.*

1. Your brother has folded and put away your laundry for you.
   You:
   Brother:

2. Your friend from work has taken some calls for you while you've been at lunch.
    You:
    Friend:

3. Your neighbor has looked after your house, collected your newspapers and mail, and fed your cat while you've been on vacation for a week.
    You:
    Neighbor:

4. A stranger has helped you change a flat tire.
    You:
    Stranger:

5. Your roommate has washed all the dishes after dinner, even though it was your turn to do it.
    You:
    Roommate:

Compliments

Although we do thank people for compliments (see Chapter 12), the person does not usually respond with a "You're welcome" after being thanked.

1. **A:** That's a beautiful necklace you're wearing.
    B: Thanks. I got it in Mexico last summer.

2. **A:** What a gorgeous flower arrangement! It's really beautiful!
    B: That's nice of you to say so. I'm really glad you like it.

3. **A:** Would you sing some more, Christos? That last song was lovely!
    B: Thank you, Mrs. Jenkins. I'm glad you enjoyed it.

4. **A:** That chicken dish was fantastic, Mahmood! You are a great cook!
    B: I appreciate the compliment, but I did have a lot of help from my sister!

5. **A:** Yumi, you did a beautiful job decorating your home. It looks wonderful!
    B: Well, thank you for saying so, but I got a lot of help from others.

PRACTICE 5

Respond to each compliment with a polite *thank you* or some variation.

1. **Ahad:** That's a nice sweater you're wearing. It looks good with your hair color!

    You:

2. **Lori:** You can really dance! I've never seen anyone move as gracefully as you!

    You:

3. **Mr. Fetner:** You did a remarkable job on the Hastings account. I want to compliment you on the way you handled it.

    You:

4. **Ben:** Your hair looks great! I know you did something different, but I can't quite tell what.

    You:

5. **Charles:** You played a fantastic game of tennis today! Your serve has never been better!

    You:

SITUATIONAL DIALOGS

The following are some ordinary situations where thanking people and responding to thanks are quite common. Choose partners, take roles, and act out the dialogs. Afterward, discuss the situations and the language used in them and answer the questions.

A. *Anna has just moved to the United States. Her next-door neighbor has brought her a basket of fresh strawberries and some helpful information about the new neighborhood.*

Beth: Well, I guess I'd better be getting home. Let me know if I can be of more help.

Anna: Oh, you've been wonderful! And thank you so much for the delicious strawberries. We'll really enjoy them!

Beth: Don't mention it. There's a farmer's market nearby where you can buy all kinds of fresh fruits and vegetables. I'll take you there sometime if you'd like.

Anna: That would be nice. Thanks a lot, Beth.

Beth: Any time. See you later.

What Do You Think?

1. *Anna thanks Beth for several things. What are they?*
2. *Beth's last comment is the informal* any time. *What does she mean by that? Change* any time *into a complete sentence.*
3. *In the United States when people move into a new house in a new neighborhood, it is common for the neighbors to bring food to the new family as a way of welcoming them. Is this common in your native country? How do you welcome new neighbors?*

B. *Carlos' English instructor has spent an extra half-hour after class with him, explaining a difficult grammar point.*

Carlos: Thank you very much, Ms. Timms. That helped me a lot.

Ms. Timms: I'm glad I could be of some assistance, Carlos. Let me know if you have any more questions later.

Carlos: I will. And thanks for giving up your **coffee break°** to help. I know you need one after teaching three classes.

Ms. Timms: Oh, I don't mind. Teaching's what I love most.

Carlos: Well, goodbye, and thanks again!

Ms. Timms: You're very welcome, Carlos. See you in class Monday.

What Do You Think?

1. *How formal or informal is this dialog? What is your evidence to support your opinion?*
2. *Carlos thanks his instructor three times. Why? Does this seem like too much to you? Why or why not?*
3. *In your native country do people take coffee breaks? Are they different from coffee breaks in the United States? If so, how?*

C. *David has stayed late to help his boss finish some important work. It's 9:00 P.M., and David's getting ready to leave.*

Mr. Wells: Thank you for staying late tonight, Dave. I appreciate your dedication to this project.

David: You're welcome. I'm sure glad we finished it! Now I can go home with a clear conscience and not have to worry about it any more.

A **coffee break** is a short rest during the workday. Sometimes these periods are set by the company, or sometimes they are taken when the worker desires.

Mr. Wells: And thanks for changing your plans this evening. I hope it wasn't too much of an inconvenience.

David: Not at all. And it's not *that* late. I still have three or four hours before bedtime. See you in the morning.

Mr. Wells: Good night, Dave.

What Do You Think?

1. *What are Mr. Wells' expressions of gratitude? How formal or informal are they?*

2. *How does Dave reply? Are they on the same level of formality as Mr. Wells's thanks?*

3. *Change the dialog so that Dave is talking with someone on his same level in the company. Did you make any changes in the way the people phrased their thanks and the way the thanks were responded to? Why or why not?*

D. *Carl would like Brenda to go to the beach with him and some friends for the weekend, but Brenda has other obligations and plans.*

Carl: Well, have you decided, Brenda? I need to tell Joan and Mark if we can **make it**.°

Brenda: I've thought about it, Carl, but I really have a lot of work to do this weekend. Thanks anyway.

Carl: Oh, come on, Brenda! At least go down with me on Saturday—just for the day. We could be back by 11:00.

Brenda: No thanks, Carl. It's a **tempting**° offer, but I really need to work on my research paper. We'll go another time.

What Do You Think?

1. *When being asked if we want something (more cake, help, a ride to work) or want to do something (go to the movies, swim, play basketball), we often reply with "Yes, thank you" or "No, thank you." We are replying to the question and thanking the person for asking us at the same time. Notice that Brenda replies "No thanks" to Carl's invitation the second time. Does she sound as if she is getting a little angry at Carl's persistence (he doesn't give up trying to convince her)? Think of some other situations where you could use "No thanks."*

2. *Thanks anyway is always a negative reply in English. Another expression used this way is Thanks just the same (usually followed by*

Make it is informal usage for "come" or "do what was planned."
Tempting means "appealing; attractive."

a but and then a reason). What are some other times these expressions might be used in everyday conversations?

3. *How well do you think Carl and Brenda know each other, and what do you think is their relationship? Are there any clues from the dialog and especially from the language used?*

E. *Ahmad is having dinner at the home of George Cain (his American classmate).*

Mrs. Cain: Would you like some more rice, Ahmad?

Ahmad: Yes, thank you. It's really delicious.

Mrs. Cain: Well, thank you. I'm glad you like it. How about some more broccoli?

Ahmad: No thanks. I have plenty, and I'm starting to get full.

George: Mom, you should taste Ahmad's cooking. It's fantastic! He makes a great chicken and rice dish!

Ahmad: Thanks for the compliment, George, but I can cook only a few things really well. My mother taught me a little bit before I came to the United States.

Mrs. Cain: How nice! I wish George would let me teach him a few things about cooking, but he won't come near the kitchen unless it's time to eat.

Ahmad: It's not that hard to learn, George. And you have such a big, modern kitchen, I'd think it would be fun—and easy—to learn here.

Mrs. Cain: Thank you, Ahmad. The kitchen is the one room of our house we have completely remodeled because cooking is something I take very seriously.

What Do You Think?

1. *In Ahmad's first two comments, how is he using* thanks?
2. *There are several compliments given by several people. What are they, and how are they responded to?*
3. *How common is it for men to cook in your native country? Can you make a comparison between men and cooking here in the United States and in another country?*

DIALOG COMPLETIONS   Choose a partner and take roles in these dialogs. Complete each one by thanking or responding to the thanks offered.

1. **Gerhardt:** I watched you at the club yesterday, Peter. Your tennis game is really improving—especially your serve.

Peter:
Gerhardt: Oh, it seems to be getting better, too. I'm giving three lessons tomorrow, but if I have time, I'd be happy to give you some help.

Peter:
Gerhardt:

2.   **Rita:** Your letter to the newspaper editor was very well written, Mr. Vann. You made some excellent points and asked some serious questions.

Mr. Vann:
Rita:
Mr. Vann: Well, I certainly appreciate your praise and support.

3. **Mohammed:**
William: Don't mention it. If I can explain anything else to you, just ask. I know how it feels to be a stranger in a new country.

Mohammed:
William: You're welcome. You can borrow it any time.

4.   **Susette:** Mike, thanks a million for lending me the money. I'll pay you back next week.

Mike:
Susette: Well, it *was* something to me! You saved me from having to live on crackers and peanut butter for the rest of the week. If I can ever do you a favor, just ask.

Mike:

5.   **Robert:** Moises, thanks for the ride home. I sure wasn't **in the mood°** to spend 45 minutes on the subway today. Thanks a lot.

Moises:
Robert:
Moises:

6.   **Koji:**
Ali: You're more than welcome. I brought it back from Oman and thought you might like it.

Koji:
Ali: Well, thanks. I'm glad you like it.

In the mood means "in the right state of mind to want to do something."

7.　**Julio:** The financial report you made to the staff on Friday was very well done, Sam. I learned a lot.

　　Sam:
　　Julio:
　　Sam: Thanks again, Julio. I appreciate the compliment.

8.　**Mashan:** The soup was delicious, Sue. My wife enjoyed it, and I know when she's feeling better, she'll want to thank you herself.

　　Sue:
　　Mashan: You've been a big help to me and the children. Thank you very much.

　　Sue:

9.　**Rosemary:** This coffee is wonderful! It must be from Saudi Arabia! It doesn't taste like anything I've ever had before.

　　Fatimah:
　　Rosemary: And the whole dinner was lovely. Thank you for inviting me. I've had a lot of fun this evening.

　　Fatimah:

10.　**Adnan:**
　　Patty: Don't mention it. You're always doing me favors—like last week when you fixed my doorbell. That saved me from having to call a repairman.

　　Adnan:
　　Patty:

ROLE PLAYS　　Here are some situations that require you and a partner to take roles and act out dialogs involving thanking someone and responding to gratitude shown. You may want to reverse roles and create different dialogs when you have finished.

1. The young boy next door, Peter Matthews, cuts Barbara's lawn for her.

2. Mrs. Lee, Samar's next-door neighbor, brings him some delicious home-made cookies.

3. John, a friend from work, asks Gloria to a jazz concert on Friday night. She accepts.

4. David's employer compliments him on the good work he's done this week.

5. Vince calls Sally, a close friend, and invites her out for pizza, but she can't go.

6. Mr. Watts finally finds someone who can babysit for him this week-
    end, even though the girl will have to change her plans. Mr. Watts is
    very grateful.

7. Jenny, the nine-year-old daughter of Yoko's friend, makes her a vase
    in art class.

8. Mr. Thompson, the gentleman who lives near Sally, offers to water
    her plants and take care of her apartment while she is away on a
    business trip next week.

9. Mary's doctor cancels another appointment so she can examine
    Mary's little boy, who has been coughing and complaining of pain in
    his chest for two days.

10. Patty brought Sam, a good friend, a cowboy hat from her trip to Texas last week.

REAL **PEOPLE,** REAL **SITUATIONS,** REAL **LANGUAGE**

Visit a shopping mall, a large department store, or any other place with various departments and salespeople. Ask each salesperson a question (described as follows), and then thank the person appropriately for the information or help. Use your notebook to record the conversation, but don't worry about recording every single word perfectly. Pay closer attention to the words leading up to the thank you, the thank you itself, and the response.

EXAMPLE: *Ask a shoe salesperson to explain the difference between two models of a Nike running shoe.*

You: *I'm interested in buying some Nike running shoes. Could you please tell me the difference between these two models?*

Salesperson: *I'd be happy to. The Nike 210s have more support for the entire foot than the Nike 100s. But the 100s are good shoes, too. They are light and very flexible. They cost $12.00 less than the 200s, and I like to recommend them to new runners who are just starting out.*

You: *Thank you very much. You've been a big help.*

Salesperson: *My pleasure. Let me know if you have any more questions.*

1. Ask a supermarket clerk if the store carries (sells) a special spice or food from your country.
2. Ask a salesperson in a department store where the restroom is.
3. Ask a cashier for change for a dollar.
4. Ask a clothing salesperson for help in finding a pair of jeans that fit.
5. Ask a movie ticket seller what the difference between *R* and *PG* is.

CHAPTER 8

MAKING, ACCEPTING, AND DECLINING INVITATIONS

- If you wanted to ask a friend to accompany you to a party next weekend, what would you say?
- If an acquaintance at school or work asked you to go to a concert, but you weren't interested, how could you say "no" without hurting his or her feelings?
- If someone you didn't know well invited you to dinner, but you weren't sure you *really* wanted to go, what would you say?

These are some typical situations that we may encounter quite often. In fact, much of our social lives involves invitations—making them and responding to them. Every day we make some sort of invitation. We may invite a friend to join us for dinner, to play tennis, to come to a concert, or to have lunch. During an average week we may also receive such invitations. Sometimes we want to accept them and are able to, but there are other times when we don't want to accept an invitation or are unable to. When we decline an invitation, we usually thank the person who has invited us and apologize for not being able to accept. Furthermore, we usually give an excuse if one is appropriate. If we are sincerely sorry that we can't accept the invitation and would like to be asked again sometime, we often say so.

We usually don't start right in with the invitation without doing a little searching to see if that person already has plans. We might say something like, "Hi, Caroline. What are you up to this weekend?" If Caroline says she's going to the beach, we can decide not to proceed with the invitation because we know she won't be able to accept. Of course, if we want Caroline to change her mind, we might say, "Oh, really? I was hoping you'd be free, so you could go with us to the lake on Saturday." Maybe Caroline will change her mind after all.

Asking if a person is busy or has plans can sometimes cause the person who is responding to be a little uncomfortable, however. If John begins an invitation with, "Hi, Laura. What are you up to this weekend?" and Laura replies, "Nothing," John may view her response as a signal meaning "I'm free." Then John may proceed with an invitation. If Laura likes John and wants to go out with him, there's no problem. But suppose she has no desire at all to go out with him. She's in a difficult situation because she's already confessed that she has no plans. What can she do? She could suddenly "remember" that she's supposed to have dinner with a friend, or she could suddenly "remember" a previous engagement. Of course, she could be truthful with John and probably hurt his feelings by saying, "No thanks, John. I really don't care to go out with you."

But sometimes we aren't completely truthful, and we may tell "a little white lie"—a small untruthful statement that is not meant to deceive necessarily but rather to keep from hurting someone's feelings. So Laura might say, "Thanks a lot for inviting me, John, but I'm not feeling very well, so I don't think I'd better go out." That's a white lie because she's not really sick; she just doesn't want to hurt John's feelings by telling him the real reason she doesn't want to go out with him.

We sometimes tell white lies, but another way to refuse someone is simply to say something like "I'm sorry, but I already have plans" or "No, I'm afraid I can't because I'm busy." "Plans" may mean curling up in front of the TV with a bowl of popcorn and watching movies all night alone, and "busy" might mean doing laundry. These are polite ways of refusing someone's invitation and avoiding doing something we don't want to do.

Making Invitations   Here are some of the more frequently used expressions that begin verbal invitations. Notice that the first several are much more formal than the last:

♣ I would like to invite you to { a reception next Sunday at my home. dinner at the new French restaurant. *(Formal)*

♣ Would you care/like to { join us for dessert and coffee? go to Washington with me next month?

♣ I was wondering if you'd like to { go to the pool on Saturday. come to dinner on Tuesday evening.

NOTE: When you begin a sentence with "I was wondering if . . . . " you follow with the SUBJECT and then the VERB: you + would like . . . . You *don't* use the typical question form of AUXILIARY + SUBJECT + MAIN VERB: Would + you + like . . . . ?

♣ Can/Will you { meet me at the gym after class for some basketball? come over tomorrow night and watch the game with us?

♣ How/What about { a movie tonight? a quick game of pool before we go home?

♣ How/What about { canoeing at the lake tomorrow afternoon? camping out at Mount Mitchell next weekend?

NOTE: After "What about . . . . ?" or "How about . . . . ?" comes a NOUN (a movie, a game) or a GERUND (canoeing, camping).

♣ Why not/don't you { jog with me this afternoon? stop by for a visit on your way home?

PRACTICE 1

Look at the given activity and form an invitation to a friend. Use a different beginning for each invitation.

EXAMPLE: *A picnic on Saturday*

Bob, I was wondering if you'd like to go with me to a picnic on Saturday.

1. Dinner at a new Indian restaurant: _____

    _____

2. A play at the Performing Arts Center on Sunday: _____

    _____

3. An exercise class on Thursday: _____

    _____

4. A soccer game tonight: _____

    _____

5. On a date this weekend: _____

    _____

Accepting Invitations

Here are some typical ways to begin acceptances of invitations. As always, this list does not exhaust all the possibilities; there are many more. Try to add a few more of your own.

* ✤ Thank you very much. *(Formal)*
* ✤ Thanks for your invitation. **I'd be delighted to/love to.**° *(Formal)*
* ✤ Thanks. I'd like to $\begin{cases} \text{have dinner with you on Monday.} \\ \text{visit you next weekend at the beach.} \end{cases}$
* ✤ Sure. That would be $\begin{cases} \text{fun.} \\ \text{wonderful.} \end{cases}$
* ✤ What a $\begin{cases} \text{nice} \\ \text{terrific} \end{cases}$ idea! I'd $\begin{cases} \text{really like that.} \\ \text{love to!} \end{cases}$
* ✤ Sounds $\begin{cases} \text{great!} \\ \text{like fun!} \end{cases}$ *(Informal)*
* ✤ Great! *(Informal)*
* ✤ Sure (thing)! *(Informal)*
* ✤ Super! *(Informal)*
* ✤ _____
* ✤ _____

I'd be delighted to and **I'd love to** are replies that are usually used more often by women than by men.

Again, notice that the responses range from very formal ("Thank you very much. I'd be delighted to come.") to very informal ("Super!"), depending on the social situation, the persons involved in the conversation, and other circumstances.

PRACTICE 2

Accept each of the following invitations by using one of the expressions we've just discussed. Choose the degree of formality carefully, according to the cues given.

EXAMPLE:

Mrs. Matthews: *I would be very pleased if you would attend the opening of the symphony orchestra with me next Thursday evening.*

You: *Thank you, Mrs. Matthews. That's very kind of you. I'd like to.*

1. **James, your roommate:** Why don't you go with me to visit my family next weekend? I know you'd enjoy meeting them.

   You:

2. **A friend:** How about a game of golf this weekend?

   You:

3. **Your teacher:** Would you care to join Maria and me for lunch? We're going to talk about the plans for the International Festival.

   You:

4. **A friend:** Can you come with Joe and me to the museum on Sunday?

   You:

5. **An elderly neighbor:** Would you like to come over for dinner next Saturday night?

   You:

FOR _Barbara King_

DATE _June 13, 1986_

TIME _12 Noon_

PLACE _5378 Pine Lane_
Boston

GIVEN BY _Millie Simmons_

R.S.V.P. _366-9841_

Declining Invitations

Here are some ways to begin a refusal of an invitation. Notice that most of these refusals are approximately the same level of formality because politeness is important when responding negatively to an invitation.

✤ Thank you, but I'm afraid I have
$\begin{cases} \text{other plans for} \\ \quad \text{that night.} \\ \text{an appointment} \\ \quad \text{that day.} \end{cases}$ *(Formal)*

✤ I'm sorry. I can't
$\begin{cases} \text{go to the movie} \\ \quad \text{with you.} \\ \text{join you in New York} \\ \quad \text{that weekend.} \end{cases}$
I . . . *(offer excuse)*.

✤ I wish I could, but I'm busy. Maybe another time, though.

✤ I hate to **turn** you **down,**° but I must . . . *(offer excuse)*.

✤ I would love/like to any other time, but I've already made plans.

✤ Thanks for asking, but . . . *(offer excuse)*.

✤ I appreciate the invitation, but I'm afraid I can't.

✤ I'm afraid I can't, but thanks anyway.

✤ I'm tied up that
$\begin{cases} \text{day.} \\ \text{night.} \end{cases}$
What about
$\begin{cases} \text{the 14th?} \\ \text{a \textbf{rain check?}}° \end{cases}$

✤ _____

✤ _____

PRACTICE 3

Decline each invitation politely, and offer some excuse if it is appropriate.

1. **Karen:** How about a game of tennis tomorrow?
   You:

2. **Harry:** Can you join me for coffee and dessert at the new café on Fourth Street?
   You:

Turn (someone or something) **down** means "refuse." We *turn down* people, invitations, requests, offers.

A **rain check** is an informal agreement in which a person may claim later something that is being offered now. Example: "I can't go to the movie now, but I'd like a *rain check.*"

3.   **Ali:**   What about getting together for lunch on Friday?
      You:

4. **Irving:**   Would you care to go to the new art exhibit at the
                City Museum on Sunday?
      You:

5.   **Alice:**   Why don't you come with Pat and me to the tennis
                matches Monday? It'll be fun!
      You:

Hesitation Strategies
Sometimes you may not want to say *yes* or *no* immediately. There are many ways to hesitate if you need some time to think over the invitation before deciding.

+ I'm not sure what my plans are at this moment. Could I let you know on Friday?
+ I may be busy that day. Do you mind if I tell you in a few days?
+ Well, I'm not sure, but I may be $\begin{cases} \text{busy.} \\ \text{playing golf.} \end{cases}$
+ My plans for that day are **still up in the air.**° I'll let you know by Tuesday, if that's okay with you.
+ I appreciate the invitation, but I might have an appointment at that time. Could I let you know later this week?
+ Thanks a lot for the invitation, but I'll have to check my calendar. Could I get back to you tonight?
+ _____
+ _____

PRACTICE 4

After each invitation, use a hesitation strategy instead of answering immediately.

1.   **Fred:**   Are you busy next Saturday night? There's a
                concert in the park that would be fun to go to.
      You:

To be **still up in the air** means "not finalized yet," "not complete," or "unsure."

2. **Mohammed:** I'd like to invite you to the final ceremony of our language program next Friday evening at 8:00. Will you be able to attend?

You:

3. **Yoko:** What about going ice-skating at the mall tonight?

You:

4. **Harriet:** I'm having a surprise party for Mary on Saturday. Can you make it?

You:

5. **Larry:** I'm going to Washington on business next Friday. Why don't you join me there for the weekend? I know we'd have a great time!

You:

SITUATIONAL DIALOGS
The following dialogs illustrate various ways of making invitations, as well as responding to them. Notice that some of the askers are quite formal and direct, whereas others are more casual. Some of the people responding accept immediately and gladly, some hesitate before accepting or declining, and others decline regretfully. Choose partners, take roles, and act out these dialogs. Then discuss the questions at the end.

A. **Steve:** Alan, what about a game of tennis after lunch?
Alan: I wish I could, Steve, but I promised Nora I'd go with her to a movie this afternoon.
Steve: Well, how about tomorrow then?
Alan: Fine with me. I really could use the exercise.

What Do You Think?
1. *Do you think Alan really wanted to play tennis with Steve when asked the first time? Why or why not?*
2. *How might Alan have responded if he hadn't wanted to accept Steve's second invitation?*
3. *Suppose Alan actually hated to play tennis. Change the conversation but try not to hurt Steve's feelings.*

B. **Pedro:** Are you busy Saturday night, Jill?
Jill: Well . . . uh . . . I don't have any definite plans yet. Why?

> **Pedro:** I thought we might go to the new movie at the Play-house Theater.
>
> **Jill:** Fantastic! I read a good review of it, and I'd love to go!

What Do You Think?

1. *Why doesn't Pedro begin his invitation immediately with "Would you like to go . . . ?"*
2. *Why do you think Jill hesitates at first? What hesitation strategy does she use?*
3. *Suppose she heard Pedro's invitation and then decided she didn't want to go. How could she have handled the invitation?*

> C. **Jamal:** Hi, Pat. What are you up to these days?
>
> **Pat:** Not much, really. I'm taking an interesting art course at the community college, though.
>
> **Jamal:** That's good. Um . . . do you think you'd be interested in going with me sometime to see the new exhibit at the Pope Gallery? It's eighteenth-century watercolors.
>
> **Pat:** I'd like that very much. When did you have in mind?
>
> **Jamal:** I don't know. How about Sunday afternoon? About 3:00?
>
> **Pat:** That's perfect! I'll be looking forward to it.

What Do You Think?

1. *Does Jamal immediately ask Pat to go to the exhibit with him? How does he handle the invitation?*
2. *What are several other ways Jamal could have asked Pat, "What are you up to these days?"*
3. *How could Pat have replied if she hadn't wanted to go with Jamal?*

> D. **Ahmed:** 'Morning, Joyce. You look tired.
>
> **Joyce:** I am! I just jogged six miles!
>
> **Ahmed:** What about coming in for a cold drink?
>
> **Joyce:** I can't, Ahmed. I've got a 10 o'clock appointment, so I've got to get home and get ready. Another time maybe.
>
> **Ahmed:** Sure. See you later.

What Do You Think?

1. *What are two or three other ways Ahmed could have worded his invitation?*
2. *As mentioned before in previous chapters, people in the United States often end a conversation by saying something like "Let's get together*

soon" or "Let's do it another time," but these "invitations" may not be genuine. By saying "Another time maybe," Joyce has gotten off the hook (an expression that means she's not obligated herself to anything), but at the same time, she's left Ahmed a little hopeful. "Another time" is very ambiguous. If Ahmed is really interested in developing a relationship with Joyce, what should he do or say?

3. *Change the conversation so that Joyce accepts Ahmed's invitation.*

E. **Hiroko:** Hi, Karen. I'm glad I ran into you. My parents are visiting me for a few days, and I'm giving a small party for them this Friday. I want them to meet some of my friends. Can you and Tony come?

Karen: That sounds great, but I need to check with Tony first and see what his plans are. What time does it start?

Hiroko: About 7:30.

Karen: If we come, we may be a little late because Tony doesn't get off work until 7 o'clock. Okay?

Hiroko: Sure. No problem. I hope you can make it.

Karen: Me, too. Thanks for inviting us.

What Do You Think?

1. *In American culture, checking with one's spouse (husband or wife) or boyfriend or girlfriend is very common when an invitation is issued to one of the partners. Thus, Karen may or may not have been using this as a hesitation strategy. Is this checking with one's partner common in your society? Would it be more common for one sex to use this reply? Discuss this with your teacher and classmates and try to think of some related situations.*

2. *In your country would it be proper for the husband or boyfriend to accept an invitation without first consulting his wife or girlfriend? What about when the roles are reversed?*

3. *Notice that Karen doesn't offer to call Hiroko and let her know beforehand if she and Tony will be at the party. In informal situations, Karen's action may be all right, but in more formal settings the inviter would probably want to know in advance if the persons were going to be able to attend, so an estimation of the amount of food and drinks could be made. Most written invitations indicate this at the bottom of the card. An RSVP means "Repondez s'il vous plaît" (French for "Please reply"), and a Regrets only means "Please respond if you cannot attend." How is this matter of replying to written invitations handled in your native country? Would Karen's way of dealing with the invitation (not letting Hiroko know for sure if she and Tony were coming) be acceptable in your culture? Why or why not?*

IT'S A PARTY

WHEN ? _May 10 - 7:30pm_
WHERE ? _Mike Smith's_
389 Vernon Dr.
WHY ? _Carol Lloyd's_
25th Birthday!!

It's a Surprise!

Regrets only - _794-3966_

DIALOG COMPLETIONS   Choose partners and take roles. Then complete the following conversations, either by extending an invitation or by responding to one. The cues in the dialogs will tell you how to respond and whether to hesitate before responding. Then switch roles and act out the dialogs again, using different words. Keep in mind the situation and the people when considering how formal or informal to be.

1. **Bernice:** 'Morning, Mario. I was looking for you to invite you to the soccer game tonight. I have two tickets. Can you come?

   Mario:

   Bernice: That's too bad. Well, don't work too hard.

   Mario:

   Bernice: Oh, you're welcome. Maybe we can go to another one together soon.

   Mario:

2. **Paul:**

   Ali: I wish I could, Paul, but I promised Louise I'd go with her to a party tonight. How about Wednesday night?

   Paul:

   Ali: Great! See you then!

3. **Linda:** Betina, I remembered you said you'd like to join an exercise class. Would you be interested in coming with me to mine? It's at 7:30 tonight in the gym.

   Betina:

   Linda: Okay. Call me when you find out.

   Betina:

   Linda: Oh, it's no problem. I can pick you up.

4. **Alice:**

   Ameed: I'm really not sure about my plans for that weekend, Alice. I'm scheduled to be in New York at that time, but my plans could change.

   Alice:

   Ameed: Okay, I will. And I really appreciate the invitation. I hope I can make it.

   Alice:

5. **Sara:**

   Mark: I'd be glad to. I don't have any plans that night.

   Sara:

Mark: That sounds like fun. What can I bring?
Sara:
Mark: Sure. No problem. I'll see you Tuesday.

6. **Harold:**
   Yasser: Sounds good, Harold, but I might have a conflict Monday morning. Can I call you and let you know something definite tomorrow?
   Harold:
   Yasser: Good. And thanks for the invitation.
   Harold:

7. **Samar:** Mari! It's good to see you! I've been meaning to call, but I've been so busy lately . . . .
   Mari:
   Samar: No, I don't have any at all. Let's go get something to eat and talk. We have a lot to **catch up on**.°
   Mari:
   Samar: Great idea! I'm in the mood for Chinese food, too. Where shall we go?
   Mari:
   Samar: No, I've never been there, but I'm willing to try it. Let's go.

8. **Marvin:** Hello, Rana. It's good to see you again.
   Rana:
   Marvin: Great! I've been staying pretty busy, though. Uh . . . my office is having its annual Christmas party next Thursday evening, and I was wondering if you'd care to go with me.
   Rana:
   Marvin: No, that's fine. Just let me know when you find out something.
   Rana:

9. **Jerry:**
   Lois: Yes, I do, Jerry. I'm going to be out of town that weekend.
   Jerry:
   Lois: Oh, really? Gee, that sounds nice. I'm sorry I've already made plans.

Catch up on means "get the latest news or information or bring up to date on the latest happenings."

Jerry:
Lois: I'd like that. Could you call me in two weeks? I can tell you definitely then.

Jerry:
Lois: Thanks, Jerry. And thanks for the invitaton, too.

10. **Florence:**
     Susan: Oh? What did you have in mind?
     Florence:
     Susan: I'd love to any other time, Flo, but I've got to take the kids to swim practice today. Could we make it another time?
     Florence:
     Susan: Excellent. I'll meet you there about 3 o'clock.

ROLE PLAYS   Here are some situations in which invitations are called for, followed by responses to them. Choose partners, take roles, and create dialogs that accurately represent the situations described. Then reverse roles and create new dialogs.

1. Pat is in an exercise class with Judy. He has had only short conversations with her, but he'd like to get to know her better. He asks her out for coffee after the class, and Judy hesitates at first, but then she accepts.

2. Martha wants Ali to go with her to see a movie. Ali's already seen it, but he'd like to go to another movie with her—another time.

3. Paul knows his friend Celina is very interested in theater, so he asks her to attend a new play with him. Celina doesn't know Paul very well and declines politely.

4. Albert has agreed to play tennis with Chen after work, but Albert remembers he has a previous appointment. He wants to reschedule the match for later in the week.

5. Frank invites his elderly next-door neighbor over for tea. She eagerly accepts.

6. Betty is having a small dinner party for a couple who are getting married soon. She invites a good friend of theirs, Ron Brown, to attend and bring a date. He is not sure if he'll be able to make it. Betty will need to know definitely by Thursday.

7. Pedro invites a friend from work to go to the mountains with him this weekend. The person has no plans for the weekend but doesn't want to go with Pedro, either.

8. Samar asks some friends to attend the Madonna concert in two weeks. Bob wants to go, Luis isn't sure he can make it, and Tom has other plans.

9. David's employer invites him to lunch to discuss his future with the company. David has already made plans to eat with his girlfriend, but he knows how important this invitation could be.

10. George asks Gloria, a friend who likes him very much, to go sailing with him on Saturday. Gloria hates sailing, but she likes George a lot and has been hoping he would ask her out.

REAL **PEOPLE,** REAL **SITUATIONS,** REAL **LANGUAGE**

1. For this task, you need to pay special attention to the people around you—*what* they say and *how* they say it. It's also a chance for you to put your new language into *real* use. In the first part of this activity, go out into your work, school, or social community and listen for people making invitations or responding to them. Take along your small notebook to record your findings. Make five observations, using the journal entry format.

    EXAMPLE: *July 15—7 P.M. at the school cafeteria—standing in line to pay the cashier*

    Boy: *Hi, Kay. Where have you been lately?*
    Girl: *Studying mostly. What about you?*
    Boy: *The same. Listen...do you want to play some tennis sometime?*
    Girl: *Sure. I'd love to. When?*
    Boy: *I don't know. Maybe next week?*
    Girl: *Any day except Thursday. Just give me a call.*
    Boy: *Okay. I will.*

2. That was the *passive* part of the assignment. Now comes the *active*. Using the tips you have received on making and responding to invitations in this chapter, go out and make at least five invitations to friends. These don't have to be elaborate invitations. They can be simple ones like inviting someone to join you for coffee and doughnuts, asking someone to come over and watch TV, or asking someone to come to your room or apartment and study with you. Using the same type of entry as in the previous exercise, try to record as accurately as you can what you say and how the persons respond. Your teacher may want you to bring your examples to class to discuss and compare them with those of your classmates.

CHAPTER 9

MAKING REQUESTS

In everyday relationships with people, we often find ourselves in situations where we need to ask someone for something: a physical object, a favor, an action. We may need to ask someone to do something (close the window) or even stop doing something (stop talking so loudly). Whatever the case, it is important to know the difference between a command and a request. The words you choose, the way you phrase them, and your tone of voice can make the difference between a rather harsh command and a polite request.

An employer speaking to her secretary might say, "Bring me the Hastings account." Since she is the boss, she is able to make such a command without her secretary thinking she is being discourteous or rude. She's simply being businesslike and direct. However, the employer could make the same request but soften it a little simply by saying, "Excuse me, Ms. Stevens. Please bring me the Hastings account." By addressing the secretary personally and by adding the polite *excuse me* and *please*, she has made the request seem a little less harsh or commanding.

But some requests are naturally in the form of commands. An Army sergeant tells his troops, "Stand up straight! Turn left! Forward, march!" An umpire at a baseball game yells, "Play ball!" A mother tells her child, "Brush your teeth and go to bed." A customer says to a waiter, "Bring me another bottle of wine." These kinds of requests are expected. They are made by persons with authority, who want immediate action, no questions asked.

Sometimes we use commands, not because we want to use our authority, but because commands are fast and to the point (direct); we can get our message across quickly, using fewer words. Look at the differences in these three requests:

> **Bob:** Bring in the paper when you come back.
> **Sam:** Bring in the paper when you come back, would you?
> **Tom:** Would you mind bringing in the paper when you come back from running?

Each speaker wants the same result: the newspaper brought to him. Bob may not even realize he's making a direct command. It could simply be his style of speech: abrupt and direct. Or if Bob were in a position of authority, the command could be intentional. By adding the words *would you* as a tag question, Sam softens the command a little. He's obviously hoping his friend will reply, "Sure. No problem." Tom is using even more tact and politeness when he begins, "Would you mind . . . ?" He's more considerate of the person's feelings, and the "Would you mind . . . ?" is a very non-threatening, pleasant way to begin a request.

Requests may also be in the form of simple declarative statements that express a desire or wish. For example,

> **Mother to child:** Laura, I want you to clean your room before supper.
> **Boss to employee:** Jenkins, I want a copy of that report on my desk by 5 o'clock this afternoon.
> **Student to librarian:** I need some help with a research paper I'm working on in history.

Naturally, each of these requests could be softened considerably simply by adding *if you don't mind* or *please* to the end of each statement. What other ways can you think of to soften requests?

PRACTICE 1

Soften each request by adding certain words or phrases to make it less direct or commanding.

1. **Father to son:** When you finish raking the leaves, I want you to take out the garbage.

   Father to son:

2. **Ali to roommate:** Turn down your stereo! I'm trying to talk on the phone!

   Ali to roommate:

3. **Teacher to student:** Rewrite this composition and correct all your errors.

   Teacher to student:

4. **Wife to husband:** Turn on the sprinkler in the front yard before you leave.

   Wife to husband:

5. **Boss to employee:** I want you to meet with me tomorrow at 4:00 about the new project.

   Boss to employee:

"Sticky" Situations

We talked about "sticky" situations in Chapter 4, "Saying Goodbye." When we find ourselves in sensitive or "sticky" situations, we need to use care, tact, and/or caution to deal with them. For example, suppose you're in a crowded elevator where smoking is never allowed. The man beside you lights a cigarette and begins puffing away. What can you say or do? You're bothered by the smoke itself and by the fact that he's breaking the law (smoking is not allowed in elevators) and creating a potentially dangerous situation (a fire in the elevator). You have several options for handling this predicament, but in any case, it requires you to make some sort of request of the smoker. If you're very angry about it, you might find yourself being a little less than courteous:

❖ Can't you read the sign, mister? No smoking allowed!
❖ It's against the law to smoke in elevators, mister!

Although in both cases you're not saying directly "Put out your cigarette!" or "Quit smoking in here!"—that's exactly what is behind your statements.

But more likely, you'll try a more polite approach:

+ Excuse me, but would you mind putting out your cigarette until you're out of the elevator?
+ I'm sorry, sir, but smoking in elevators isn't allowed.
+ Please don't smoke in here, sir. It's against the law, and it's also very annoying to nonsmokers.

Notice that in the polite approach, *sir* (rather than *mister*) is used. *Sir* shows more respect and formality than *mister*. Notice, too, that although the last example is a direct command, it is not meant to be harsh or rude. The speaker has begun with a polite *please* and ended with a reminder of the law. However, the speaker is definitely serious in making the request and wants the smoker to stop immediately.

PRACTICE 2

In each situation described, make two different kinds of requests: a *direct* one, in which you get your message across immediately, and a *polite* one, in which your request is less urgent and more tactful.

> **EXAMPLE:**   *You're at a restaurant and need more coffee.*
>
> (Direct)   *Bring me some more coffee when you come back.*
> (Polite)   *Could I have some more coffee, please?*

1. You want your roommate to clean up his or her dirty dishes.
   (Direct)
   (Polite)
2. You're at the gym and you want your friend to pass you a towel.
   (Direct)
   (Polite)
3. A man behind you in a theater is talking rather loudly during the movie.
   (Direct)
   (Polite)
4. You want Bassim to remember to bring his swimming goggles to the pool tomorrow so you can use them.
   (Direct)
   (Polite)

5. You're having dinner at an older couple's house, and you want the hostess to pass you the chicken.
(Direct)
(Polite)

Requesting

To request something (to have, to borrow, or to use, for instance), you may use many polite forms. Most of them begin with auxiliaries. Here are a few common ways:

+ May I have
  - an apple?
  - a Coke?
  - another helping of rice, please?

+ Could I borrow
  - ten dollars?
  - your rake?
  - that book, please?

+ Can I use
  - that umbrella?
  - your hairdryer?
  - the phone, if you don't mind?

+ Would you mind if I
  - had a sandwich?
  - borrowed your newspaper?
  - used your car this afternoon?

+ _____

+ _____

PRACTICE 3

You want to borrow, have, or use the following items. Make a polite request, and try to use a different beginning for each one.

EXAMPLE: *Your roommate's iron*

You: *Charlie, may I borrow your iron this afternoon, please?*

1. Your co-worker's telephone book
   You:

2. The last piece of pie in the refrigerator
   You:

3. Your classmate's dictionary
   You:

4. Your neighbor's garden hose
    You:

5. Your employer's business magazine
    You:

To request some type of action, the following forms are often used, but there are many others, as the Situational Dialogs will illustrate. Try to think of others.

✦ Could I trouble/bother you to
{ get me a cold drink?
  help me with this?
  answer the phone? }

✦ Will you
{ answer the phone while I'm out, if you don't mind?
  hand me that picture frame, please?
  please clean your room before going outside? }

✦ Would you mind
{ not smoking **at the table**?°
  speaking more slowly, please?
  retyping this letter before you leave? }

✦ How/What about
{ helping me with the dishes?
  picking up° some soft drinks on your way home?
  turning your stereo down a little? }

NOTE: A gerund (VERB+ING, used as a NOUN: *smoking, speaking, retyping,* etc.) follows the phrases "Would you mind . . . ?" and "How/What about . . . ?"

✦ _____

✦ _____

PRACTICE 4

Request the following action. Be polite and use a different beginning for each request.

EXAMPLE: *You want help with cooking dinner.*

You: *How about some help with dinner, Paul? Could you make the salad, please?*

At the table here means "at the dinner table" or "while eating."
Picking up means "buying" or "getting."

1. You want your roommate to turn down the heat in the apartment.
    You:

2. You would like the man at the table next to you in the restaurant to stop smoking his cigar.
    You:

3. You want your neighbor to stop walking across your freshly planted grass.
    You:

4. You would like your friend to give you a ride to the airport tomorrow.
    You:

5. You want your teacher to explain a grammar problem to you.
    You:

Responding to Requests

We can respond positively (yes) or negatively (no) to requests. But we usually do not simply say *No!* and leave it at that. We often offer some kind of apology or excuse (see Chapter 10, "Apologizing and Responding to Apologies," and Chapter 11, "Making Excuses") to explain why our reply to the request is negative. Here are some typical ways to begin responses to requests.

Positive Responses

+ Yes, I'm more than willing to . . . (contribute to the Cancer Society). (*Formal*)
+ Certainly . . . (I'd love/like to help with the dance decorations). (*Formal*)
+ Of course, it's no problem to . . . (change your appointment to Friday).
+ No, it wouldn't be any trouble to . . . (get you more tea).
+ Not at all. (In response to "Would you mind . . . ?")
+ I don't mind **one bit**° . . . (watering your plants while you're away).
+ Sure. I'll be glad to . . . (help you fix dinner).
+ No problem. (I'll be happy to pick up the kids after school). (*Informal*)
+ No sweat. I don't mind . . . (lending you my skis). (*Very informal*)

One bit means "even a little" or "at all" and is used with a negative: "It didn't hurt *one bit*!"

✤ **Piece of cake!°** (I'd be glad to show you how to use the key.) (*Very informal*)

✤ _____

✤ _____

Negative Responses

✤ I'm afraid I can't . . . (lend you that book) because . . . (offer excuse). (*Formal*)
✤ I wish I could . . . (let you borrow $20.00), but . . . .
✤ I'm sorry, but . . . .
✤ It's impossible for me to . . . (change your appointment) because . . . .
✤ I can't . . . (pick up your drycleaning) because . . . .
✤ Sorry, but I . . . . (*Informal*)

✤ _____

✤ _____

PRACTICE 5

Choose partners for this exercise. Then look at the clues, make a request, and have your partner respond positively (+) or negatively (−), according to the signal given.

> **EXAMPLE:** *roommate/jacket/borrow (−)*
>
> **You:** *Could I wear your tan jacket tonight, Mary?*
>
> *Mine's at the cleaners.*
>
> **Roommate:** *Sorry, but I'm going out, too, and I plan to wear it.*

1. friend/some milk/borrow (+)
   You:
   Friend:

2. co-worker/assignment/help with (−)
   You:
   Co-worker:

3. landlord/leak in the bathroom/fix (+)
   You:
   Landlord:

Piece of cake! is a very informal expression that means the same as "No sweat," "No problem," or "It's easy!"

4. classmate/chewing gum/have (−)
    You:
Classmate:

5. friend/typewriter/use (−)
    You:
Friend:

SITUATIONAL DIALOGS

Here are some situations showing different ways of making requests and responding to them. Choose partners, take roles, and read the short dialogs. Then answer the questions or do the tasks requested of you.

A. **Michael:** Hey, José, would you mind lending me your accounting book this evening? I left mine at school.

José: Sorry, Mike, but I've got to use mine tonight to study for a big test tomorrow. Maybe you can borrow Robert's.

What Do You Think?

1. *What does Michael need to borrow from José and why? Change Mike's request slightly by using the word* borrow.
2. *What excuse does José offer by saying* no? *Does it seem valid to you?*
3. *Change José's response to* yes *but add a condition (something that is necessary for his request to be granted) to his response. For example, "You can use my car as long as you put gas in it."*

B. **Pat:** I'd like you to pick up a quart of milk and a loaf of whole-wheat bread on your way home from work, if you have time.

Chen: No problem. Anything else?

What Do You Think?

1. *Can you tell what kind of relationship Pat and Chen have from the way Pat phrases the request? How close is their relationship? How do you know this?*
2. *Change Pat's request and make it less polite and more commanding.*
3. *Change Chen's reply to a negative one and give an excuse.*

C. **Frank:** Would it be all right if I drank this last Diet Coke, Carl? I'll get some more tomorrow.

Carl: Go ahead. But buy **a six-pack°** because Joyce and Mona are coming over to study with me, and I want to have plenty to offer them.

Frank: Sure. No problem.

What Do You Think?

1. *What does* go ahead *mean literally? How is it being used in this example? What are some other situations in which we might use this expression?*
2. *Change Carl's request and make it a little more polite.*
3. *Change Carl's reply to* no *and give Frank a reason.*

D. **Abdulla:** Could I trouble you for a cigarette, Thomas?
Thomas: I'm all out. Sorry.

What Do You Think?

1. *Rephrase Abdulla's request and make it less formal.*
2. *What does* all out *mean? What are some other ways Thomas could have said the same thing?*
3. *Change the dialog so that Thomas is a little offended by Abdulla's request because Thomas quit smoking a month ago.*

E. **Sam:** I want to bring Karen to dinner on Sunday. Okay?
Mother: Of course. She's welcome any time.

What Do You Think?

1. *Change Sam's request and put it in the form of a polite question.*
2. *Change his mother's response to a polite but firm* no *and give a reason.*
3. *In your society, would it be considered normal or acceptable to ask someone of the opposite sex to dinner at your family's home? Why or why not?*

DIALOG COMPLETIONS
Choose partners and complete the following dialogs by making requests or responding to requests made.

1. **Mrs. Tyson:** Would you mind picking up some bread at the store on your way home?
Mr. Tyson:

A six-pack is a carton or container that holds six bottles or containers of drinks.

Mrs. Tyson: I'd really appreciate it if you could. I'm going to be tied up all day.

Mr. Tyson:

Mrs. Tyson: Thanks a lot, honey. I really do appreciate it.

2. **Valerie:**

Ahmed: I wish I could, Val, but I've got a class at 4:00. How about another time?

Valerie:

Ahmed: Sure! That would be great!

3. **Terry:**

Mark: If you had told me earlier, I could have, Terry, but I've already made plans.

Terry:

Mark: Yes, Monday is fine. Let's meet at the gym around 6:00.

4. **Linda:** Would you mind if I switched to channel 8? I want to watch a baseball game.

Sandy:

Linda: Oh, I didn't know you were watching anything. I can wait till it's over.

Sandy:

Linda Thanks, Sandy. I appreciate it.

5. **Kelly:**

Aziz: Oh, no. It's no trouble at all. I'll be glad to take you there.

Kelly:

Aziz: You're welcome. I'm glad I can help.

6. **Yoko:** May I have another piece of cake, Lynn? It's really delicious!

Lynn:

Yoko: Oh, that's okay. I didn't realize that everyone hadn't been served yet.

Lynn:

Yoko: No, I couldn't take yours! You eat it. I don't need another one anyway!

7. **Mrs. Dobbs:**

Secretary: I'll do my best. When do you need it finished?

Mr. Dobbs:

Secretary: I don't think that will be any problem.

8. **Celina:**
   Laura: I don't have time to listen to it right now, Celina. How about tonight when I come home from work?
   Celina:
   Laura: Sure, I'll be glad to. Anything else you need?
   Celina:
   Laura: Okay, No problem. I'll see you around 6:30.

9. **Joel:** Could I borrow your tennis racket, Mary?
   Mary:
   Joel: Oh. That's okay. Maybe I can borrow Nick's. Do you happen to have his number?
   Mary:
   Joel: Okay. I'll give him a call. Thanks.

10. **Betty:**
   Elena: I'm afraid I can't today, Betty. I'm busy.
   Betty:
   Elena: Let me look at my schedule, and I'll call you back tomorrow, okay?

ROLE PLAYS

Choose partners, take roles, and act out the following situations that require some kind of request and response—positive (+) or negative (−). Then switch roles and re-create different role plays, expressing the requests and responses in different ways.

1. Sarah would like to change her haircut appointment from Tuesday to next Friday. She calls her hairdresser. (−)

2. Tom would like to borrow his neighbor's lawn mower on Saturday. (+)

3. Pat would like her roommate to cook dinner tonight (even though it's her turn), since Pat's getting home late and won't have time. (−)

4. Bassim would like his companion to pay for lunch this time, since he's short on cash. (+)

5. Laura would like her neighbor to keep his dog out of her yard. (+)

6. Margarita would like to have an extra day to finish the assignment her boss has given her. (−)

7. Yuki would like her neighbor to give her a ride to work in the morning. (+)

8. Enrique would like the man sitting next to him at the lunch counter to **refrain from**° smoking while Enrique is eating. (+)

9. Jean is at a restaurant, and she'd like some cream of broccoli soup. (−)

10. Jamal would like his roommate to turn off the TV so he can go to sleep. (−)

Refrain from means "keep oneself from doing (something)."

REAL **PEOPLE**, REAL **SITUATIONS**, REAL **LANGUAGE**

Now it's your chance to go out into your community and make some real requests of real people. Using your notebook, record both the requests and the responses as accurately as you can.

> **EXAMPLE:** *To roommate: TV is too loud (or not loud enough)*
>
> **Me:** *Bonnie, would you mind turning down the TV a little? I'm talking on the phone, and I'm having a hard time hearing.*
>
> **Bonnie:** *Oh, sure! I'm sorry about that.*

1. To librarian: help finding information on "blood poisoning"
2. To your boss or teacher: help with an assignment
3. To a fast-food restaurant worker: extra ketchup
4. To a neighbor or friend: help moving a piece of furniture
5. To a friend or roommate: loan of a piece of clothing

When you have finished, your teacher may ask you to bring in your findings and compare them with those of your classmates.

CHAPTER 10

APOLOGIZING AND RESPONDING

What would you say to the person if

- you accidentally stepped on the foot of the man sitting beside you at a concert?
- you turned in your homework a day late to your history professor?
- you were 20 minutes late to meet a friend for dinner?
- you backed your car into your neighbor's fence and broke the gate?

It is difficult to write rules that tell exactly when you should apologize, but it is not difficult to learn *how*. If we have done something to hurt someone's feelings, or if we have been impolite or rude, we should apologize. An apology indicates that we realize we've made a mistake, and we're sorry for it. It's a way of expressing our regret or sorrow for something. When we apologize, we admit our wrongdoing or discourtesy (impolite action), usually offer a reason for it, and express regret.

The simplest way to apologize is to say, "I'm sorry," but often that is not enough. Let's take a common situation. Mario is late for class and enters the classroom, interrupting the instructor in the middle of her lecture. What does he do? The most polite action is usually to take a seat as quietly as possible and apologize later. But if the instructor stops and waits for him to say something, he could apologize simply ("I'm sorry I'm late"), ask permission to take his seat, and sit down. Naturally, more than this—a reason for the tardiness—is needed, but this is not the time or the place for it because he has already caused one interruption and doesn't need to make it any longer or worse than it already is.

After class, when he can speak to the teacher privately, Mario can apologize again, this time giving his excuse. He might say, "Professor Johnson, I'm sorry I was late for class this morning. I'm afraid I overslept and missed the bus." When we give an excuse or reason to the person to whom we are apologizing, we are admitting responsibility. Of course, sometimes the situation arises in which we apologize for another person, not ourselves. For instance, a mother in a supermarket might say to the cashier, "I'm sorry my little boy opened that candy bar. I'll gladly pay for it." The mother is accepting the responsibility and blame for her little boy's wrongdoing, and thereby teaching the child a lesson in responsibility.

After the excuse there sometimes (but not always) comes a promise to change, improve, or not to let the action happen again. For example, after Mario gives the reason for his tardiness, he might add, "I won't let it happen again" or "I promise I'll be on time from now on." This last part of the apology may also include an offer or a promise to **make up for**° the mistake, or it may include a question or comment about **rectifying**° the mistake. When the mother says that she will gladly pay for the candy bar her little boy unwrapped, she is trying to make amends or do something to repair the damage caused by her son's behavior. But Mario has nothing to offer his professor as a means of rectifying the situation, so his apology stops with a promise to do better in the future.

PRACTICE 1

Look at each apology. Try to add to it with a reason or excuse that might fit the situation; offer to compensate the person for the problem; and/or

Make up for means "compensate (give something in return) for a wrongdoing or mistake."
Rectifying a problem or mistake means "correcting it or making it right."

make a promise to change, improve, or not to let the action happen again. All three steps (the *excuse*, the *compensation*, and the *promise*) may not always be necessary or appropriate. Be ready to defend your choices for including or omitting the steps in your apologies.

> **EXAMPLE:** *Laura to an acquaintance in English class:*
>
> (Apology)   *Margaret, I'm really sorry, but I lost the pen you let me borrow yesterday.*
>
> *I put it down on the seat beside me on the bus, and I guess I forgot to pick it up when I got off. Here. (She offers Margaret another pen.) I bought you another one. I hope it's okay. And I'm really sorry. I'll be more careful next time.*

NOTE: Although all four parts of the apology are included, the promise is really not necessary because Laura has expressed her regret quite sincerely.

1. Daughter to father:

    (Apology)   Dad, I'm really sorry I got a D in math this semester.

    _____

    _____

    _____

2. Student to teacher:

    (Apology)   Ms. Pratt, I want to apologize for acting so rudely in class

    today. _____

    _____

    _____

3. Peter to roommate:

    (Apology)   Tom, I'm sorry about disturbing you last night with the

    stereo. _____

    _____

    _____

4. Waiter to customer:

    (Apology)   I beg your pardon, ma'am, but I'm afraid we're out of

    swordfish tonight. _____

_____

_____

5. Husband to wife:

    (Apology) Darling, will you forgive me for **snapping at**° you on the

    phone this morning? _____

    _____

    _____

   After someone apologizes to us, how do we respond? Naturally, it depends on the nature of the wrongdoing or discourtesy and the mood we
are in when we receive the apology. If the professor is in a bad mood or is
simply tired of Mario's constant tardiness, she might let her anger show
when she responds:

> I'm tired of your excuses, Mario! From now on, if you're going to
> be 20 minutes late, don't bother coming and interrupting the whole
> class. It's very annoying and distracting for me and for the students
> as well!

The instructor has a legitimate or valid reason for being so angry with
Mario, since he has obviously been late several times before; thus, her negative response to Mario's apology is understandable. Sometimes we *don't*
want to accept a person's apology. In that case, we let the person know why
and still try to keep our anger or annoyance under control. But more often,
we *do* accept another person's apology, and there are several polite ways of
doing so. If the professor is forgiving and accepts Mario's apology, she
might say something like, "That's all right this time, Mario, but please try to
be on time in the future."
   Here are some commonly used expressions for beginning apologies and
for responding to (accepting) them. Of course, there are variations on
these expressions. See if you can think of others. Notice the difference
between the very formal and the informal ones. Can you think of situations
where one would be more appropriate than another? What are some?

_____

Snapping at someone is speaking in a fast, usually annoyed, way. We sometimes
   snap at people when we're in a bad mood or when something bothers or annoys
   us.

Apologies

* I beg your pardon, sir. (I didn't realize you were speaking to me.) (*Formal*)
* Pardon me, please, for . . . (stepping on your foot). (*Formal*)
* I hope you'll forgive . . . (my absence yesterday. I was ill). (*Formal*)
* Excuse me for . . . (being late. I forgot about the time).
* I apologize for . . . (knocking over your cup. I didn't see it).
* I'm $\begin{cases} \text{very} \\ \text{really} \\ \text{awfully} \end{cases}$ sorry . . . (that I woke you).
* Sorry . . . (about the steak. I'll be glad to prepare you another one).
* Sorry about that. (*Informal*)
* _____
* _____

PRACTICE 2

Here are some situations where an apology is necessary. Use a different beginning for each one you make. Add other parts of the apology if they are appropriate.

1. You dropped and broke your friend's saltshaker.
   You:

2. You're fifteen minutes late picking up a friend because you got a phone call as you were going out the door.
   You:

3. You forgot to buy the milk your roommate asked you to get at the supermarket.
   You:

4. You borrowed and then forgot to return your friend's dictionary.
   You:

5. You felt sick yesterday and yelled at a friend for no reason. Today you feel bad about it.
   You:

Acceptances
Accepting an apology is usually quite simple. We often use one of the following responses:

+ That's quite all right. (*Formal*)
+ Think nothing of it.
+ It's all right.
+ Don't worry about it.
+ No harm done.
+ That's okay.
+ Forget it. (*Informal*)
+ No problem. (*Informal*)
+ **No big thing.**° (*Informal*)
+ No sweat. (*Very informal*)
+ _____
+ _____

PRACTICE 3

Respond to each of the five apologies you gave in Practice 2. Try to use a different beginning for each acceptance.

1. **Friend:**

2. **Friend:**

3. **Roommate:**

4. **Classmate:**

5. **Friend:**

SITUATIONAL DIALOGS
Here are some common situations that call for apologies. Most of the responses represent polite ways of accepting apologies. Only one of them is a little negative. Try to explain why. Choose partners, take roles, and read and discuss each dialog. Then answer the questions that follow.

No big thing means "It's not important at all, so there's no need to worry about it."

A.   *In the driveway between their homes:*

Carmen: Oh, Doris! I'm so sorry about Fido tearing up your newspaper again. I'll have George get you another when he comes home.

Doris: Thanks, Carmen, but I wish you'd **keep a** better **eye on°** your dog. He's always getting into my flower beds and digging up my petunias.

Carmen: I really *am* sorry he's caused so much trouble lately. I'll have the fence repaired this week, so he can't get out of the yard. I promise it won't happen again.

Doris: I hope not.

What Do You Think?

1. *Carmen makes two apologies. What are they? What kind of compensation for the first problem does she offer? What does Carmen promise to do to make sure the problem doesn't happen again?*

2. *How is Doris probably feeling when she says, "I hope not"? Is she completely accepting Carmen's apology? Why or why not?*

3. *We don't say, "I kept an eye on TV last night," but we do say, "I'll keep an eye on your house while you're on vacation." What's the difference? What other things do you* keep an eye on?

B.   *In the living room, after Janice has eaten dinner without her husband:*

Janice: Excuse me for not waiting for you, honey, but I didn't know how long you'd be, and I was **starving!°**

Henri: No problem. I had a late meeting and grabbed a bite on the way home.

What Do You Think?

1. *If Janice had been really angry at her husband, what might she have said? How might he have responded? Create a short dialog and have him offer an apology for being so late.*

2. *If you are going to be late for dinner in your country, what do you do? What is the polite thing to do in the United States if you're going to be late—for anything?*

Keep an eye on means "watch carefully."

Starving, in this sense, means "very hungry." Literally, it means "dying from lack of food or nutrition."

3.   *When do you sometimes* grab a bite (to eat)? *Where do you do this and what do you usually have?*

C.   *At the library, after Carla sits in someone's seat by mistake:*

Carla: Oh, I beg your pardon. I didn't know this seat was occupied. I'll move.

Rob: That's all right. I'm leaving anyway.

What Do You Think?

1.   *What does* occupied *mean? Can you think of other ways we use this word?*
2.   *If Rob had been angry with Carla, what do you think he might have said, and how might she have responded?*
3.   *How does Carla offer to make up for her mistake? Would some sort of promise from her have been appropriate? Why or why not?*

D.   *In Ms. Lowery's office at the accounting firm:*

Ms. Wilson: I apologize, Ms. Lowery, but I'm running a little behind schedule. May I bring you the contract tomorrow instead of today?

Ms. Lowery: That's fine. I won't need it until late tomorrow afternoon anyway. But please make sure I have time to review it before my 4 o'clock meeting tomorrow.

What Do You Think?

1.   *If Ms. Lowery were angry at Ms. Wilson, she might have replied differently. Give at least two examples of how she might have responded if she hadn't accepted the apology and the excuse.*
2.   *If Ms. Wilson had wanted to reassure Ms. Lowery that her tardiness was not going to be a habit, what could she have added to her apology?*
3.   *Everyone sometimes* runs behind schedule. *When do you?*

E.   *At a cafe, after the waiter has just spilled coffee on a customer's jacket:*

Waiter: Oh! Excuse me, sir! I'm sorry I'm so clumsy! I'll get something to clean your jacket right away!

Martin: No great harm done. I just hope it doesn't **stain.**°

Waiter: I'll be glad to have your jacket dry-cleaned for you, sir. I do apologize!

Martin: Well, thank you very much. I appreciate it.

Stain means "make a permanent mark or spot usually on fabric."

What Do You Think?

1. *What does* clumsy *mean? How is the waiter clumsy? Could he have used another (perhaps a better) excuse for the accident?*
2. *Martin's reply, "No great harm done" is informal. What kind of formal reply could he have made?*
3. *Would this situation be handled differently by the waiter if this had happened in a restaurant in your country? Explain.*

DIALOG COMPLETIONS   Choose partners and take roles. Then complete the following dialogs by apologizing, accepting an apology, or refusing to accept it. Remember, you may find it necessary to give an excuse or reason, offer some compensation, and/or make a promise about future action or performance.

1. *In a doctor's waiting room:*

Mr. Olson: I beg you pardon, ma'am. I didn't realize this was your newspaper.

Mrs. Sims:

Mr. Olson: Well, thank you very much.

2. *In their dorm room that night:*

Margaret: Sorry about not waiting for you this morning, Leila, but I had to be on time for my 8 o'clock class.

Leila:

Margaret: Well, I *said* I was sorry! I'm not your mother, and I'm not going to stand over you to make sure you get up on time. It's your responsibility—not mine!

Leila:

3. *After class in the classroom:*

Iris: I hope you'll forgive me for not typing my paper, Professor. I'm afraid I don't own a typewriter, and I couldn't find anyone in my dorm to type it for me.

Prof. Lee:

Iris: Yes, sir. I won't wait till the last minute next time. I'm sorry.

Prof. Lee:

4. *In their apartment after Anna returns from a date:*

Anna:

Yoko: No harm done. It was an old blouse anyway. I hardly ever wear it.

Anna:

Yoko: That's really not necessary, you know, but if it will make you feel better—well, okay.

Anna:

5. *At work:*

Ellen:

Hashim: Forget it. I haven't needed to use it. But next time, would you mind telling me when you borrow something?

Ellen:

Hashim: Don't worry about it. It's okay.

6. *At a nice restaurant:*

Waiter: I apologize for the **mix-up°** in your order, ma'am. I'll have your dinner out very shortly.

Wanda:

Waiter: Yes, I know. This is my first day on the job, and I'm having a few problems.

Wanda:

Waiter: Well, thank you for being so understanding. I appreciate it.

7. *In the kitchen of their apartment the next morning:*

Sanora: Sorry if I kept you up last night, Joan. My friends and I were a little noisy, I know.

Joan:

Sanora: Well, I really do apologize. I'll try to be quieter from now on.

Joan:

8. *In their kitchen:*

Dean: What's all this mess in here, Joel?

Joel:

Dean: That's okay, but I need to use the kitchen in a couple of hours. I'm having a few friends over for dinner tonight, remember?

Mix-up means "mistake caused by poor planning or poor communication."

Joel:
Dean: Thanks. I'd appreciate it.

9.   *In Ms. Hill's office at the newspaper:*

Ms. Hill:
   Terry: Yes, ma'am. That was my mistake, and I hope you'll forgive me. I've corrected it now, I think.
Ms. Hill:
   Terry: I realize I've been making a few mistakes lately. But I promise I'll concentrate better on my work. You won't have to reprimand me again, I assure you.
Ms. Hill:
   Terry: Certainly. I understand.

10.   *At work:*

Frederic: Were you able to get us those concert tickets, Dan?
   Dan:
Frederic: You don't have to apologize. You tried. Next time, I won't ask you so late. Thanks anyway.

   Dan:

ROLE PLAYS   Choose partners, read the situations carefully, and prepare a short dialog for each, including an appropriate apology and an acceptance (or you may wish *not* to accept the apology). Remember the various parts of an apology and include those that you think are important or fitting.

   1.   Yoko has just accidentally knocked over and broken her friend's expensive vase from France.

2. Laura **lost her temper**° yesterday and said some very angry words to a friend and co-worker, Paul Daniels.

3. When Maria is pouring a cup of tea for Mrs. Griffin, her next-door neighbor, Mrs. Griffin bumps Maria's arm, and Maria spills some tea on her arm and skirt.

4. Mohammed arrives at the tennis courts 20 minutes late for his match with Ned. This is not the first time Mohammed has been late.

5. Mario's library books were due yesterday, but he was in such a hurry that he forgot them. Now, today, he takes them back to the desk where the librarian is sitting.

Lost her temper means "became angry and showed strong emotions (perhaps by shouting)."

6. Sam and Barbara were supposed to go out for dinner together tonight, but she feels as if she is getting the flu.

7. Harry and Koji were supposed to play racketball tomorrow, but Koji's boss has asked him to go out of town unexpectedly on business.

8. Ahmed was talking to a classmate while the teacher was trying to explain an important grammar point. After class, he scolds Ahmed.

9. Melissa's cat has torn a large hole in her roommate's bedspread. This is not the first time her cat has caused her roommate problems.

10. A friend was supposed to call Paul on Sunday about going swimming at the lake. Paul waited all morning, and he never called. Now it's the next day, and Paul sees him at the bookstore. Paul's a little angry.

REAL **PEOPLE,** REAL **SITUATIONS,** REAL **LANGUAGE**

Go out into your work, school, or social community and listen for people apologizing. Try to record at least five dialogs, using the journal entry format in your notebook. If an excuse, offer of compensation, or promise to change is given, record them as best you can.

EXAMPLE: *Monday, April 9—in my dorm room*

Roommate: *I'm sorry about waking you last night when I turned on the lights. I didn't realize you were already in bed.*

Me: *That's okay. I had just gone to bed anyway.*

Your teacher may ask you to bring in your examples to share and discuss with the other class members.

CHAPTER 11

MAKING EXCUSES

We have already discussed making excuses quite a bit in Chapter 4, "Saying Goodbye"; Chapter 8, "Making, Accepting, and Declining Invitations"; and Chapter 10, "Apologizing and Responding" because three of the most common situations for using excuses are when we say goodbye, when we decline an invitation, and when we apologize to someone. When we're ready to leave, we don't simply say, "Goodbye." We preface our leaving with a reason or an excuse: "It's late, and I have to get up early in the morning." We don't just say, "No, I can't go to the mountains next weekend." We give an excuse: "I already have plans to go to the beach"—to help soften the rejection. And we don't simply say, "I'm sorry I lost your book." We add an excuse to help explain the apology: "I left it in the classroom, and when I returned to get it, it was gone."

Now let's examine some situations that may require excuses. Even though other chapters have dealt with some of these areas in detail, it will be good to review how to make excuses when necessary.

Excuses for When We Refuse Someone Something (a Favor, a Request, an Invitation, for Example)

Suppose Carl wants his neighbor Nancy to drive him to work tomorrow while his car is being repaired. If Nancy can't (or won't) oblige him, she might say, "I wish I could, Carl, but I'm not going into the office until late because I have some clients to call on in the morning." Just saying "No, I can't" would be abrupt and impolite. An excuse softens the rejection. Here are some typical ways of beginning rejections (most have been mentioned in previous chapters) and making excuses:

+ I wish I could, but . . . (offer excuse).
+ Sorry. I can't. I . . . (offer excuse).
+ I'd like to go/help, but I can't. I . . . (offer excuse).
+ _____
+ _____

PRACTICE 1

A friend has asked you for a favor or request or has given you an invitation. Tell your friend *no* and then add a reason or an excuse to soften his or her disappointment.

1. **Martin:** Could I borrow your car for a few hours? Mine's being fixed, and I need to do some shopping.
   You:

2. **Mahmood:** Could you help me move the couch into another room? It's really heavy, and I need some hslp.
   You:

3. **Barry:** How would you like to go on a bicycle ride this Sunday? I think the weather is going to be beautiful, and we could have lunch along the way.
   You:

4.   **Ali:** Would you mind mailing a package for me on your way to work?

   You:

5.   **Nancy:** Would you please slow down a little? You're driving too fast!

   You:

Excuses for When We Apologize for Some Wrong-Doing or Accident or When We Make a Mistake

Suppose Bill accidentally breaks Hernando's coffee mug. Bill might say, "I'm sorry about your cup, Hernando. I wasn't looking where I was going, I knocked it against the refrigerator, and it broke. Of course I'll buy you another one." As mentioned earlier in Chapter 10, we often offer to compensate a person for the wrongdoing or accident. Bill offers to replace Hernando's coffee cup. If Hernando accepts Bill's apology and excuse, he might say, "That's all right, Bill. Don't worry about it" or "You don't have to. It wasn't expensive." Of course, Hernando could also say, "Well, thanks, Bill. I'd appreciate it" (meaning he is accepting the apology, the excuse, *and* Bill's offer to compensate him for the broken cup). The previous chapter dealt with accepting and rejecting apologies in greater detail.

PRACTICE 2

Here are some situations that describe mistakes that have been made. With a partner, create a short dialog and give appropriate excuses and responses to them.

1. Perry, Tom's roommate, played his stereo very loud last night.
   Perry:
   Tom:

2. Joe is late for an important meeting because he overslept; however, he doesn't want his client to know this.
   Joe:
   Client:

3. The cashier keeps a customer waiting a long time.
   Cashier:
   Customer:

4. Melanie forgets (for the third day in a row) to bring Koji the book he asked to borrow. She feels embarrassed about her forgetfulness.

   Melanie:
   Koji:

5. Jason knocks over and breaks a bottle of Marlene's expensive perfume.

   Jason:
   Marlene:

Excuses for When We Want to Leave or to Get Out of a Difficult or Uncomfortable Situation

"Difficult" or "uncomfortable" situations can be quite varied. Suppose Heinz is at a friend's house. His friend Robert is talking nonstop, and Heinz is very bored and uncomfortable. He sneaks a glance at his watch and sees that it is nearly 1:30 A.M. He might say (surprised), "Gosh, I can't believe how late it is! I need to be leaving. I have a long day tomorrow." His excuse is a perfectly acceptable one, since it is very late, and he has a difficult day ahead (usually the meaning of *a long day tomorrow*). In other situations, where the person wants to leave but doesn't have a completely valid reason, the person might use vague excuses like "I have some things to do" or "I need to get back to work" as preludes (beginnings) to saying goodbye.

PRACTICE 3

Here are some situations dealing with leaving and getting out of difficult predicaments. Choose a partner and create a short dialog for each, with appropriate excuses and responses to them.

1. Diego wants to leave a boring, unimportant business meeting and go play tennis. Of course, he doesn't want his boss to know the real reason for leaving.

2. Carol has a terrible headache and wants to cancel her date with Rob, whom she is not very fond of anyway.

3. It's very late, you're tired, and you want to go home. However, you're at Enrique's house, and you rode with Sam, who is having a great time and obviously doesn't want to leave yet.

4. Maxine is with Greg on their first date. They're at a movie that has lots of violence and sex. Maxine is very uncomfortable and embarrassed and wants to leave.

5. Ana Marie is having dinner at her boss' house with him and his wife. They want to show her their pictures and slides of the Grand Canyon, but Ana Marie is ready to go home. However, she doesn't want to offend them or hurt their feelings.

There are other situations that may require excuses. Can you think of some? Can you think of certain predicaments that require excuses in your country but not in the United States? And what about other cases, where an excuse may not be needed or required in your country but is in the United States? Discuss these with other members of the class and your teacher.

SITUATIONAL DIALOGS

Here are some examples of how excuses are used in common, everyday situations. Choose partners, take roles, and read the dialogs. Next, discuss the language used and how successful, polite, and appropriate the excuses and responses are. Then answer the questions or do the tasks that follow.

A. *Diana invites Ameed to a dance that her club is having. Ameed really wants to go, but he can't.*

Diana: Ameed, you know the Spanish Club is having a dance next Friday night, don't you? Well, I was wondering if you'd like to go with me.

Ameed: I'd really like to, Diana, but I can't. I'm going out of town for the weekend. If I'd known sooner, I might have been able to change my plans. I'm really sorry.

Diana: Me, too. Well, I hope you have a nice time.

Ameed: Thanks. And I hope you do, too.

What Do You Think?

1. *What is Ameed's excuse for not being able to go? Does he appropriately express his regret? If so, how?*
2. *If Diana had really wanted Ameed to accompany her, what might she have said to try to make him change his mind and his plans?*
3. *Change the dialog and the excuse that Ameed uses.*

B. *Jimmy mistakenly takes Rudi's book bag from a cluttered table in the student lounge. The bags are very similar in appearance.*

Rudi: Ummm . . . Jimmy. I think that's my bag.

Jimmy: Are you sure?

Rudi: Yes, I think so. Mine has an ink stain on the bottom, and this one doesn't—so it must be yours.

Jimmy: You're right. I'm sorry about that. I was in such a hurry to get to class that I guess I grabbed the wrong one.

Rudi: That's okay. I'm just glad I realized it now—before we went to our separate classrooms.

What Do You Think?

1. *What is Jimmy's reason for taking Rudi's book bag? Does Rudi accept the reason and the apology?*
2. *What other excuses could Jimmy have used?*
3. *Think of a similar situation (such as walking away with someone else's shopping cart by mistake in the supermarket) and create a short dialog between you and the other person.*

C. *Margarita has not finished her essay that is due today in writing class. After class, she goes up to the professor.*

Margarita: Dr. Wells, I'm sorry, but I didn't turn in my essay today.

Dr. Wells: Oh? Why not?

Margarita: I've had a lot of personal problems lately, and I just haven't been able to concentrate very well on my school work.

Dr. Wells: Well, Margarita, since this is the first time you've been late with an assignment, **I'll let it go** °—but I expect you to have it ready on Thursday. All right?

Margarita: Certainly, Dr. Wells. It'll be ready. Thank you for understanding.

Dr. Wells: Well, I hope you solve your problems soon.

What Do You Think?

1. *Margarita's excuse is vague—perhaps on purpose. What do you think* personal problems *mean?*
2. *Margarita was lucky that Dr. Wells accepted her excuse. How might he have responded if he hadn't believed her excuse or if he simply hadn't accepted it?*
3. *Change the dialog: Margarita gives an excuse that Dr. Wells finds unacceptable, and he responds.*

D. *Chen is having dinner at an American family's home. Mr. and Mrs. Rogers keep offering him more food, but Chen really doesn't like it. However, he doesn't want to seem impolite or ungrateful.*

Mr. Rogers: What about some more peas, Chen? I grew them in my own garden, you know.

Chen: Did you? How nice. But really, I can't eat any more. I still have lots on my plate.

I'll let it go means "I won't punish or penalize you this time."

Mrs. Rogers:	You haven't even tried the bread. Would you like some?
Chen:	No thank you. I try not to eat too much bread or too many sweets. I've put on a lot of weight since I came to the United States.
Mrs. Rogers:	Oh, you look fine, Chen. I don't think you need to lose a pound.
Mr. Rogers:	Neither do I. Have some carrot and raisin salad. It's good for you.
Chen:	Oh, I couldn't. I'm very full.

What Do You Think?

1. *What are the three excuses Chen makes when he is asked to have more food? How successful is he at convincing his host and hostess that he doesn't care for any more?*
2. *What do you say in your country when you are offered more food, and you really do not like it at all?*
3. *In the United States a guest is usually offered food only once. If it is refused, the host might say, "Are you sure?" but it is usually not offered a second time. How does this custom compare with offering food in your country? Discuss this topic with other members of the class.*

E. *Renée, the baby-sitter, has some questions to ask before Mrs. Jackson leaves her with Mike for the evening.*

Renée:	Would it be all right if I took Mike to the park, Mrs. Jackson?
Mrs. Jackson:	I wish you wouldn't today, Renée. He's just getting over a bad cold, and I think it's too damp and cold for him outside.
Renée:	Okay. I understand. What about his bedtime? 9 o'clock, as usual?
Mrs. Jackson:	No. Put him to bed earlier—about 8 o'clock—because he didn't have a nap this afternoon, and he seems a little tired.
Renée:	That's fine. Oh—and Mrs. Jackson. Do you think you'll be home around midnight?
Mrs. Jackson:	Yes. I don't plan to be out much later. Why?
Renée:	Well, you know I usually don't mind baby-sitting until 1 o'clock or 2 o'clock, but tomorrow's a school day, and I have a big exam at 8 o'clock.
Mrs. Jackson:	That's fine, Renée. I promise to be back before midnight.

What Do You Think?

1. *The excuses Mrs. Jackson offers in her first and second comments are a little different from the ones we've just studied. Mrs. Jackson answers Reneé's questions, and then gives reasons for these answers. She could have just said, "No, don't take him to the park" without explaining why, but she chose to offer Reneé a reason or excuse for saying no. What are the two reasons she uses in response to Reneé's questions, and are they logical and acceptable? Is there any way to tell if they are real reasons or simply excuses to hide another reason?*

2. *Expand the dialog so that Mrs. Jackson makes two or three other excuses for certain instructions she wants Reneé to follow.*

3. *What is Reneé's excuse for needing to go home earlier than usual? How does Mrs. Jackson respond to it?*

DIALOG COMPLETIONS   Here are some unfinished dialogs that deal with excuses for all types of situations. Choose partners, take roles, and complete the dialogs, using appropriate reasons and excuses and responding to them if necessary. Pay special attention to background information and to clues within the dialogs. Then change roles and complete the dialogs differently.

1. *Jennifer invites George to a concert. He doesn't have any plans, but he likes another girl and doesn't want to go out with Jennifer.*

Jennifer: George! Guess what? I have tickets to the Prince concert next Friday! Can you go with me?

George:

Jennifer: Oh? What kind of plans?

George:

Jennifer: That's too bad. Can't you change them? This is going to be a great concert!

George:

Jennifer: Okay. I see.

2. *Ahmed has been late several times lately. He doesn't have a very valid excuse this time.*

Ms. Callahan: Ahmed, this is the third time this month you've been late for work. What's your excuse this time?

Ahmed:

Ms. Callahan: Really? That's what you told me last week. Why don't you get your car fixed then?

Ahmed:

Ms. Callahan: Well, Ahmed. Payday is this Thursday. I certainly hope you'll be able to have your car repaired soon. Your lateness to work is going to have to stop.

3.   *Brad would like Fay to help him fix dinner, but Fay is exhausted and wants to finish a good book she's reading.*

Brad: Fay, I really could use some help in the kitchen. I'm not really sure about the instructions in this salmon recipe.

Fay:

Brad: Well, could you at least set the table? How much energy could that take?

Fay:

Brad: I don't believe you! You have an excuse for everything!

4.   *Barbara was supposed to call Walid last night about a composition assignment he missed, but she didn't.*

Walid: What happened last night, Barb?

Barbara:

Walid: I thought you were going to call me last night and give me the assignment?

Barbara:

Walid: That's no excuse, Barbara. Couldn't you have used a pay phone to call?

Barbara:

Walid: Well, okay. But I don't know what I'm going to do when Mr. Rosewall asks me for my composition.

Barbara:

Walid: Are you kidding? I couldn't say that. I can't lie.

Barbara:

Walid: Yeah. I think the truth is best, too.

5.   *Luis asks Vicki out on a date, but she doesn't feel well.*

Luis: The new *Rocky* movie starts tonight, Vicki. Would you like to go?

Vicki:

Luis: Oh, that's too bad. What about tomorrow night if you're feeling better?

Vicki:

Luis: Sure. I understand. I'll call you tomorrow and check on you. I hope you feel better.

6. *Harvey is having a boring time at an informal gathering at Ahmad's house. He wants to leave, but he hasn't been there very long.*

Ahmad: Would you like another diet drink, Harvey?
Harvey:
Ahmad: But you just got here!
Harvey:
Ahmad: Would you like some aspirin?
Harvey:
Ahmad: Well, okay. I wish you wouldn't go, but I understand.

7. *Bart wants Masumi to teach him some Japanese, but she doesn't feel confident enough to do it.*

Bart: Say, Masumi. Would you be interested in teaching me some Japanese once or twice a week? I could help you with your English in return.
Masumi:
Bart: Oh, I'm sure you'd do a good job. I just want to learn some elementary grammar and conversation skills.
Masumi:
Bart: Well, okay. I guess I understand, but I wish you'd change your mind. It wouldn't have to take up *that* much of your time.

8. *Wanda borrows Lillian's jacket, and someone at a party spills some sauce on it.*

Wanda:
Lillian: You did? How did it happen?
Wanda:
Lillian: It didn't come out?
Wanda:
Lillian: I use the Pinecrest Cleaners about a mile from here.
Wanda:
Lillian: Don't worry. It doesn't look so bad. The cleaners can probably get it out.

9. *Abdulla and Danny just bought a microwave oven for their apartment, and Abdulla* **tried it out** ° *on a dinner. He asks Danny to be in charge of fixing dinner tomorrow night, but Danny declines.*

Tried (something) **out** means "tested (something) by using and experimenting with (it)."

Danny: That was a great dinner you fixed in the microwave, Abdulla. I can't believe how quick and easy it was.

Abdulla:

Danny: My turn? Tomorrow?

Abdulla:

Danny:

Abdulla: Well, I thought that was what we decided on, Danny— we would take turns cooking dinner each night. I think you need to change your plans.

Danny:

10. *Deborah wants to borrow a silk dress that belongs to her roommate, Claudia, but Claudia is hesitant about lending her clothes to anyone.*

Deborah: Claudia, I was wondering . . . could you do me a big favor?

Claudia:

Deborah: Well, Joel asked me to dinner tomorrow night at a very elegant French restaurant, and I don't have anything appropriate to wear. Could I possibly wear your blue silk dress? It would be perfect!

Claudia:

Deborah: Oh, couldn't you make an exception this time, Claudia? I promise I won't let anything happen to it! I'm just going out to dinner! I'll even have it dry-cleaned for you.

Claudia:

Deborah: Well, I'm not Mary! I won't ruin it—I promise!

Claudia:

Deborah: Thanks a lot, Claudia! I'll be *really* careful with it! You can trust me!

ROLE PLAYS   Here are some situations dealing with all sorts of predicaments where reasons and excuses need to be used. Choose partners, take roles, and act them out, using appropriate excuses and responses. When you finish, change roles and redo the dialogs a little differently.

1. Carla doesn't go to her 8 o'clock class because she hasn't done her homework for that class. That afternoon, she runs into her teacher, who asks her why she wasn't in class that morning.

2. A new waiter spills hot coffee on a customer's arm because he isn't watching carefully and because the customer bumps him when turning to speak to his dinner companion.

3. Yasser needs to pick up his brother at the airport in an hour. His car won't start, so he asks Diane to lend him hers. Diane doesn't know Yasser well and doesn't want to lend him her car, but she doesn't want to hurt his feelings.

4. Bob invites Nadia to the beach with his family for a week in July. She really wants to go, but she has some work schedule conflicts.

5. Anton can't repay Barry the $25 he borrowed from him last week, and he knows Barry needs the money. Anton's real reason for not being able to pay it back is that he spent the money taking his girlfriend out to dinner, but he doesn't want to tell Barry.

6. Yoko's aunt has invited her to Miami for the weekend. Yoko doesn't want to go because she thinks she'll be bored with her aunt and her aunt's friends.

7. Margarita must cancel a tennis game—for the third straight day—with Hassan. She has to go out of town on business.

8. Lillian is eating dinner with Rosemary, who has cooked an elaborate but unappealing meal. Rosemary offers her more food, but Lillian refuses politely.

9. Patty needs some help cleaning the apartment, but Marta, her roommate, always has some excuse. Patty is angry that Marta always avoids helping.

10. Joe, a friend of Susan, wants her to hurry to complete her university application and send it in. But Susan keeps giving Joe excuses for not doing it.

REAL **PEOPLE,** REAL **SITUATIONS,** REAL **LANGUAGE**

Take your notebook with you for the next several days as you go about your daily activities. Listen to people talking (in school, at work, in the community) and record excuses you hear them using. As usual, use the journal entry format, and try to record at least five.

EXAMPLE: *Monday, Feb. 24—standing in line at the post office*

Girl 1:   *Did you send Irene a birthday card?*

Girl 2:   *Oh no! How could I be so stupid? I bought a card for her last week and forgot to mail it.*

Girl 1:   *Well, you could call her tonight, couldn't you?*

Girl 2:   *No, I can't! She's on a business trip, and I don't know where she's staying.*

CHAPTER 12

COMPLIMEN-TING AND RESPONDING

Compliments are expressions of admiration, respect, or praise. Everyone likes to receive compliments; they make us feel good about ourselves. Complimenting people and responding to compliments given us by others are major parts of our daily lives. It's sometimes easier to *tell* someone we like his or her new shirt than it is to *respond* when someone says, "I really like the cologne you're wearing." If the compliment is too personal, some people become flustered, nervous, or embarrassed; they don't know how to reply. Responding doesn't have to be difficult.

Responses to Compliments

Here are some beginnings of responses to compliments. These may vary with the situation and the particular compliment. Try to think of others.

✤ You're too kind. (*Formal*) (Compliment: The dinner was delicious.)

✤ Thank you for saying so. (Compliment: You did a fine job on the report.)

✤ I appreciate the compliment. (Compliment: That's a beautiful belt!)

✤ Thank you. I'm glad you { like it. (Compliment: Your hair looks nice.)
enjoyed it. (Compliment: The cake was wonderful.)
think so. (Compliment: Your car drives great!)

✤ Thanks. I like your _____, too. (Return the compliment.)

✤ _____

✤ _____

We all get embarrassed by compliments sometimes, but we should try to be gracious when receiving them in order to make the giver feel good. It's all right to show disagreement with a compliment; just try to do it in a polite, nonthreatening way.

PRACTICE 1

Read each compliment and response. Then change the rejection to a more gracious, accepting response. You can show that you disagree, but don't be quite so negative.

EXAMPLE: **Abdulla:** *You're a great dancer, Doris! I wish I could do half as well as you!*

(Reject) **Doris:** *You've got to be kidding! I'm an awful dancer!*

(Accept) **Doris:** *Thanks, Abdulla. That's nice of you to say so, but sometimes I don't feel I'm very good at all!*

1. **Tom:** Your necklace is pretty, Pat. Is it sterling silver?
    (Reject) **Pat:** Oh, I've had this old thing for years—it's not real silver.

(Accept)   **Pat:**

2.   **Jamal:**   You look really nice tonight, Vicki.
    (Reject)   **Vicki:**   No, I don't! I look as awful as I feel!
    (Accept)   **Vicki:**

3.   **Janet:**   I thought your tennis game was a lot better today,
                                 Anne!
    (Reject)   **Anne:**   You've got to be kidding! I thought it was terrible!
    (Accept)   **Anne:**

4.   **Frank:**   Your new hairstyle is quite attractive, Mary.
    (Reject)   **Mary:**   I hate it, Frank. I think it makes me look 10 years
                                 older!
    (Accept)   **Mary:**

5.   **Earl:**   Chen, this chicken dish is very nice! I really wish
                                 you'd make it more often!
    (Reject)   **Chen:**   I think it tastes terrible, Earl! I put too much salt in
                                 it, and I didn't cook it long enough!
    (Accept)   **Chen:**

To make it easier to learn how to give and accept compliments, we can put them into different categories, depending on what we are complimenting. For example, we often compliment people on their physical or personal appearance, skills or talents, work accomplished, and possessions. Each category will be examined, and some typical compliments and responses to them will be provided.

Compliments on Appearance
There are some aspects of a person's appearance that are fine to compliment and there are others that should be avoided. The more intimate we are with a person, the more personal our compliments can be. Men and women compliment each other in friendship, dating, or marital relationships, and this is quite normal—and even expected. A man may compliment a woman on her eyes, hair, smile, figure, or general appearance. However, it would not be in good taste to compliment a woman on more personal parts of her body—unless the two people were very intimate with each other. Women compliment men, too, and generally on some of the same aspects of their appearance—a nice haircut, a warm smile, a good tan—but, again, very personal parts of the body should not be the subject of compliments.

Here are some typical compliments on physical or personal appearance and responses to them:

1. **Robert:** You really have beautiful eyes, Barbara. I've never seen such a gorgeous **shade°** of blue.
   Barbara: Thank you, Robert. That's a nice compliment.

2. **Abdulla:** Gosh, you look great, Beverly! Have you lost weight?
   Beverly: That's nice of you to notice—I've lost about 10 pounds, but I still need to lose another 5 or 6.

3. **Gene:** Your new hairstyle is terrific, Cindy!
   Cindy: Thanks, Gene. I think I've finally found a style that looks decent and is easy to handle.

PRACTICE 2

Here are some aspects of a person's physical or personal appearance. Make a compliment for each, and then have the person respond to it in a positive way.

1. José's new haircut
   You:
   José:

2. Carol's pretty lipstick
   You:
   Carol:

3. Margaret's teeth (Her **braces°** have just been removed.)
   You:
   Margaret:

4. Ahmed's appearance (He's wearing formal clothes to a dance.)
   You:
   Ahmed:

5. Karen's long, pretty fingernails
   You:
   Karen:

A **shade** is a degree of color.
Braces are devices that a special dentist puts inside the mouth to straighten teeth.

Compliments on Skills or Talents   Complimenting people
on their skills or talents is a common, natural activity. Here are some typical
compliments and responses to them:

1.   **Pat:**   I didn't know you could play the guitar so well, Nak.
                   Your song was lovely!

      Nak: Thanks, Pat. I'm glad you enjoyed it.

2.   **Yumi:**   Joe, your **backhand**° is getting stronger every time
                  we play!

      Joe: Do you really think so? I've been practicing every
                  day, and I'm pleased you can see an improve-
                  ment.

3.   **Maxine:** Bud, your photographs are unbelievable! I really
                  wish you'd give me some advice to help my pic-
                  tures come out better. [Asking for someone's
                  help, advice, or suggestions on something that
                  person is good at is a type of compliment itself.]

      Bud: Thank you, Maxine. I'm not sure how much help I
                  can be, but I'd be glad to give you a few **tips.**°

At this point it might be good to mention the difference between *complimenting* someone and *flattering* somebody. Compliments are given with no
ulterior motives (no hidden reasons and with nothing to gain). Flattery,
however, is usually insincere complimenting for specific (sometimes hidden) purposes (to please a person, to get something from a person, etc.).
For example, suppose José wants his roommate Jack to help him with his
English homework, but he knows that Jack is busy with his own work. José
may try to use flattery to help persuade Jack to help him. Look at the
following dialog and see if you can tell how José is more than complimenting Jack—he's flattering him with a specific purpose in mind:

José: You know, Jack, your English is much better than most
            Americans'.

Jack: Thanks, José, but really, mine's not so good. I make a lot of
            mistakes—like most people.

José: But you really understand the rules of grammar better than
            most people. And you're so patient with people—like

---

A **backhand** is a tennis stroke made with the back of the hand turned in the same
   direction as the movement.

Tips (or *pointers*) are helpful pieces of advice.

with my Spanish friends. When they're visiting and they ask you a question, you take the time to answer and explain it. Not many Americans do that. Well, I was . . . uh . . . wondering, Jack, could you take a look at my composition and let me know if I've made any big mistakes? I'd really appreciate it.

Jack: Well, er . . . I don't know, José. I really think you ought to do your own work.

José: I've *done* the work! It's just that you're a lot better at spotting grammar mistakes than I am, and I'd really appreciate your helping me out.

Jack: Well, okay. I guess I could point out a few of your big mistakes, but I want you to try to correct them yourself. Okay?

José: Sure! And thanks a lot, Jack.

Did you notice how José buttered Jack up (an idiomatic expression that means "used flattery to gain something") before actually asking him the favor? What are some of the ways José used flattery on Jack? Was he successful at getting Jack's help? Can you sometimes tell when people are flattering you? Relate an incident you remember that involved someone flattering you—or you flattering someone—with an ulterior motive. What was that motive and was the flattery successful?

PRACTICE 3

Now let's practice some more sincere complimenting—this time on the person's skills or talents, and then have them respond graciously.

1. Lynne's skill at handling the children at the kindergarten where she works
   You:
   Lynne:

2. Your employee's ability to deal with a delicate and difficult situation
   You:
   Employee:

3. Linda's talent for sewing
   You:
   Linda:

4. Johan's talent for public speaking
   You:
   Johan:

5. Maria's skill at driving in the mountains
   You:
   Maria:

Compliments on Work Accomplished

When someone has done a job well or has performed a task in such a fine way that it deserves to be recognized, we often compliment the person. Sometimes we use the word *congratulations* in our praise: "Congratulations on getting that new position, Paula! You really deserved it!" Offering congratulations is a way to compliment someone. Here are some other typical ways and responses to them.

1. **Millie:** You did a fine job on the room, Mike. I don't think I've ever seen it that clean!

   Mike: Oh, it was nothing. I'm glad I could help.

2. **Mr. Jones:** Congratulations, Barry! That report you wrote was excellent! I'd like to use it as a model at the staff meeting Friday.

   Barry: Thank you, Mr. Jones. I'd be **flattered°** for you to use it.

3. **Wang:** I don't know how you did it, Carl, but the stereo works beautifully now. **You deserve a medal°** for your work.

   Carl: It wasn't hard at all. I'm an electronics major—remember?

PRACTICE 4

Compliment each of the following people on the job completed. Then let your partner respond to the compliment graciously.

1. Bassim wrote a fine composition in writing class, and the teacher read it aloud.
   You:
   Bassim:

In this case, **flattered** is being used in a positive way; it means "honored."
You deserve a medal (or *an award*, *a pat on the back*, *a hand* [applause]) means that the person deserves some recognition and praise for a job well done.

2. Pedro cleaned out the closets in the apartment you share.
   You:
   Pedro:

3. Marilyn typed your term paper for you, and she did an excellent job.
   You:
   Marilyn:

4. Mark, a co-worker, made a delicious cake for you and brought it into the office for your birthday.
   You:
   Mark:

5. Hans, a neighbor, planted a beautiful flower garden.
   You:
   Hans:

Compliments on Possessions

It's nice to compliment someone on something owned by that person—a piece of jewelry, a car, a shirt, a piece of artwork—but be careful how far you go. It is considered impolite to pry into people's personal business. For instance, it's fine to say, "That's a beautiful watch, Greg!" but it's *not* all right to add, "How much did you pay for it?" If you know the person extremely well, you may be able to ask *some* personal questions without offending the person, but you should preface your question with "Do you mind my asking . . . ?" You need to be careful not to ask very personal, direct questions of just anyone—especially if the questions relate to money, age, or sex. If the person wants to reveal more (how much the watch cost, where it was purchased, etc.), the person will usually do it without having to be asked directly. In summary, it's fine to compliment someone on a possession, but know when to stop. Don't go too far and begin asking personal questions that the person may prefer not to answer and may cause both of you some embarrassment.

Here are some examples of acceptable compliments on possessions and responses:

1. **Abdul:** Your new sweater is very pretty, Sue.
   Sue: Thank you. My sister gave it to me for my birthday. I like yours, too. Is it new?

2. **Yoko:** Your house is lovely! I especially like what you've done to the front yard.
   Lynn: Really? That's nice of you to say so.

3. **Arthur:** You know, I *do* like your new glasses, Bob. I don't know exactly what it is, but **they make you look older**.°

Bob: Thanks. I take that as a compliment, I guess. I think they help my new image as a banker, don't you?

PRACTICE 5

Compliment each of the following people on their possessions. Then, your partner should reply politely and graciously.

1. Diana's new blouse
   You:
   Diana:

2. Hernando's sailboat
   You:
   Hernando:

3. Betty's briefcase
   You:
   Betty:

4. Aziz's new running shoes
   You:
   Aziz:

5. Satoshi's flower arrangement in her apartment
   You:
   Satoshi:

Finally, complimenting *should* be a pleasant activity, but what do you do about people who search for compliments? These are people who directly ask, "How do you like my new dress?" or "What do you think about my new hairstyle?" These people want you to compliment them and make them feel good about themselves.

They make you look older: Be careful how you use phrases such as this or the reverse, ". . . make you look younger." Some people are offended by these "age" compliments; others may be flattered. A 50-year-old woman might like to be told she looks younger, but a 20-year-old woman may be offended (if she is trying to look older).

Honesty is *not* always the best policy when responding to these compliment-seekers, but we can often hedge (refuse to answer directly) by using words such as *interesting* or *different*. If you're not particularly fond of the dress, you might say, "Oh, it's very interesting" or "I like the color." (Pick one positive thing about it—if you can—and compliment it.) The better you know the person, the more honest you can be. For instance, if you're not too fond of your friend's new hairstyle, you could say "It's nice, but I really liked the other way, too." Try not to hurt the other person's feelings—especially when it's obvious he or she is looking for a compliment from you. Chapter 18, "Hiding Feelings," gives more explanation on this very delicate subject.

SITUATIONAL DIALOGS
The following dialogs show various situations where complimenting (as well as flattering and congratulating) and responding to the compliments take place. Choose partners, take roles, and act out the dialogs, using any gestures or facial expressions you feel are appropriate. Then discuss each dialog and try to answer the questions that follow.

> A. *Yoko is standing at the bus stop, and Carol, an acquaintance, joins her.*

> **Carol:** Hi, Yoko. I almost didn't recognize you with your hair fixed that way. It looks great!
> **Yoko:** Do you really like it? I wasn't too sure about it yesterday when I had it done.
> **Carol:** It really looks nice. It flatters you—especially your eyes.
> **Yoko:** Well, thanks. I was nervous about having it done, but I guess I'm glad I did.
> **Carol:** I know what you mean. I'm always reluctant about changing anything about my appearance. But I'm serious—your hair really looks cute!

What Do You Think?

> 1. *Why does Yoko question Carol's compliment with "Do you really like it?"*
> 2. *What does Carol mean about being* reluctant? *What are some things she might be reluctant to change?*
> 3. *How does Carol build up Yoko's confidence again and again?*

> B. *Marian is trying on a pair of pants and comes outside the* **dressing room°** *to look at herself in the mirror. A salesclerk comes up to her.*

A **dressing room** is a small room in a clothing store for trying on clothes.

Salesclerk: Those pants look lovely on you. Do you like them?
Marian: Well, I don't know. They fit fine at the waist, but don't you think they're a little **baggy°** on my hips?
Salesclerk: Not at all! That's exactly how they should fit—a little loose on the hips. That's the style this season.
Marian: I know, but I really think they make me look fat.
Salesclerk: You must be joking! You have a **darling°** figure, and the pants look wonderful! With a wide belt, they'd look even better.
Marian: Well, I don't know. I think I'll look around a little more before deciding.

What Do You Think?

1. *The salesclerk tries to use flattery to convince Marian to buy the pants. How does she do this? Is she successful?*
2. *In the United States, many salespeople are paid on commission; that is, they often receive a small salary for working, but the big money comes when they sell something to someone—and the larger the sale, the more money (commission) they make. Can you understand why people who work on commission may seem to be more aggressive than those who work just on straight salary? Is working for a commission common in your country?*
3. *What direct and indirect compliments does the salesclerk give Marian?*

C. *Laura has spent a lot of money on a new suit, and Brenda, her roommate, does not like it very much.*

Laura: You haven't said a word about my new suit, Brenda. Don't you like it?
Brenda: I'm sorry I didn't say anything about it sooner. It certainly is unique; I don't think I've seen anything like it before.
Laura: I know. That's why I bought it. I hate wearing the same styles everybody else is wearing. Do you think it makes me look too big?
Brenda: Well, horizontal stripes always make people look larger than they really are. But I really like the fabric. Is it silk?
Laura: Silk and linen. I love the way it feels.
Brenda: And the color is very unusual.

Baggy means "hanging loosely."
Darling, as used here, means "cute" or "nice." It's an adjective that women usually use more than men. Others are *sweet, precious,* and *adorable.*

Laura: Thanks. That's another reason I like it. You don't see much peach and brown this season.

What Do You Think?

1. *Notice that Brenda doesn't answer Laura's question directly about how the suit makes her look. What does her answer tell you, though? And how does she change the subject?*
2. *By using the word* unusual *in reference to the color, Brenda may be hedging. Can you think of other adjectives that can have either positive or negative interpretations? How do you think Laura interpreted Brenda's response about the color?*
3. *Brenda does find one aspect of the suit to compliment. What is it?*

D. *Larry and Bashar are sitting in their dorm room, watching a tennis match on TV.*

Bashar: By the way, Larry, I was walking by the tennis courts this afternoon and saw you and Hernando playing. Your serve was unbeatable!

Larry: Thanks, Bashar. I don't know what happened, but I **aced°** him five times!

Bashar: Wow! That's super! And your backhand wasn't bad, either!

Larry: Well, it still needs some work. I don't feel as comfortable with it as I do my forehand. *You* ought to give me some **pointers°** on that part of my game! Yours is incredible!

Bashar: Aw—It's okay, but I don't think it's *that* good.

What Do You Think?

1. *How is Bashar using* wasn't bad *in his second comment? It's a positive expression that we sometimes say in a joking way, but we're being very complimentary. Do you have expressions like this in your native language?*
2. *What opportunity does Larry use to compliment Bashar?*
3. *How does Bashar respond to the compliment? Do you think he is embarrassed by it?*

E. *David and Olive are having dinner together and talking about their day at the law office. They work together and are good friends.*

Aced means (in tennis) "served an unreturnable ball and won the point."
Pointers are helpful suggestions or advice.

David: I heard Mr. Thomas complimenting your work on the Jackson case, Olive. He was talking to John Peterson next door.

Olive: Really? Well, I wish he'd compliment *me*! He has never said a word to me about it.

David: I know. That's the way he is. He never compliments anyone face to face, but I know he's proud of you. From what I heard, you must have done a terrific job.

Olive: Oh, I worked pretty hard on it, but I know I didn't work as hard as you did on that big case in January. I don't know if I told you, but I thought you did a superb job.

David: Thanks, Olive. I hope you don't think I was fishing for a compliment. I just wanted you to know that your good work has not gone unnoticed.

What Do You Think?

1. *Olive takes the opportunity to compliment David in her own response to his compliment. How does she do this?*

2. *What does David mean when he uses the expression,* fishing for a compliment? *Why does he say this? What are some ways people* fish for compliments?

3. *Pretend it is the next morning, and Olive is in her office. Mr. Thomas comes in and compliments her. Create a short dialog between Olive and her employer.*

DIALOG COMPLETIONS   Choose partners and complete each dialog as you think it needs to be by making compliments, congratulating, flattering, and responding. Be sure to look for clues to help you know how to respond. Then change roles and act out the dialogs again, using different lines.

1. *At home (Sara and Tom are wife and husband):*

Sara:

Tom: It's pretty, honey. Where did you buy it?

Sara:

Tom: No, it looks great—especially with your nice tan. I think you should keep it.

Sara:

2. *In their dorm room:*

Chris: What do you think about my new leather jacket, Yuki?

Yuki:

Chris: Does it look too big to you?
Yuki:
Chris: Thanks. I knew I had to have it the moment I saw it in the window.

3. *On the tennis court:*

Edward: That was fun, Brian! You played a great game!
Brian:
Edward: Thanks, but I don't know. My serve didn't have the power I wanted it to have. I don't know what I was doing wrong.
Brian: At least you didn't hit it into the net four times in a row—like me!
Edward:
Brian: Thanks. I've been trying to do more running lately to get my legs in better shape. I guess that's helped.

4. *In the classroom:*

Naomi: I love your shoes, June. Did you get them here?
June:
Naomi:
June: Thank you, Naomi. I got it for my birthday last week.

5. *At the disco (Asim and Doris have just met):*

Asim:
Doris: That's a nice compliment. Thank you.
Asim:
Doris:

6. *In the office at work:*

Manager:
Luigi: You're very kind, Mr. Sloan. Thank you for the compliment.
Manager: You deserve it, Luigi. And your work on the new shopping mall project has been very fine, too. Keep up the good work.
Luigi:

7. *In a shoe store:*

Salesclerk:
Lillian: I don't know. I think they look kind of funny on my feet, don't you?

Salesclerk:
 Lillian: I guess you're right. Okay. I'll take them.
Salesclerk:
 Lillian: Thank you.

  8. At dinner at Masumi's house:

 Celina:
Masumi: I'm glad you like it, Celina. It's called *yakitori*, and it's
    made with chicken livers.
 Celina:
Masumi: Sure, I'll be glad to. It's really easy to fix.

  9. After a big basketball game in the locker room:

Coach: Congratulations, Juan! You played a great game!
 Juan:
Coach:
 Juan: Thanks, Coach, but I don't deserve all the praise. If it
    weren't for Carl, I'd have been in big trouble.
Coach:

  10. On a second date:

Samir: What have you done to your hair, Paula? It looks differ-
    ent.
Paula:
Samir: No, I think it makes you look more sophisticated but not
    really older.
Paula:
Samir: No, really! I like it. It's just hard for me to get used to it
    like that.

ROLE PLAYS Choose a partner and take roles to act out the following situations. They require complimenting, congratulating, flattering, and/or responding appropriately. When you finish, switch roles and create a different role play, changing the dialog.

 1. For your birthday, your mother has bought you a sweater that you don't like, but you don't want to hurt her feelings.

2. An acquaintance from the university has had a poem published in a small magazine. You really like the poem.

3. You're driving your new car, and a friend stops you to compliment you on it.

4. You're having dinner at a friend's house, and he has fixed a delicious meal.

5. A friend from the Newcomer's Club asks you how you like her new purple lipstick and nail polish. You hate it, but you don't want to hurt her feelings.

6. Your employer thinks you've done an excellent job on a difficult assignment.

7. Your best friend has painted a lovely picture for her art class, but she isn't completely satisfied with it. You think it's beautiful.

8. Your next-door neighbor won a prize for the roses that she grew in her garden.

9. A colleague from work wants some help from you on an assignment, so he tries to flatter you.

10. After returning from a trip, you find your roommate has completely rearranged the furniture in the apartment. You like a few things about it, but you're very unhappy about the rest of the changes.

REAL **PEOPLE,** REAL **SITUATIONS,** REAL **LANGUAGE**

At a party, an evening with friends, or just a day at work or school, record compliments and responses made to them by friends or people you happen to hear. If it becomes difficult to find five, you can make some *genuine* compliments to people and listen to their responses. Make your observations in the form of journal entries in your notebook.

EXAMPLE: *Monday, Jan. 11—cafeteria at lunch—Hernando complimented Sara on her new sports watch.*

Hernando: *Can I see your watch for a minute, Sara? Wow! That's nice! Did you get it here?*

Sara: *No, I got it in Switzerland last year.*

Hernando: *Well, I really like it! It's different from most I've seen.*

Sara: *Thanks. I like it a lot, too.*

Your teacher may want you to bring in your examples to discuss and compare with those of your classmates.

CHAPTER 13

COMPLAINING

Complaining is expressing pain, discontent, or dissatisfaction. We complain every day about the weather, the food we eat, the traffic, our work, money problems, and other areas of our lives. Although we can certainly be rude when we complain ("This steak tastes like leather!"), we usually try to be more tactful and polite ("This steak seems to be overdone."). We also do not usually complain just to complain (although some people do). There's almost always a reason for the complaint. The man complaining about his steak being overcooked might add a request: "Could you please have the cook prepare me another one—medium rare, as I requested."

Complaints take many forms, but the most common are simple statements of fact, followed by a question or request (or vice versa):

This report is incomplete. Finish it, please.
Complaint: incomplete report
  Request: make it complete

Do you mind if I **skip**° the meeting tonight? I'm very tired.
Complaint: being tired
  Request: not to attend the meeting

Sometimes we don't *directly* offer or ask for a solution to our problem. We just complain:

Alan: What's wrong?
 Bob: I have a terrible sore throat and cough.
Alan: Have you seen a doctor?
 Bob: A doctor? I don't have time! I'm so busy I can hardly take the time to eat!

Bob first complains about how he feels. When Alan asks if he's been to a doctor, Bob complains that he doesn't have time. Notice, there's no request made or wanted—at least no *obvious* or easy-to-see request. But perhaps Bob is complaining because he wants Alan to say, "I'm sorry to hear that" or "Well, don't work so hard," or even "I'll **take over**° for you while you go to the doctor." The speaker may have any number of intentions behind the complaint, and often, the only way of knowing what these intentions are is to know more about the situation and/or the person complaining. Here's an example:

A husband has been watching a football game on TV for the past two hours. A program on drug abuse is coming on soon, and the wife would really like to watch it.

   Wife: That program on drug abuse is supposed to be excellent, honey. Is the game almost over?
Husband: About 30 more minutes—maybe more.
   Wife: It seems like you've been watching it all night. I hope it's over by 9:30.
Husband: It probably won't be, but I don't mind if you want to change channels. It's not a very good game.

Skip can mean "miss," "pass over," or "leave out." Here, it means "miss."
Take over means "take control of or responsibility for something."

> **Wife** Are you sure?
> **Husband:** I'm sure. San Francisco's going to lose anyway.

In this situation, the wife doesn't directly complain about the football game, but she does make several comments—"It seems like you've been watching it all night" and "I hope it's over by 9:30"—to let her husband know that she's ready to switch channels and watch something *she*'s interested in. Her complaint is very indirect and tactful, and it *works*—her husband agrees to change channels.

PRACTICE 1

Now you try it. Here are some situations. Choose partners and together write a short dialog for each situation, but make your complaint as indirect or as tactful as you can—without hurting the person's feelings.

1. Your roommate has opened the window, and you think it's too cold in the room.

2. Your friend offered to type a report for you. You get back the finished product, and it's full of errors.

3. Your date fixes dinner for you and offers you more chicken, which you don't like.

4. Your son cleaned his room without being asked, but he didn't do a very good job.

5. Your neighbor's dog is cute, but it is constantly digging in your flowers and messing up the yard.

Assigning Blame

A common way of complaining is to put the blame on someone or something else. We often accomplish this by using the passive voice. Look at these examples:

- ✦ This cake was cooked too long, I think. It tastes pretty dry.
- ✦ Someone took the "wet paint" sign off before the paint was dry. Now I have paint all over my hands!
- ✦ My racket wasn't strung tightly enough. No wonder I'm not playing well today!
- ✦ My new shirt seems to be missing. I wonder if someone borrowed it without asking.

Notice in the first and third examples, the passive voice is used to imply that someone else is responsible for the problem. In the tennis racket example, the person is placing the blame for his or her poor performance on the racket and that *someone* didn't string it properly. This is a common way of shifting the blame—by complaining about something else, not the real cause of the problem. In the last example, *seems* (instead of *is*) is often used to soften the complaint. We use *seem* and *appear* when we want to make our complaint less harsh: "Does it *seem* a little chilly in here to you? Would you mind if I closed the window?" or "The paper *appears* to be a little messy. Maybe it should be retyped." The person complaining uses the passive voice in the last example and says, "It should be retyped," without saying who will do the retyping. Again, this is a mild way of avoiding placing the blame but complaining, still.

PRACTICE 2

Read the situation and make a complaint in which you put the blame on someone or something else.

> **EXAMPLE:**   *You were absent yesterday and didn't do the homework assignment. The teacher is annoyed with you, but you don't think it was your fault.*
>
> **You:**   *Well, I was sick yesterday, and nobody told me about the homework.*

1. You knocked over a lamp on a shelf in a department store, and you don't think it was your fault.
   You:

2. You lost a tennis match to Sam. You're wearing new shoes, and there are a lot of leaves on the court.
   You:

3. You're late for an appointment. Your alarm didn't go off.
   You:

4. You're on a plane. You asked for a pillow a half hour ago, and the flight attendant still has not brought you one.
   You:

5. Your film was ruined. Your roommate loaded your camera for you a few days ago.
   You:

Handling Complaints
In American business, there's a motto: "The customer is always right." Thus, when a customer complains that his potato is undercooked, the waiter *should* respond, "I'm very sorry, sir. I'll bring you another one right away." Or when a customer at her hairstylist's shop says, "You didn't cut my hair short enough last time in the back," the hair cutter *should* say something like, "Oh, no? Well, I'll definitely make sure I get it right this time."

Handling complaints requires as much tact as—maybe even more than—making them. This is especially true if the person who is complaining (the customer who is "always right") *isn't* always right. Look at these examples of responding to complaints:

1.   **Joe:**   Ali, I wish you'd asked me before you borrowed my jacket. I wanted to wear it last night, but I couldn't find it.

      Ali: I'm really sorry about that, Joe. I didn't think you'd mind. You let me borrow it once before, remember?

2.   **Luis:**   Carl, do you mind turning off the overhead light? I've got a big day tomorrow, and I really need to get some sleep.

      Carl: Sorry. I'll turn it off in a second. I just need to finish reading this chapter.

3.   **Mahtab:**   Joyce, there seems to be a little too much salt in the meat. Would you mind not salting it before you cook it next time?

      Joyce: Sure. I forgot you don't like salt. I'll remember next time.

PRACTICE 3

Now try to respond to these complaints as tactfully as the people in the three examples did.

1.   **Teacher:**   I think you forgot some punctuation rules when you were writing your essay, Pedro.

      Pedro:

2.   **Ms. Williams:**   When I put my car in for **a tune-up,**° I also asked that my left front light be fixed, and it wasn't done.

      Mechanic:

3.   **Mr. Jackson:**   Carol, I was supposed to be at my meeting 20 minutes ago. I thought I asked you to be here at 6:00?

      Babysitter:

A tune-up is a general adjustment made on a car (in this case) to assure efficient performance.

4. **Ahmed:**   The clock didn't go off, and I missed my first class. I thought you were supposed to set it last night, Paul?

   Paul:

5. **Customer:**   I ordered french fries, not a baked potato.

   Waiter:

SITUATIONAL DIALOGS
Here are some typical situations involving complaining and handling complaints. Choose partners, take roles, and read the dialogs. When you have finished, discuss them, answer the questions and do the tasks that follow.

> A.   *Karen feels that her roommate isn't doing her share of the housework.*

Karen: Jane, I think it's your time to do the dishes, isn't it?
Jane: Is it? I don't remember.
Karen: Well, I did them last night and Sunday. Your turn is today and tomorrow.
Jane: Okay. I'll get to them soon.
Karen: And could you also help me keep the bathroom and dining room a little neater? It's embarrassing sometimes to have guests over when the apartment looks so bad.
Jane: You just need to remind me more, Karen. I've never been a very good housekeeper.
Karen: Okay. I really do hate to complain, but sometimes I feel like I do all the work around here.
Jane: Well, I'm really sorry. I promise I'll try to do better from now on. Just give me a swift kick sometimes to remind me.

What Do You Think?

1.   *Karen doesn't complain immediately to Jane. How does she handle the first problem—about the dirty dishes?*
2.   *How does Karen lead up to her real complaint? Notice that she judges Jane's reaction first before she complains more strongly.*
3.   *What is Jane's reaction to Karen's complaints? How sincere do you think she is?*

> B.   *Aziz thinks it's too hot in the office that he shares with Marian.*

Aziz: Is it just me, or is it hot in here to you, too?
Marian: I feel very comfortable, Aziz.
Aziz: I don't know. Maybe I'm coming down with something, but I feel really hot.

Marian: Well, why don't you turn on the air conditioner? I don't mind.

Aziz: Are you sure you won't be too cool?

Marian: If I am, I'll just put my suit jacket back on.

Aziz: Thanks. I appreciate it. But let me know if it bothers you.

What Do You Think?

1. *How does Aziz mention his discomfort? What is his purpose in asking, "Is it just me, or is it hot in here to you, too?"*

2. *How does Marian react to Aziz's complaints about the heat? Suppose she didn't want the temperature any cooler in the room. How might she have handled Aziz's complaint?*

3. *Aziz wants to make sure Marian doesn't think he's being selfish in his desire to cool the office, so what does he do? Change the dialog so that Aziz is much more direct in his complaining.*

C. *Ms. Jensen asked for a report to be written by today, but Doug doesn't have it ready.*

Ms. Jensen: Where's the report I asked you to finish for today, Doug?

Doug: I'm really sorry, Ms. Jensen, but it's not quite ready. I'll have it by tomorrow.

Ms. Jensen: Tomorrow is *too late*, Doug. You've been working on it for three weeks now! Why can't you have your work done on time?

Doug: I've just had a lot of other things to do. And I still haven't **caught up with**° the work I missed while I was on vacation.

Ms. Jensen: Well, I'm really tired of your excuses, Doug. Your work has been **slipping**° for the past several months. I've said a few things about it in the past, but nothing seems to help.

Doug: I really am sorry. I know I'm not working up to my capabilities. You'll see a real improvement in my work from now on, Ms. Jensen. I can promise you that.

Caught up with means "brought something up to completion."
Slipping means "becoming worse and worse."

Ms. Jensen: I certainly hope so. I know you're capable of doing much better than you've shown in the last few months.

What Do You Think?

1. *Ms. Jensen uses this opportunity to complain about what other parts of Doug's performance?*
2. *On a scale of 1 to 10 (10 being "extremely angry"), how angry do you think Ms. Jensen is? What evidence in the dialog supports your opinion?*
3. *What is Doug's excuse? Does Ms. Jensen accept it or not? What other ways could she have complained a little more softly?*

D.   Pedro and Barbara are talking over lunch.

Barbara: What's wrong, Pedro? You look terrible!

Pedro: I've had a headache all day, and my nose is stopped up. I can't breathe very well.

Barbara: Well, you ought to go home and go to bed. You could be coming down with the flu or something. A lot of people in my office are sick.

Pedro: I can't Barbara. I have a lot of work to do, and my assistant is out this week.

Barbara: Well, you need to get some rest, Pedro, or you'll be really sick!

What Do You Think?

1. *What is Pedro's first complaint, and how does Barbara respond?*
2. *He complains again when Barbara offers a suggestion. Why does he complain this time, and what is his excuse?*
3. *What other ways could Barbara have said, "You could be coming down with the flu or something"?*

E.   Chen is upset about the amount of work he has in one of his classes.

Chen: My reading teacher gives us so much work that I don't have time to do anything anymore!

Marie: Do other students feel the same way?

Chen: They sure do! They complain more than I do about it!

Marie: Well, maybe you should talk to your teacher about it.

Chen: I've tried, and a few others have, too, but it doesn't do any good. She doesn't listen to anyone! She's so *stubborn*!

Marie: Well, it's her class, and she can run it the way she wants to. I'm afraid you're at her mercy.

What Do You Think?

1. *What is the first item Chen complains about, and why does he complain? What do you think Chen and Marie might have been talking about before, which led to Chen's first complaint?*
2. *What other complaint does Chen have about his teacher?*
3. *What does Marie mean when she says, "You're at her mercy"? Can you tell from the context? When are you sometimes* at another person's *mercy? Give some examples.*

DIALOG COMPLETIONS   Choose a partner and, remembering what you have learned about complaining and handling complaints, complete the following dialogs appropriately.

1. *Nancy and Marge are studying. Marge is* **humming**° *to herself, and this sound is annoying Nancy.*

Nancy:
Marge: Oh, I'm sorry, Nancy. I didn't realize I was doing it.
Nancy:

2. *George was supposed to have the stereo repaired, but he forgot. Larry wanted to listen to some music tonight.*

Larry: George, I turned on the stereo, but it still doesn't work. What's wrong?
George:
Larry: But that was your responsibility. You said you'd do it!
George:

3. *Ahmed's boss doesn't like the way he's written his report.*

Boss:
Ahmed: I apologize. I know I didn't spend as much time on it as I should have.
Boss:
Ahmed: Right away! I'll have it rewritten and on your desk by 5:30.
Boss:
Ahmed: Yes, sir. I understand.

Humming means "singing music softly with the lips closed."

4.   *In a restaurant Mr. Brown is unhappy because there have been several things wrong with the food he ordered.*

Mr. Brown: Excuse me, but I believe I ordered my steak rare. This steak is medium.

Waitress:

Mr. Brown: Yes, there is. This bread appears to be somewhat stale. I'd like some that is fresh, please.

Waitress:

5.   *Ken is in a hotel room, and there are no towels or soap in the bathroom. He calls* **Housekeeping.°**

Ken:

Housekeeping: I'm terribly sorry about that. I'll send someone up with fresh towels at once.

Ken:

Housekeeping: Certainly. And I apologize for the inconvenience.

Ken:

6.   *Martin doesn't want to hurt his girlfriend's feelings, but he doesn't like the new perfume she's wearing.*

Martin: Suzette, what's that perfume you're wearing now?

Suzette: It's "Night and Day." Do you like it?

Martin:

Suzette: Oh, really? Well, I was just tired of the other and thought I'd try something new.

Martin:

Suzette: Well, don't worry, Martin. I'm not throwing out the other perfume.

7.   *Terry is typing her term paper at 2:00 A.M. Greta is trying to sleep.*

Greta:

Terry: I'll close the door, then. I didn't realize I was disturbing you.

Greta:

Terry: Sorry, Greta. I'll do it earlier next time.

Housekeeping is the maid service in a hotel that is responsible for cleaning the room, changing linens and towels, and taking care of the room in general.

8. *Mrs. Franks bought some milk from the supermarket, and the next day it was sour. She takes it back to the supermarket.*

Mrs. Franks: I'm sorry to have to complain, but I bought this milk yesterday, and when I had some this morning, it was sour.

Clerk:

Mrs. Franks: Yes, I did. **The expiration date°** is next week!

Clerk:

Mrs. Franks: I'd like to exchange it for some fresh milk.

Clerk:

Mrs. Franks: That's okay. Those things happen sometime.

9. *Essam ordered a cheeseburger with tomato and lettuce, but when he bites into the sandwich, he discovers there is no cheese on it.*

Essam:

Clerk:

Essam: That's okay. I'll wait.

Clerk:

10. *Jim is waiting in line to buy tickets to a movie. He sees a friend come up, and Jim motions for the friend to get in line in front of him. The woman standing behind Jim does not like this.*

Woman:

Jim: Well, he's my friend.

Woman:

Jim: Well, there's no reason for him to have to get in the back of the line if we're planning to sit together in the movie, is there?

Woman:

Jim: Well, I'm sorry, but I've been waiting in this line longer than you.

Woman:

The expiration date is the date stamped on perishable items—foods that spoil quickly—to tell the customer how long they are fresh.

ROLE PLAYS   For each situation described, choose partners and create a short dialog in which a complaint or complaints are made and responded to appropriately.

1. Peter is very cold in his hotel room, but he doesn't know how to turn on the heat.

2. Bob's reading the newspaper and discovers his roommate has cut out many articles, making it impossible to read the newspaper thoroughly.

3. Sarah has been standing in line at a movie theater for 20 minutes. A teenager cuts (breaks) in line and starts talking to the person in front of her.

4. It's 2:00 A.M., and Betty's trying to sleep, but the people next door are having a wild, noisy party.

5. Carl's sister cleaned his kitchen for him, but she rearranged all the items, and now he can't find anything.

6. Ali gives the drugstore cashier a $20 bill, but she gives him change for only $10.

7. Pedro ordered pancakes with bacon and orange juice, but the waiter brought him sausage and grapefruit juice instead.

8. When Yoko lent her friend her car this morning, the gas tank was full, but when the friend returns the car, the tank is almost empty.

9. Sarah's teacher returns her homework assignment and tells her it's full of grammar and spelling mistakes.

10. Maria's husband has rearranged the living room furniture in an awful way. Maria liked it the way it was.

REAL **PEOPLE,** REAL **SITUATIONS,** REAL **LANGUAGE**

A. This is a rating card that some restaurants use to gather comments and complaints from their customers. Take this form (or a copy of it) with you to a restaurant and fill it out after a meal. If you check *average* or *poor* for any of the areas, write your complaints under "Comments."

How Do We Rate?

	Excellent	Good	Average	Poor
FOOD	————	————	————	————
Comments:				
SERVICE	————	————	————	————
Comments:				
ATMOSPHERE	————	————	————	————
Comments:				
CLEANLINESS	————	————	————	————
Comments:				

After you have finished, tell a friend about your experience at this restaurant and record the dialog in your notebook as accurately as you can, showing how you expressed any complaints and how your friend responded.

B.   Joe and Elizabeth ate dinner last night at Pizza City and didn't have a very good experience. Here's the rating card they filled out when they finished their meal. Create a short dialog between Joe and Moises, Joe's roommate, who is thinking about going to Pizza City tonight for dinner. Then create another dialog in which Joe and Elizabeth complain to the manager of the restaurant as they are leaving.

PIZZA CITY
HOW DO WE RATE?

What do you, our valuable customer, think about our...

FOOD   ☐ Excellent   ☐ Good   ☒ Average   ☐ Poor

Comments: *Pizza could have been hotter. There weren't very many onions on it, and we ordered extra onions.*

SERVICE   ☐ Excellent   ☐ Good   ☐ Average   ☒ Poor

Comments: *Waitress didn't bring enough water. She forgot our salads, so we had to remind her. She wasn't very friendly.*

ATMOSPHERE ☐ Excellent   ☐ Good   ☒ Average   ☐ Poor

Comments: *The music was too loud. There needs to be a non-smoking section.*

CLEANLINESS ☐ Excellent ☐ Good   ☒ Average   ☐ Poor

Comments: *The table & floor were dirty when we sat down.*

Other:

_____ ☐ Excellent   ☐ Good   ☐ Average   ☐ Poor

_____ ☐ Excellent   ☐ Good   ☐ Average   ☐ Poor

C. When you return merchandise to a store and ask for a *refund* (your money back), *credit* (the store *credits* your account with the money you spent, so the next time you make a purchase, you have to pay only the balance), or an *exchange* (replacement of one item with another), you usually have to fill out a form, explaining your complaint with the merchandise and the reason for returning it. Look at this example, and then answer the questions that follow.

The Parkwood Men's Store
Merchandise Return

NAME _Tom Jackson_

ADDRESS _413-H Harrison Drive   Chicago, Illinois_

DATE OF PURCHASE _3/2/86_

DATE OF RETURN _3/7/86_

DESCRIPTION OF MERCHANDISE:

_Men's red wool sweater -
size medium._

REASON FOR RETURN:

☐ SIZE
☐ COLOR
☑ DEFECT   TYPE: _hole in left sleeve and_
☐ OTHER _____ _poor sewing around neck._

_____
_____
_____
_____

Tom Jackson
CUSTOMER SIGNATURE

- -

METHOD OF PAYMENT:

☐ CASH   ☑ CHECK   ☐ CREDIT CARD   ☐ VISA
☑ REFUND ☐ CREDIT   ☐ EXCHANGE   ☐ MASTERCARD
                                       ☐ AMERICAN
                                         EXPRESS

TOTAL AMOUNT REFUNDED _$53.58_

1. Why does Tom return the sweater?

2. What does *defect* mean?

3. What does Tom want to be done about the problem?

4. Create a short dialog between Tom and the salesperson, with Tom making his complaints and the salesclerk responding.

5. Suppose Tom had checked "Other" under "Reason for return." What could *other* mean? Give some examples of other reasons we return merchandise. Create a short dialog between you and a salesperson, giving a different reason for returning a piece of clothing that was given to you as a gift.

CHAPTER 14

EXPRESSING OPINIONS, AGREEING, AND DISAGREEING

How often have you been in a situation where somebody says, "What do you think about . . . ?" The person expects you to express an opinion on a subject, and probably a discussion (with agreement and disagreement) will follow. Learning how to express opinions, to agree, and to disagree are verbal and social strategies that require knowledge of some fixed expressions and a certain amount of tact. Let's discuss offering opinions first.

Expressing Opinions

Here are some typical ways of starting to let a person know what you think about a topic. Remember, though, that these are only beginnings; you must add a statement of opinion after each. For example, if you start with "I feel that . . ." you might say, "the new seat belt law should be more strictly enforced."

❖ The point I'm making is . . . . (*Formal*)
❖ In my opinion . . . .
❖ It seems to me that . . . .
❖ I $\left\{\begin{array}{l} \text{believe} \\ \text{think} \\ \text{feel} \end{array}\right\}$ that . . . .
❖ As I see it . . . .
❖ If you ask me . . . .
❖ $\left.\begin{array}{l} \text{Personally,} \\ \text{Frankly,} \end{array}\right\}$ I think . . . .
❖ _____
❖ _____

Of course, you can add adverbs (*strongly, really, firmly, wholeheartedly*) that intensify an opinion (make it stronger), as in "I *firmly* believe inflation will get worse during the next ten months!" Your voice also stresses the adverb.

Sometimes if we're not 100 percent sure in our opinions, we can modify our opening statements by adding certain expressions. Here are some examples:

❖ Well, I'm not quite sure, but I believe . . . .
❖ I still have some doubts, but my feeling is that . . . .
❖ Although I'm not 100 percent sure, I still think that . . . .
❖ Well, I don't know, but I'm beginning to think that . . . .

These statements let the listener know that we *do* have an opinion, even though it may not be a strong one, and there may be some doubt. Nevertheless, it *is* an opinion.

PRACTICE 1

Use some of these opening statements to offer an opinion on the following topics. The topics are broad, so you can narrow them as you wish. If you have a little doubt, feel free to express it.

EXAMPLE: *Television*

(Opinion)   *If you ask me, children in the United States watch too much TV!*

1. Homework
    (Opinion)_____

2. Alcoholic beverages
    (Opinion)_____

3. Economy cars
    (Opinion)_____

4. Learning a second language
    (Opinion)_____

5. New York City
    (Opinion)_____

   To find out what another person thinks about a topic, we often ask questions like "What do you think about the Middle East situation?" Here are some beginnings of questions about other people's opinions:

   ✦ Are you $\left\{ \begin{array}{l} \text{opposed to} \\ \text{in favor of} \end{array} \right\} \ldots$?
   ✦ What do you think about . . . ?
   ✦ What's your opinion on/about . . . ?
   ✦ How do you feel about . . . ?
   ✦ I'd be interested to know your thoughts on . . . .
   ✦ _____
   ✦ _____

PRACTICE 2

Choose a partner. Let one person ask a question about the other person's opinion on the subject indicated, and have the other person reply, using some of the opening expressions that have been discussed. If the topic is too broad, you can narrow it as much as you wish.

   EXAMPLE: *Basketball*

   A: *What do you think about the university's new basketball team?*

   B: *Well, I think we may finally have a winning season!*

1. The women's movement
    A:
    B:

2. Violence in movies
   A:
   B:

3. The 55 mph speed limit on interstate highways
   A:
   B:

4. The parking situation at . . . (the university, for example)
   A:
   B:

5. Capital punishment
   A:
   B:

Agreeing

Agreeing with an opinion or a statement is a lot easier than disagreeing, and there are lots of ways to express agreement. Here are a few. See if you can think of others.

+ I couldn't agree more!
+ How true!
+ You're
  That's } exactly right!
+ I agree wholeheartedly with what you say!
+ That's exactly { what I was thinking!
                   what I believe!
                   how I feel!
+ There's no doubt about it.
+ That's my opinion, too.
+ Absolutely!
+ Definitely!
+ You can say that again! (*Informal*)
+ For sure! (*Informal*)
+ You bet! (*Informal*)
+ And how! (*Informal*)
+ I'll say! (*Informal*)
+ Right on! (*Informal*)
+ _____
+ _____

Remember that the very informal expressions of agreement are not appropriate for all situations. They are fine in informal settings with peers or close friends, but care and consideration should be given before using them in formal business or social settings. In addition, remember that there are degrees of agreeing (from the 100 percent agreement—"I couldn't agree with you more!"—to the reluctant or hesitant agreement—"Well, I'm not completely sure, but I generally agree."), so you can vary your responses with the situation and the way you feel.

PRACTICE 3

With a partner, practice expressing an opinion and then agreeing with it. You can add an intensifier or a statement after the agreement phrase to make it stronger and clearer if you'd like. You can also make your agreement reluctant if you care to.

> **EXAMPLE:** *Spring*
>
> **A:** *Personally, I think spring is the most beautiful time of year in Washington.*
> **B:** *I definitely agree! It really is lovely!*

1. Horror movies
   A:
   B:

2. Traveling by bus
   A:
   B:

3. Video cassette recorders
   A:
   B:

4. Summer vacations
   A:
   B:

5. Reading
   A:
   B:

Getting People to Agree with Us   There are many times when we want to get people to agree with us, and we manipulate the language (use it to our advantage) to try to lead a person to our side. One

common way to do this is to make a statement of opinion, and then add a tag question:

+ It's hot in here, isn't it?
+ That was a fantastic burger, wasn't it?
+ San Francisco is certainly a beautiful city, isn't it?
+ That surely wasn't a very interesting movie, was it?

The tag question is usually spoken with a falling intonation (. . . isn't it?) when the speaker is almost sure that the listener will agree or is hoping to get the listener to agree.

Other ways of getting people to agree with us involve phrasing the question in such a way that the person responding *knows* what we want to hear. For example:

+ Don't you think it's hot in here?
+ Don't you agree that was a fantastic burger?
+ Isn't San Francisco a beautiful city?
+ Wasn't that a boring movie?

In the first two examples, the speaker leads the listener to the desired response by beginning with "Don't you think/agree . . . ?" In the last two examples, negative questions are used to indicate the speaker's idea, belief, or attitude. The listener can tell from the question (and perhaps the tone of voice) how the speaker *wants* the listener to respond.

Disagreeing

Disagreeing with someone's opinion is a little harder because there are several factors to take into consideration when deciding how to express the disagreement. First, and probably most important, is our relationship with the other person. If we know the person very well, we can be stronger and more direct in our disagreement. Here are some examples of ways to begin a disagreement with people we know well:

+ You've got to be { joking! / kidding! }
+ Are you { joking? / kidding me? / crazy? }
+ Don't make me laugh!
+ That's { absurd! / ridiculous! }

+ You can't really $\left\{ \begin{array}{l} \text{be serious!} \\ \text{believe that!} \\ \text{think that!} \end{array} \right.$

+ Oh, come off it! (*Very informal*)
+ Oh, **get out of here!**° (*Very informal*)
+ _____
+ _____

Please remember that these are very direct and rather informal ways of disagreeing. We use these only with very close friends in informal situations. It would be considered inappropriate and perhaps even rude to use these in a discussion with people we don't know very well or in very formal settings.

But suppose we're not in informal situations with intimate friends. For example, we're with someone in a respected position of authority in a business setting. Then we need to tailor (fit) our language to the situation. We soften the disagreement so that we don't appear rude or hurt the other person's feelings. In the examples that follow, notice that the strongest disagreements (but they're still *polite*) are the first two, and the milder ones—the softened disagreements—come last:

+ I disagree with what you're saying.
+ I don't $\left\{ \begin{array}{l} \text{see it that way.} \\ \text{think so.} \\ \text{agree with you.} \end{array} \right.$

+ I respect your opinion, but I think . . . .
+ I'm not sure if I agree with you completely on . . . .
+ Well, you have a right to your opinion, but I . . . .
+ I understand what you're saying, but in my opinion . . . .
+ Yes, that's true, but my feeling is that . . . .
+ $\left. \begin{array}{l} \text{You could be right,} \\ \text{You have a point,} \end{array} \right\}$ but don't you think that . . . ?
+ I hate to disagree with you, but I believe . . . .
+ _____
+ _____

In the last seven examples, notice that we acknowledge the other person's opinion (we may even agree with part of it), but then we disagree politely in the end by offering our own opinion. In any kind of disagreement, whether it is an abrupt, direct "You've got to be kidding!" or an indirect,

---

Get out of here! is not a command for the person to leave; it simply is a very informal (but friendly) way of saying, "I can't believe you really believe that!"

softened "Well, I see your point, but I still don't quite agree," we almost always offer a reason for our disagreement. It's important to let the person know we're not merely disagreeing to disagree—that there's a reason for it. For example, if Paul says, "That new James Bond movie is the best one I've ever seen!" and José says, "Come off it!"—he would usually follow immediately with a reason: "*Goldfinger* was the best James Bond movie ever made. There was a lot more excitement and spy action in it."

PRACTICE 4

Here are some opinions. Disagree with them in two ways: first, very *directly*, and then, by softening the disagreement and making it more *indirect*. Don't worry if you aren't familiar with all the subjects of the opinions; you don't need to know them to be able to make appropriate kinds of disagreements.

> **EXAMPLE:** *Don't you think Marian looks better than she's ever looked?*
>
> **(Direct):** *You must be joking! I think she looks terrible!*
> **(Indirect):** *I can't agree with you. She seems tired and pale to me.*

1. I think that Bruce Springsteen is the greatest living American singer!
   (Direct):
   (Indirect):

2. I firmly believe that the legal drinking age should be lowered to 16.
   (Direct):
   (Indirect):

3. Personally, I think the Honda Prelude is the best Japanese car built!
   (Direct):
   (Indirect):

4. That grammar test was the hardest one we've had this semester!
   (Direct):
   (Indirect):

5. In my opinion, Disney World is the best vacation spot in the United States.
   (Direct):
   (Indirect):

SITUATIONAL DIALOGS   Choose a partner or partners, take roles, and then act out the following dialogs, using appropriate tone of voice and gestures. Afterward, discuss the dialogs and the questions that follow.

A. **Alicia:** I think Brad and Susan have the cutest house I've ever seen. And they've decorated it so nicely, don't you think?

Naomi: Well, I do like the house, but personally, I hate the way they've decorated it. And I don't like the colors at all!

Alicia: Are you kidding?! The pink and blue look gorgeous together!

Naomi: I'm sorry, Alicia, but it just doesn't appeal to me. And I don't like that kind of furniture. I like more modern things.

Alicia: Well, I couldn't agree *less*! I think it's all lovely!

What Do You Think?

1. *What clue in Alicia's first comment lets you know that she's hoping Naomi agrees with her opinion?*
2. *Does Naomi agree with any of Alicia's opinions? If so, which one(s)?*
3. *Change the dialog so that Naomi agrees with everything Alicia says.*

B. **Maria:** I'm not sure about this soup, Karl. It tastes like something's missing.

Karl: No, I don't think so. It tastes fine to me.

Maria: Well, I still think it needs something. Salt?

Karl: No—definitely not. What about garlic? If anything, I think it could use a little more of that.

Maria: Now you're talking! That's *exactly* what it needs! And how about some more onions, too?

Karl: I don't know about that, Maria. I think you might be going overboard on the spices.

What Do You Think?

1. *What expression does Maria use to agree with Karl's suggestion about the garlic? Have you ever heard this used before? Think of some other situations where it might be used.*
2. *Notice that Maria uses the word* still *in her disagreement with Karl. What is its function?*
3. *Karl uses the idiom* going overboard *in his last comment. Can you tell what it means from the context? What other things do people sometimes go overboard on?*

C. **Asim:** Well, in my opinion, Maria should not have spoken so rudely to the teacher. I know she was angry, but that's still no excuse for rudeness.

Dave: I disagree, Asim. I think she had a right to say that. The teacher was wrong to have accused her of cheating in front of the whole class!

Asim: You've got to be joking! It's the teacher's right to say anything she wants, and if she saw Maria cheating, she certainly had the right to say it.

Dave: I agree she had a right to say something, but I feel she should have done it privately—after class in a conference with Maria. There was no need to have involved the whole class.

What Do You Think?

1. *What are the main points that Asim and Dave disagree on? Is there anything they agree on?*
2. *Change the dialog to make them basically agree with each other.*
3. *How would a cheating situation like this be handled by a teacher in your native country? Are there any factors that need to be considered as you discuss this issue?*

D. **Enrique:**   That new Chevy Chase film was hilarious!

Melanie: Oh, come off it, Enrique! I didn't think it was funny at all! Chevy Chase is a great comedian, but he **sure**° didn't show it in that movie!

Enrique: I can't believe you feel that way! I never laughed so hard in all my life!

Melanie: Well, I'm sorry to disagree, but his so-called humor did nothing for me in that film. I liked his performance in *Vacation* much better.

Enrique: Are you kidding me? He was funny in *Vacation*, but he was hilarious in his new film.

What Do You Think?

1. *Do Melanie and Enrique agree on anything? If so, what?*
2. *What is their main source of disagreement? Which person seems to have the strongest opinions and why? Do you have any clues concerning what Melanie and Enrique's relationship might be?*
3. *What does Melanie mean by* so-called *in her second comment to Enrique? In what other ways do we use this expression? Give some examples.*

Sure (instead of *surely*) is often used in informal speech.

E. **Lloyd:**   Ameed, what do you think about the new company rule prohibiting smoking in the office building?

Ameed: Personally, Lloyd, I'm greatly in favor of it. It's very annoying—not to mention unhealthful—for me to be in our small room, trying to work, with four people puffing on **cancer sticks°** around me.

Lloyd: Oh—I'm in total agreement with you! I absolutely *detest* having to sit next to smokers, but I wonder how the office smokers are going to take it? I feel kind of sorry for them.

Ameed: I don't at all! They're going to have a smoking lounge, so if they have to smoke, they can go there or outside. That's more than enough for them!

What Do You Think?

1. *What are Ameed's and Lloyd's opinions about smokers and about the new office policy?*
2. *What are they in disagreement about?*
3. *Change the dialog so that the two men disagree strongly with each other on the subject.*

DIALOG COMPLETIONS   Choose partners and take roles, completing the dialogs appropriately. Be sure to consider the relationship between the speakers and the setting (if known) as you choose ways of expressing opinions, agreeing, and disagreeing. When you finish, change roles and complete the dialogs a little differently.

1. *Doug and Hans are classmates at the university.*

Doug: What's your opinion of the psychology professor?

Hans:

Doug: Me, too. I couldn't agree with you more.

Hans:

Doug: I don't know. I guess she's okay. It's still a little early to tell.

Hans:

2. *Julio and Alice are husband and wife, discussing their summer vacation plans.*

Alice:

Cancer sticks (and *coffin nails*) are slang terms for cigarettes.

Julio: I don't agree, honey. I think Florida would be too hot that time of year.

Alice:

Julio: That's true, but remember, we went there two years ago, and it rained four out of six days.

Alice:

Julio: Now that's a good idea! I'll have our travel agent look into it.

    3.   *Nancy, a customer, is talking with a cashier at her neighborhood supermarket.*

Nancy: Well, how do you like your new computer cash register?

Cashier:

Nancy: Oh, really? I'm sorry to hear that. I thought it would make it a lot easier on you.

Cashier:

Nancy: That's too bad. Do the other cashiers feel the same way?

Cashier:

    4.   *Theresa and Samar sit next to each other in sociology class, but they don't know each other very well.*

Theresa:

  Samar: No, I don't agree with you. I thought it was a waste of time.

Theresa: Well, what did you think about the film on alcohol abuse?

  Samar:

Theresa:

  Samar: Well, at least we agree on something!

    5.   *Don, Tom, and Betty are co-workers in an engineering office.*

Don: Don't you like Betty's new hairstyle?

Tom:

Don: Me, too. And it makes her look more sophisticated.

Tom:

Don: I'm not so sure I agree. I like it long.

Tom:

Don: You've got a point there. It does **show off**° her eyes better that way.

Show off in this case means "emphasize in a positive, attractive way."

6. *Gerhardt and Valerie are classmates and good friends.*

Gerhardt: What's your opinion on the new book we're reading in the Great Novels class, Val?

Valerie:

Gerhardt:

Valerie: No, I'm not joking! I really like it. It's exciting and the characters are interesting and seem very real.

Gerhardt:

Valerie: Well, you've got your opinion, and I've got mine.

7. *Rose and Sara are friends having lunch together in a restaurant.*

Rose: Aren't you a little chilly, Sara?

Sara:

Rose: Well, maybe something's wrong with me, but I think it's cold in here.

Sara:

Rose: Maybe you're right. I'm sitting closer to the air conditioner than you are.

8. *Harvey and Steve are friends driving home together after seeing a rock concert.*

Harvey:

Steve: I thought they were terrible! That was the worst concert I've been to in a long time!

Harvey:

Steve: I'm glad you agree. What did you think about the first singer?

Harvey:

Steve:

Harvey: How can you say that? I could understand every word she sang!

Steve:

9. *Ms. Blanchard is William's employer in an architectural firm.*

William: I'd be interested to know what you thought of my report on the new office complex, Ms. Blanchard.

Ms. Blanchard:

William: Thank you, but did you agree with my evaluation of the heating system?

Ms. Blanchard:

William: Really? Why not?

Ms. Blanchard:
 William: Oh ? What do you mean?
Ms. Blanchard:
 William: Oh, I see your point, and I think you're right about that.

10. *Wang and Max are friends discussing last night's soccer match.*

Wang:
 Max: You can say that again! It was the best game I've seen all season!
Wang:
 Max: Are you crazy?! Hawkins was better by far!
Wang:
 Max:
Wang: Why don't you agee with me? You know I'm right!
 Max:

ROLE PLAYS

ROLE PLAYS   Here are some situations that require you and a partner or partners to take roles and act out dialogs, expressing opinions, agreeing, and disagreeing. The strength of the agreements and disagreements and the words you choose will depend on how well you know the people and the kind of settings you're in.

1. Larry and his roommate Greg are discussing their new chemistry teacher. Larry likes her; Greg doesn't.

2. Janice and her boyfriend have just returned from a movie. Janice didn't like it, but her boyfriend did.

3. Ali bought a new kind of laundry detergent. Both Ali and his room-
    mate Ken detest it, but for different reasons.

4. Patty just bought the new Hall and Oates album. She likes it, but her
    friend hates it.

5. Two friends, Chris and Sandra, are discussing favorite vacation spots.
    They agree and disagree on various points.

6. Dave and a co-worker are discussing the new work schedule. Neither
    one is completely happy with it, but the co-worker is more dissatisfied
    than Dave.

7. Deborah, Anna, and Hiroko are discussing the latest summer fashions. All three generally agree, but there are two or three points they disagree on.

8. Mark and his employer are at lunch discussing sports cars. They don't agree with each other at all.

9. Harry and his best friend are eating at a Mexican restaurant. Harry doesn't like it; his friend does.

10. Melissa and her next-door neighbor, whom she knows only casually, are discussing a new office complex being built a block away from their apartment building. The neighbor is against its construction for several reasons, but Melissa doesn't have much of an opinion on the subject.

REAL **PEOPLE,** REAL **SITUATIONS,** REAL **LANGUAGE**

With the help of your instructor, find out when a city council meeting, a public hearing, a student government meeting, or some kind of other group meeting will be held and attend it. Listen to the people as they express their opinions, agree, and disagree on the issues presented. In your notebook, record the dialogs as well as you can, paying special attention to the particular expressions and phrases used. Use the journal entry format you are now familiar with. Try to record about five.

> **EXAMPLE:**   *Tuesday, March 14 —student government meeting. Issue: more student parking places needed*

> **Student A:**   *It is the opinion of most of those living in Moore Hall that we need at least 30 more parking places in front.*

> **Student B:**   *I agree. Sometimes we have to park almost a mile from our own dorm! That just isn't fair.*

> **Student C:**   *I hate to disagree, but do you really think it's necessary to encourage so many students to bring cars to campus?*

Your instructor may ask you to bring your examples to class to discuss and compare with those of your classmates.

CHAPTER 15

REQUESTING AND OFFERING ASSISTANCE

What would you say if

- you were being chased by a vicious dog, and you needed help?
- you saw an elderly gentleman struggling to carry three large bags of groceries?
- you couldn't find a particular brand of running shoes you were looking for in a sporting goods store?
- you noticed a woman having trouble starting her car?

In each situation some kind of assistance is needed. This chapter will deal with appropriate ways to ask for help and to offer assistance.

Requesting Assistance

When we need help, we ask for it—unless, of course, we're content to struggle by ourselves. *Assistance* is a broad word, and the kind of assistance requested depends on the kind of situation—from an emergency (like a fire or a thief stealing someone's handbag) to an ordinary situation (like needing help to paint the kitchen or fix the washing machine).

In real emergencies we don't think about being polite; we want to get our message across as fast as we can to our listeners. Suppose you're on the subway, and someone has just **picked your pocket°** and is running away with your wallet. You need help. You might call out:

+ Help! I've been robbed!
+ Help me! Stop that thief!
+ Quick! Don't let that man get away! He stole my wallet!

These commands are signals to those around you that you need immediate help to catch the person who is fleeing.

In another case, suppose you're in a restaurant, and your dinner companion suddenly starts gasping for breath and choking. He signals that he can't breathe. You might ask for help by shouting:

+ Help! He's choking! Does anyone know **the Heimlich maneuver?°**
+ Help me! Is there a doctor? It's an emergency!
+ Someone! Quick! Get a doctor! He's choking!

Fortunately, both of these situations are *not* common, everyday ones. But it's good to know how to ask for emergency assistance when the need arises. Being direct and explicit is very important in emergencies because quick action is usually vital.

PRACTICE 1

Read each situation. What would you say and/or do to request assistance? Discuss your answers with your classmates and teacher to find out if they agree.

Picked (someone's) **pocket** means "stolen something from your pocket—usually in a crowd."

The Heimlich maneuver is a first-aid technique used to aid a choking victim. It is named after the doctor who devised it.

EXAMPLE: *You're skiing down a steep hill and see another skier take a bad fall. You ski over and see that she is in very bad pain and has probably broken her leg.*

I would try to attract the attention of the ski patrol° or of another skier and say, "Bring help! It's an emergency! There's an injured skier!"

1. You're standing outside and see a strange man trying to break into a neighbor's car.

2. You're swimming in a lake with friends. Suddenly you have terrible **cramps°** and can't stay afloat. You feel as if you're drowning, and you're far from shore.

3. You are alone in your house and are suddenly awakened in the middle of the night by the sound of someone trying to open the back door by force.

4. You're alone in an elevator, and suddenly it stops between floors and doesn't move anymore. It is stuck. There's an emergency phone on the wall.

5. You're walking alone late at night, and you're sure someone's following you.

A **ski patrol** is a group of expert skiers whose job is to look for and help injured skiers or skiers in trouble.
Cramps are severe pains caused by the tightening of muscles, which make movement very difficult.

If the situation is not as dangerous and doesn't require emergency action, we can request assistance in a calmer, more polite way. For example, suppose you need some help carrying a heavy box to the car. You might say to your roommate, "José, if you're not busy, would you mind helping me a minute?" Or if you're having trouble with some vocabulary in a reading, you might ask, "Patty, would you please give me some help with this article I'm reading? I'm having some trouble understanding all these words."

Here are some common ways to begin requests for assistance. Notice the use of modals (*would, could, can, will*) in the examples:

+ If it's not too much trouble, could you . . . ?
+ Could I impose on you to . . . ?
+ Could I ask you a favor? Would you . . . ?
+ I hope you don't mind, but could . . . ?
+ Would you mind $\begin{cases} \text{helping me?} \\ \text{doing something for me?} \end{cases}$
+ I have a favor to ask. Would you . . . ?

+ $\left.\begin{array}{l} \text{Could} \\ \text{Would} \\ \text{Can} \\ \text{Will} \end{array}\right\}$ you $\begin{cases} \text{help me?} \\ \text{lend me a hand?} \end{cases}$
+ How about assisting me with . . . ?
+ _____
+ _____

PRACTICE 2

Choose a partner and read the following situations. Have one person ask for assistance and the other reply either positively (+) or negatively (−). If a negative reply is given, supply an excuse or a reason.

EXAMPLE: *Laura wants her roommate Ana to help fix her hair.*

Laura: *Ana, could I ask you a big favor? I've got a date in 30 minutes, and my hair's a mess! Could you please help me with it?*

Ana (+): *Sure, Laura. I'd be glad to. Why don't we put some mousse° in it and make it kind of funky°?*

Mousse is a foam used in styling hair, named for a frothy dessert.
Funky is an informal word for "good—in a contemporary or modern way."

Ana (−):   *I wish I could, Laura, but Jeff's picking me up in just a minute. We're going to a 7:30 movie.*

1. Khalid isn't having any luck fixing his stereo. His friend George enters the room.
   Khalid:
   George (−):

2. Maria doesn't understand the meaning of some of the words and ingredients in a recipe she's trying to make. She goes next door to a friendly neighbor's apartment and asks Shelly for some help.
   Maria:
   Shelly (+):

3. Theresa has to have a report typed by the morning. She doesn't type, so she asks her friend Paul for some assistance.
   Theresa:
   Paul (−):

4. William needs some help with his new personal computer, so he asks an acquaintance Betty, who is a computer science major.
   William:
   Betty (+):

5. Frank is having difficulty raising a window, so he asks Ken for some assistance.
   Frank:
   Ken (+):

Offering Assistance

We don't always wait for someone to ask us for help to offer our assistance. Suppose you notice Wong, a classmate, standing in front of a posted bus schedule, looking very confused. You might go up to him and say, "What seems to be the trouble, Wong? Do you need some help?" Or what if you see a young woman on her hands and knees, searching frantically on the floor for something? You might approach her and offer your assistance by saying, "Hi. Do you need some help?" or "Can I help you look for something?"

Other very common examples of offering assistance can be found in sales settings. For instance, salesclerks in stores often greet their customers with "Hello. Is there anything I can help you with today?" or simply, "May I help you?" (If assistance is needed, the person would tell the salesclerk what it is, but if no help is required, a common reply is "No thanks. I'm just looking" or "No thank you. I'm just browsing.")

Here are some typical ways of beginning offers of assistance. Remember that situations vary, so these openings may not be appropriate in all settings. Your teacher can give you some specific examples.

- May I help you?
- Would you like
- Do you need   } some { help?
- Can I give you   { assistance?
- What can I do for you?
- How may I help you?
- What seems to be the { matter?
                       { trouble?

More direct:

- Here! Let me help you!
- Let me give you a hand with that.
- _____
- _____

PRACTICE 3

Here are some situations where someone needs help. With a partner, offer assistance, and then let him or her respond positively (+) or negatively (−).

> **EXAMPLE:** *You see a friend with an armload of books and groceries, trying to unlock his door. Some of the items are spilling from the bags as he fumbles for his key.*

You: *Hi, Carl. It looks as if you could use a hand. Let me hold those for you.*

Carl (+): *Thanks a lot! You're a lifesaver!*

Carl (−): *Oh, that's okay. I think I've got it.*

1. You notice a young woman in the library who seems lost.
   You:
   Woman (+):

2. Your roommate seems to be having touble with his or her cassette player.
   You:
   Roommate (−):

3. You notice an elderly woman having trouble opening a heavy door.
   You:
   Woman (+):

4. A little boy in your neighborhood is crying because the wheel of his **tricycle°** came off.
   You:
    Boy (+):

5. You're at the swimming pool and see a young girl get stung by a bee.
   You:
   Girl (+):

SITUATIONAL DIALOGS   The following dialogs show various ways of asking for and offering help in both emergencies and ordinary situations. Choose partners, take roles, and act out these situations. When you finish, discuss them and answer the questions or do the tasks.

> A.   *Paul's car is stuck in the snow near his apartment. He sees a neighbor come out of his home to get his evening newspaper.*
>
> **Paul:**   Hey, Claude! Claude! (He waves.) Could I ask you a big favor?
> **Claude:** What is it?
> **Paul:**   I drove into a **snowbank°** and I'm stuck. Will you give me a push and help me get out?
> **Claude:** Well, uh .... Could you wait a few minutes while I change my clothes? I don't want to ruin my new suit.
> **Paul:**   Of course. Thanks a lot. Oh—and Claude, could I borrow your ice scraper to clean my windshield? Mine broke.
> **Claude:** Sure. Be right back.

What Do You Think?

> 1.   *In what other ways could Paul have asked Claude for assistance?*
> 2.   *Change the dialog so that Claude refuses to help Paul. Give a good reason.*

A **tricycle** is like a bicycle, but it has three wheels (one in front and two in back) and is used by young children until they are coordinated enough to ride a bicycle.
A **snowbank** is a big pile of snow, usually on the side of a road.

3. *How eager is Claude to help Paul? What are some clues from the dialog that show this?*

B. *Carol walks into Betty's house and sees her struggling with a window blind.*

Betty: Gosh, I'm glad to see you. Could you do me a favor?
Carol: Sure. What is it?
Betty: I need some help putting up these blinds. Would you mind?
Carol: Not at all.
(Later)
Carol: I think that does it. Anything else you need help with?
Betty: No, that's it. I really appreciate your help, Carol.
Carol: Any time.

What Do You Think?

1. *In what other ways could Betty have asked Carol for help?*
2. *Carol offers more assistance to Betty when the first job is finished. How does she do this, and what other words or expressions could she have used?*
3. *Change the dialog and have Carol refuse to help Betty—for a good reason.*

C. *Patrick is in the drugstore, looking around, confused.*

Clerk: May I help you?
Patrick: Yes, please. I'd like to buy some toothpaste.
Clerk: It's over there by the back entrance—on your right.
Patrick: Thanks a lot. Oh—and would you mind telling me where the furniture polish is?
Clerk: Ummm . . . furniture polish? I don't believe we sell any. You should try a supermarket.
(Clerk turns and accidentally knocks over a display of film.)
Patrick: Here! Let me give you a hand.
Clerk: Thank you. I wasn't looking where I was going.

What Do You Think?

1. *What are some other ways a clerk might greet a customer in a store?*
2. *If Patrick had not needed any assistance, how might he have responded?*
3. *When the clerk knocks over the display, Patrick doesn't ask if help is needed; he just immediately offers his assistance. How? In what other ways could he have done this?*

D. *Luis is struggling to lift a heavy box from his car when Amin walks by and sees him.*

Amin: Luis, it looks like you could use another pair of hands and a strong back!

Luis: Whew! I sure could! I'm glad you came along.

Amin: This is heavy! What's in it?

Luis: My new stereo equipment. I just bought it.

Amin: Great! Would you like some help setting it up?

Luis: Thanks anyway, Amin, but I think I can manage. The salesclerk explained how to do it in great detail. And anyway, I don't have time to do it right now. I've got an appointment.

What Do You Think?

1. *Another pair of hands and a strong back is one way of saying what? How else could Amin have phrased his offer of assistance?*

2. *Change the dialog. This time, Luis asks for help before Amin has a chance to offer it.*

3. *What do you think about Luis' refusal of Amin's offer to help set up the equipment? Is it polite? Why or why not?*

E. *Harry is walking down the street and sees an old man stumble and fall over the curb. His leg appears to be caught in the drain of the* **gutter**.°

Man (to Harry): Help! My leg is caught! Can you help me?

Harry: **Hang on**!° Let me see if I can move the drain cover, so I can get your leg out.

Man: It's in there pretty tight. You might need to get some more help.

Harry: Does your leg feel as if it's broken?

Man: I can't tell. It really hurts a lot, though.

(A teenager approaches.)

Harry: Hey! Can you help me? I need some help moving this cover to get his leg out!

Boy: Sure. Just tell me what to do.

What Do You Think?

1. *Are there any other ways the old man could have asked for help in this emergency?*

A **gutter** is the narrow ditch that runs along a street to collect and carry rainwater. The *drain* is the opening that allows the water to flow into an underground sewer or pipe.

Hang on means "Wait a minute; be patient."

2. *Harry's quick action is his answer to the man's request for help. What else could he have said to reply directly to the man's request?*
3. *Change the dialog so that an elderly man sees a little boy become caught in some way but is unable to help him.*

DIALOG COMPLETIONS
Choose partners and complete the following dialogs, asking for help, offering assistance, or responding to an offer or request. Then reverse roles and complete them again, using different words and expressions.

1. *Inez sees Pete struggling to light a fire in the fireplace in the living room.*

Inez: Pete, what's the matter? You look as if you need some help.
Pete:
Inez: Sure. I'd be glad to. I learned how from camping in the mountains.
Pete:

2. *Mike is having trouble with his new typewriter.*

Mike:
Amin: I don't know much about typewriters, but I can give it a try.
Mike:

3. *Henry has locked himself out of his apartment. He goes to the apartment office.*

Secretary:
Henry: I hope so. I feel a little silly.
Secretary:
Henry: Well, I locked myself out of my apartment by accident, and I can't get back in.
Secretary:
Henry: Thanks. I'd really appreciate it.

4. *Juan goes to turn on the faucet in the sink, and the handle comes off in his hand. Water bursts everywhere and he can't cut it off. He begins shouting.*

Juan:
Aziz: What's wrong?
Juan:
Aziz: I don't know how to fix it. Should I call somebody?
Juan:

Aziz: Okay! Okay! I'm hurrying as fast as I can! Where's the phone book?

5. *Hans doesn't understand his reading assignment. He calls Diego, a classmate.*

Hans:
Diego: Oh, hi, Hans. What's happening?
Hans:
Diego: I wish I could help, but I really don't understand it myself. I was thinking about calling Mari. She always knows what's going on.
Hans:
Diego: Sure. I'll be glad to. I'll pick you up about 7:30.

6. *Mohammed is walking down the street when suddenly a dog starts running after him and barking viciously. He recognizes the dog's owner standing on her porch.*

Mohammed:
(Owner doesn't look up.)
Mohammed:
   Owner: Here, Beebee! Come here, Beebee! Leave that man alone!

7. *A clothing store salesperson approaches a customer.*

Salesperson:
  Customer: No thank you. I'm just looking.
Salesperson:
  Customer: Thank you. I will.

8. *The little girl next door is crying because a dog tore off the head of her doll. Yoko approaches the sobbing girl.*

Yoko:
 Girl: That mean dog just broke my doll.
Yoko:
 Girl: Do you think you can?
Yoko:
 Girl: Oh, thank you! You fixed my doll!

9. *Elizabeth has climbed up on the roof of her house to adjust her TV antenna, and the wind has blown down the ladder. Her boyfriend Adam is in the house.*

Elizabeth:
(Adam doesn't answer.)
Elizabeth:
    Adam: What is it? What's the matter?
Elizabeth:
    Adam: How did that happen?
Elizabeth:
    Adam: Okay. Hold on. I'll set the ladder up in a second.

10.   *Yumi and Paula are having a party tonight at their apartment, and there is a lot to do to get ready. Paula is doing all the work, and Yumi is watching TV.*

Paula:
Yumi: Can I help you later? I just want to finish watching this movie.
Paula:
Yumi: I know. I know. But this is a great old movie, and it's only 30 more minutes. Can't you wait?
Paula:
Yumi: Okay. What do you want me to do?

ROLE PLAYS

Here are some situations that require requests for assistance or offers of help. After choosing partners, take roles, and act out the role plays. Use some of the words and expressions presented in this chapter and others that are appropriate to request and offer assistance. Then reverse the roles and change the dialog in the situations.

1.   Ingrid is walking by the playground near her house and sees a small boy by himself, crying.

2. A police officer notices a car stopped on the side of the road. The driver is looking under the hood of the car.

3. Harry is looking for a book in the library, but he doesn't know how to find it. A librarian is sitting at the Information Desk.

4. Ken needs some help with fixing a broken light switch. The hardware clerk wants to help him.

5. Steve is trying to fix a broken chair and needs some help. He asks Asim, but Asim can't help him.

6. Marcia is in the produce section of the supermarket and is very confused. She wants to buy a vegetable from her native country but can't find it. A clerk is nearby.

7. Juan is waiting at the bus stop and sees a car swerve and hit a youngster on a bicycle. The car keeps going, and the child lies in the street without moving.

8. Louisa needs some help with a chemistry problem. Her friend Mark is watching TV.

9. Samuel is taking care of his two children. One of them opens a bottle of laundry **bleach**° and starts to drink it. She starts coughing and crying. Samuel opens the door and yells to his neighbor to help him.

Bleach is a substance used to make clothes whiter. It is poisonous if swallowed.

10. Eduardo hits a telephone pole and cannot drive his car because the fender has cut into the tire. He sees a car coming slowly toward him and begins to wave.

REAL **PEOPLE,** REAL **SITUATIONS,** REAL **LANGUAGE**

Go out into your neighborhood, school, or work community and listen for people asking for and offering assistance. In your notebook, record at least five dialogs as well as you can, paying special attention to the ways people phrase their requests for and offers of assistance. Use the journal entry format as you usually do.

EXAMPLE: *Saturday, November 2—supermarket—customer needing assistance*

Customer (*at meat counter*): *Excuse me, sir. Could you help me?*

Butcher: *Yes, ma'am. What can I do for you?*

Customer: *I'd like to buy a roast beef, please, and I'd like you to cut it into small, bite-sized pieces.*

Butcher: *I'll be glad to. Anything else?*

Customer: *Yes, please. I'd like a pound of turkey — sliced very thin.*

Butcher: *Certainly. Just a moment, please.*

CHAPTER 16

ATTRACTING ATTENTION AND WARNING

What would you do and/or say if

- you wanted to get your teacher's attention in class to ask her a question?
- you saw a friend across a crowded auditorium and wanted to ask her to sit with you?
- you needed to ask someone a question, but she was busy reading a newspaper?
- you saw a car coming down the street fast, and a young girl was getting ready to step out into its path?
- you noticed your friend about to knock over a cup of coffee with her elbow?

Would you

- raise your hand and wave?
- shout, "Hey!" and her name?
- whistle and clap your hands?
- hit her on the back?
- look at her and try to **catch her eye**?°
- grab her sleeve and pull?
- take her hand and squeeze it?
- clear your throat and say, "Excuse me . . . "?
- shout, "Look out!"?
- say, "If I were you . . . "?

Of course, each of these five situations is very different and requires a different response. The ten examples of attracting attention or warning that follow the situations are also very different. Some are acceptable; others are not. As always, usage depends on the type of setting and the people involved. This chapter is devoted to two related areas: attracting people's attention and warning people.

Attracting Attention: Nonverbal Cues   To attract some-
one's attention so that we might speak to that person, we often use both verbal and nonverbal communication. Let's discuss nonverbal communication first. Probably the most common way of attracting someone's attention is by waving. For example, if we're at a noisy party and we see Joan, a friend, come in the door perhaps 20 or 30 feet away, we might raise our hand and wave to her as a signal that we see her or that we want her to join us.

But just how hard do we wave in situations like this? Here are some examples. Suppose Lynn is at the airport, and she sees her brother get off the plane and begin walking toward her. If she's very excited, she might jump up and down and wave as hard as she can to attract his attention. Or if Pat's brother is swimming alone far out in the ocean, and she sees a shark approach him, she's going to jump up and down, wave frantically, and shout to try to attract her brother's attention so she can warn him of the approaching danger. These are two instances where some big, obvious nonverbal signals are quite appropriate.

But let's look at some less frantic social and business situations where

---

To **catch** (someone's) **eye** is to look at the person and try to get his or her attention.

smaller nonverbal attention getters are more appropriate. In a restaurant if we want to attract the attention of our waiter, we have several choices. We can wait until he passes near us, catch his eye, and nod slightly to let him know we would like him to come to our table. Or we can raise our hand slightly to show that we need assistance. We do *not* whistle, clap our hands, or snap our fingers to get the person's attention. That is considered impolite and even rude.

In most social and business situations where some informality is allowed, a brief raise of the hand and a small wave is fine. For instance, if you're walking across campus and see your professor approaching you, a small, friendly wave to attract his or her attention is appropriate. Here's another situation. What if you are sitting or standing beside a friend and something happens so that you need to get your friend's attention quickly—but you can't say anything? You can do several things. You can softly poke or nudge your friend in the side by gently raising your elbow and letting it hit the person. Or you could take hold of your friend's hand or arm and give it a gentle squeeze. (Note: Two men would probably not choose to do the latter, but two women or a man and a woman might.) This is a silent signal that says, "Hey! Look!"

Once you've gotten your friend's attention, however, you shouldn't point at the person or thing you want her to look at. A slight nod or a brief word will do. Pointing at someone is usually considered rude. Of course, there are times when pointing is perfectly acceptable, such as when a teacher wants to get someone's attention in class. The teacher often points to the student and says, "Ahmed, would you read the next sentence, please?" Pointing here is not impolite; it's simply a way to get someone's attention or to indicate which person is being called on.

These are not all the ways of attracting attention without using words, but they are the most common. Sometimes we use our voices without using words; for instance we might say, "Ummm . . . " or clear our throats to make a person notice that we would like some attention. Can you think of other ways? Does the nonverbal signal depend on the situation? If so, how? Do you have different ways of attracting people's attention in your native country? What are they, and would they be acceptable here? Why or why not?

PRACTICE 1

Choose a partner from a different country. Now look at each situation and describe ways that people in your country use nonverbal signals to attract attention. Discuss these with your partner and try to discover if people use the same gestures and signals or if they are different and why.

What would someone in your country do to

1. get the attention of a forgetful waiter or waitress?

2. attract the attention of someone standing in line in front of him or her at a theater?

3. attract the attention of a manager leading a business meeting?

4. get the attention of a friend who is across the room at a noisy, crowded party?

5. attract the attention of someone standing next to him or her in a crowd of people, waiting to see a famous rock group come out of their hotel?

Attracting Attention: Verbal Cues
The nonverbal signals for attracting attention are often accompanied by verbal ones. Let's take some typical situations and examine some fixed expressions for attracting people's attention.

In a formal setting, such as a business meeting, a classroom discussion, or a dinner party, where one person is speaking (your manager, a classmate, or the hostess, for example), it is best to wait until that person is finished or there is a break in the conversation before trying to attract that person's attention. In other settings where someone seems to be busy, and you must talk with that person, you nccd first to attract that person's attention. As mentioned earlier, you could clear your throat or begin with "Ummm . . ." as a way of letting the person know you would like some attention. Or you could say:

+ Uh, excuse me, but . . . .
+ Pardon me, Mr. Jenkins, ...
+ Um, $\begin{cases} \text{Harold? . . . .} \\ \text{Sir? . . . .} \\ \text{Ma'am . . . .} \end{cases}$
+ _____
+ _____

In an informal setting, such as a party, a lunch with several people, or a conversation with several people, you can use any of the previous openers, or you can be a little more informal with "Hey, Joan?" or just the person's name. If the person is far away, we sometimes shout the person's name, say, "Yoo hoo! Laura!" (used by women more than men), "Yo! Paul!" (used by men more than women), or "Hey! Tom!" (used by both men and women). If you're in a setting where you need to be fairly quiet, you could whisper, "Pssst. Jose!" to get his attention, but this should be used only in informal situations.

PRACTICE 2

Read each situation and tell what kind of *verbal* and/or *nonverbal* signals you might use to attract the person's attention. Be ready to support your answers with reasons, and discuss them with a partner.

1. You're in the Miami airport, and you see your tennis coach several hundred feet ahead of you, getting ready to board a plane.
     (Verbal)
   (Nonverbal)

2. You're in the library and see your classmate going into the elevator.
     (Verbal)
   (Nonverbal)

3. You're in an airplane, and you need a blanket. All the flight attendants are busy.
     (Verbal)
   (Nonverbal)

4. You're in a business meeting, and your boss is talking about the project you have been working on. You have something important to say about it.
    (Verbal)
    (Nonverbal)

5. The cashier at a restaurant is reading a magazine and doesn't see that you are standing there, ready to pay your check.
    (Verbal)
    (Nonverbal)

Warning

Occasionally we find ourselves in situations that require us to warn a person of something dangerous or bad about to happen. Naturally, how we word the warning depends on how dangerous, threatening, or impending the situation is. In a very serious, dangerous situation, such as when a car appears to be coming straight toward an unobservant pedestrian, we might shout:

*   ✤ Hey! Look out!
*   ✤ Watch out! There's a car coming!
*   ✤ Get out of the way! Quick!

Some physical gestures that might accompany these exclamations of warning might be waving the arms, jumping, pointing toward the approaching car (we don't think of politeness at times like this), and even perhaps pulling the person away from the danger. In any kind of threatening situation, the most common warnings are in the form of commands: "Move!" "Look out!" "Be careful!" "Watch out!" "Get out of the way!" "Run!" "Duck!" (bend down to get out of the way of an object about to hit). We don't take the time to make a polite request. We shout instructions to let the person know it's an emergency.

PRACTICE 3

Read each situation, and with a partner, discuss how you would make an appropriate warning. You will want to include verbal and nonverbal signals.

1. An old man is just about to walk into an uncovered **manhole°** in the street.

A **manhole** is an opening through which workers can enter to repair underground wires and pipes.

2. A little girl is chasing her ball and is about to run into a fence.

3. An angry dog is just about to bite the leg of a woman at the bus stop.

4. A large, powerful wave is about to knock down a man as he stands waist-deep in the ocean, looking back toward the shore.

5. Some construction workers are dropping roof tiles and bricks to the ground, and an elderly woman is walking very near the site.

   If the situation is not as life-threatening as the previous ones, we don't have to be as direct or use hard commands. For instance, suppose your friend has been drinking a lot and has to drive home. You might say, "Andy, you'd better not drink any more. You have to drive home, remember?" or "Andy, if I were you, I'd slow down on the beer drinking. You've got a long drive home." Some ways to begin situations not quite as life-threatening or as dangerous as previous ones mentioned are as follows, from very blunt or direct to softer, advicelike warnings:

   ✦ You must . . . (stop smoking so much).
   ✦ You ought to . . . (eat less sugar and less red meat).
   ✦ You need to . . . (**think twice°** about spending all that money on a stereo).
   ✦ You'd better . . . (not drive so fast).
   ✦ You should . . . (study harder or you might not pass).
   ✦ If I were $\left\{ \begin{array}{l} \text{you,} \\ \text{in your shoes,} \\ \text{in your situation,} \end{array} \right\}$ I would . . . (not waste my time on that).

Think twice means "think hard and seriously before doing something; consider the results several times before acting."

♣ I think it would be a good idea if you . . . (exercised more).

♣ Don't you think you $\begin{cases} \text{had better . . .} \\ \text{ought to . . .} \\ \text{should . . .} \end{cases}$ (unplug the toaster before fixing it)?

♣ Perhaps you should think about . . . (studying more and playing video games less).

♣ Maybe you ought to . . . (drive more carefully at night).

♣ _____

♣ _____

Notice the number of modals (*must, ought to, should, had better*) used in making warnings.

Obviously, people in positions of authority can use strong warnings with those who work or are in positions under them. For example, a manager could say to her salesperson, "Joe, your sales are slow this month. You need to get out there and **hustle°** more!" A vice-president might say to his employee, "Henry, this is just a warning, but you need to **shape up°** if you expect to stay in your position!" Or a mother could say to her daughter, "Laura, you had better study harder, or I'm going to have to **ground°** you during the week."

Notice in the second and third examples, the speakers accompany the warnings with consequences that will or might result if the warnings aren't heeded (followed). The vice-president warns his employee about the possibility of losing his position in the company, and the mother uses the possibility of the daughter's having to stay inside the house during the week as a likely consequence if the daughter doesn't heed her mother's warning. There is no direct threat made or consequence mentioned with the first warning, but the employee probably has an idea what will happen if he doesn't perform better.

PRACTICE 4

Give each person some kind of direct or friendly warning and state a possible consequence (if appropriate) if the warning is not followed.

1. It's dark and raining, and your sister is driving very fast.
   You:

Hustle means "work very hard."
Shape up means "improve."
To **ground** someone is to restrict the activities of that person as a punishment.

2. Paula, a good friend, is thinking about investing a lot of money in a house that you don't think is worth the money.
   You:

3. Your dinner companion is getting ready to put salt on the meat. You've already tasted it, and it has a lot of salt.
   You:

4. Steven, your employee, has been writing poor reports during the last few months.
   You:

5. A neighborhood boy is playing dangerously close to a very busy highway. You don't see his parents anywhere.
   You:

SITUATIONAL DIALOGS

Choose partners, take roles, and act out the following dialogs. Verbal and/or nonverbal clues will be used in each situation to attract attention and warn. When you finish, discuss the questions that follow.

A. *A little girl is running along the slippery edge of a swimming pool.*

Mrs. Stone: Honey, you shouldn't run so fast.
Girl: Why not?
Mrs. Stone: It's very slippery and you might fall down and hurt yourself.
Girl: But I'll be careful.
Mrs. Stone: I know, but there are pool rules you must obey, and one of them is no running in the pool area.

What Do You Think?

1. *If the little girl had been in greater danger, how might Mrs. Stone have handled the situation? What do you think their relationship is?*
2. *Older people (especially women) sometimes use* honey *or* sweetheart *with children, even though they may not know them. Is this a custom in your country?*
3. *Mrs. Stone doesn't really threaten the girl with her warning, but she does give some reasons and possible consequences. What are they?*

B. *Koji and Brian, his American roommate, are standing on a golf course, watching some people play golf.*

Golfer: Fore!
Brian: (pulling Koji aside) Look out, Koji! You might get hit.

Koji: (moving fast as the ball comes toward him) Thanks for the warning, Brian. But why didn't the golfer say something?

Brian: He did. He said, "Fore!"

What Do You Think?

1. *Obviously,* fore *is a special word used by golfers to mean "Heads up! Look out!" Can you think of other special warning terms that people in the United States or in your native country use?*
2. *What else could Brian have said and/or done to warn Koji?*
3. *Change the dialog and have Koji warn Brian about the bones in a piece of fish they are eating.*

C. *Ahmed's professor has asked him to come to her office. He knocks on her open door, but she doesn't hear him at first.*

Ahmed: (clears throat) Uh, excuse me, Professor Mills.

Professor Mills: Oh, yes, Ahmed. Come in.

Ahmed: You asked me to see you after class.

Professor Mills: Yes, I did, Ahmed. I just wanted to have a few words with you about your performance in class lately. Your last three test scores have been very disappointing.

Ahmed: I know I've gone down. I just haven't been studying as much as I ought to.

Professor Mills: Well, I'm glad you realize it, Ahmed, because if you don't improve, you're going to lose the B average you had at midterm.

What Do You Think?

1. *How does Ahmed go about getting the professor's attention?*
2. *How strong is the warning the professor gives Ahmed? Is it accompanied by a consequence that might occur if he doesn't heed the warning?*
3. *If the professor had been a lot angrier, how could she have expressed her warning?*

D. *Mr. Lewis is very angry with his neighbor's little boy for riding his bicycle through his newly planted flowers.*

Mr. Lewis: Tommy! Come here this instant!

Tommy: Yes, sir?

Mr. Lewis: Haven't I warned you about being more careful when you ride your bike?

Tommy: What do you mean?

Mr. Lewis: I mean, if you don't stop riding that bike through my flowers, I'm going to speak to your parents and you know what they will do! Do you understand?

(Tommy isn't looking at him.)

Mr. Lewis: Tommy! I'm speaking to you! Did you hear what I just said?

Tommy: Yes, sir.

What Do You Think?

1. *Mr. Lewis is extremely mad at Tommy. How can you tell by his words?*
2. *Mr. Lewis does more than warn Tommy; he almost threatens him. How and why? What might be the consequence if Tommy doesn't listen to his warning?*
3. *How does Mr. Lewis get Tommy's attention? Can you think of any gestures that might accompany his words?*

E. *At a business meeting, Steve feels his boss is overlooking something very important having to do with a product the company is trying to sell.*

Boss: . . . and so, I think we need to . . .

Steve: Excuse me, Mr. Franks. I hate to interrupt, but I think we've overlooked a vital point.

Boss: Oh? What's that?

Steve: Well, if we continue to use the same marketing techniques we've been using, we'll lose a very big market.

Boss: And who is that?

Steve: The under 25-year-old crowd. They are as interested as anyone else because of the impact of television. We'd better consider aiming the product at them, or we'll lose a lot of money.

What Do You Think?

1. *Steve feels he has to interrupt his boss to make an important point. How does he do this and get his attention? How polite is he?*
2. *What type of warning does he issue? How strong or direct is it?*
3. *What sort of bad results does he predict if his suggestions aren't followed? Would this type of dialog occur in a business meeting in your country? Why or why not?*

DIALOG COMPLETIONS

Choose partners and complete the dialogs. All the situations deal with attracting people's attention and warning people. You may need to provide nonverbal as well as verbal signals. Look carefully

at the parts of the dialogs given to help you decide how to complete them.
When you finish, change roles and act out the dialogs again, using different
expressions and gestures.

1. *Paul is about to* **scorch**° *the shirt that he is ironing, and Carol sees it
just in time.*

Carol:
Paul: Thanks, Carol. I wasn't paying attention.
Carol:
Paul: I will. It's just that I'm not used to ironing my own shirts.

2. *A police officer turns on the blue light and pulls Frank over.*

Officer:
Frank: Was I? I thought I was only going about 60.
Officer:
Frank: Yes, I know, officer.
Officer:
Frank: Thank you, officer. I promise I'll slow down.

3. *Hernando sees an elderly gentleman about to walk into the path of a
speeding taxi.*

Hernando:
Man: Thank you, young man! You saved my life!
Hernando:
Man: I know. I know. I wasn't paying attention. Thank you
for your concern.
Hernando:
Man: Yes, I realize that. I'll be more careful.

4. *Ed and Maria are watching their four-year-old daughter play in the
living room.*

Ed: Maria, Renee is awfully close to that glass vase. Shouldn't
we move it over?
Maria:
(Ed sees the child begin to pull down the vase.)
Ed:
Maria: Thank goodness you said something, or I never would
have noticed!

Scorch means to "burn something slightly."

5. *Janine is talking to her dentist about her tooth problems.*

Dentist:
Janine: Two cavities? I can't believe that!
Dentist:
Janine: But I already do! I brush at least once a day—and usually twice!
Dentist:
Janine: Three times? But I don't have time to brush three times a day!
Dentist:
Janine: Yes, I understand. I'll try to do better.
Dentist:
Janine: And what might happen?
Dentist:
Janine: Okay. Thank you for the warning. I'll take your advice.

6. *Mr. Parks is having a serious talk with his son about his recent bad behavior in class.*

Mr. Parks:
William: But I tried, Dad. I really did!
Mr. Parks:
William: Yes, sir. I understand.
Mr. Parks:
William: No, sir. I don't want to be punished.
Mr. Parks:
William: I'll do better. I promise.

7. *Frances has been called in by her employer for not obeying certain company policies.*

Employer:
Frances: No, I didn't. I didn't know I was supposed to.
Employer:
Frances: I understand. I won't do it again.
Employer:
Frances: Thank you. I appreciate the warning. I'll be more careful.

8. *Mrs. Barton is very upset because her neighbor's dog has been tearing up her newspaper and bothering her cat. She has complained to Mr. Lawson, the owner of the dog, several times already.*

Mrs. Barton:

Mr. Lawson: I'm sorry to hear that. I'll try to watch Barney better in the future.

Mrs. Barton:

Mr. Lawson: Yes, Mrs. Barton. I understand. And as I said, I'll keep him out of your way.

Mrs. Barton:

Mr. Lawson: That won't be necessary. Your first warning was enough.

9. *Mark and Ellen are roller skating on a bumpy sidewalk in the park.*

Ellen:

Mark: Whew! Thanks for the warning! I almost didn't see it in time.

Ellen:

Mark: Yes, I see it. I'll get over it, even if I have to walk.

Ellen:

Mark: Don't worry!! I'm doing fine.

10. *Patty's exercise instructor is watching her do some abdomen exercises.*

Teacher:

Patty: Oh, are you speaking to me?

Teacher:

Patty: Really? I didn't realize that I was doing that. Could it cause any damage to my back?

Teacher:

Patty: Okay. I'll try that.

Teacher:

Patty: Yes, that's much better. Thanks for the warning.

ROLE PLAYS   Choose partners and compose short dialogs, complete with appropriate verbal and nonverbal cues for attracting attention and/or warning. Act out the role plays in front of a small group or your entire class and let the audience evaluate your performance and how you handle the situation.

1. Dr. Thompson is disturbed because her new patient, Lynne Jennings, has very high blood pressure and is quite overweight. The doctor gives her at least two warnings.

2. Ms. Munn is angry with one of her employees who has not been performing his job well and who has been leaving the office before quitting time lately.

3. As Barbara is about to cross the street, she notices a truck about to back into a small car. The truck driver isn't paying attention to what he's doing.

4. Betty is late for an appointment. She needs to pay the check for her lunch, but the waiter is across the room. Her companion warns her about being late.

5. Susan needs to get her boyfriend's attention to warn him that the roast he's cooking may be burning. He's very interested in a good TV program.

6. Gina, Maria's roommate, has been jogging alone late at night recently. Maria has heard about a strange man seen sitting in a parked car at various places in the neighborhood. She warns Gina, who is very absorbed in reading a book.

7. The mechanic has examined Pedro's car and has found two or three serious problems that could result in some real danger if Pedro doesn't have it fixed soon.

8. Don has bare feet and is standing outside in a puddle of water. He's trying to fix his electric leaf blower, which is plugged into an outlet. He's listening to music through his headphones and doesn't hear Jean trying to warn him.

9. Nancy has had only a few hours of sleep the past few nights because she's been working on her term paper. Sara, her roommate, is very concerned that Nancy will get sick if she doesn't rest. She doesn't hear Sara trying to get her attention.

10. A police officer stops Tom for going through a yellow light and for following another car too closely. The officer gives Tom some strict warnings but no ticket.

REAL **PEOPLE,** REAL **SITUATIONS,** REAL **LANGUAGE**

A. Go out into your community and listen for people attracting attention of other people and warning them. In your notebook, make at least five journal entries that record the words and expressions used by the people you observe.

EXAMPLE: *Sunday, June 24—at a playground*

Mother to child: *Bobby, be careful on the swings. Don't go too high.*

Child: *It's okay, Mommy. I won't hurt myself.*

Mother: *Bobby! I'm not warning you again! Don't swing so high!*

B. Here are some common household and medicinal products you can find in a drugstore or supermarket. The label of each product has a warning on it. Read each warning and explain what it means. Compare your interpretations with those of your classmates.

EXAMPLE: *Marlboro cigarettes*

(Warning) *The Surgeon General has determined that cigarette smoking is dangerous to your health.*

(Interpretation) *If you smoke, you're endangering your health. Smoking can cause cancer.*

1. *Lysol Brand Disinfectant Spray*
   (Warning)
   (Interpretation)

2. *Regular or Extra-Strength Tylenol (pain reliever)*
    (Warning)
    (Interpretation)

3. *Sweet 'N Low (sugar substitute)*
    (Warning)
    (Interpretation)

4. *Duration Nasal Spray*
    (Warning)
    (Interpretation)

5. *Tilex (instant mildew stain remover)*
    (Warning)
    (Interpretation)

CHAPTER 17

EXPRESSING AND RECEIVING SYMPATHY

We offer sympathy to people who have experienced something unfortunate or bad, such as a disappointment, an illness, an accident, a loss, or the death of someone close to them. It is often hard to know what to say—or how much to say—at a difficult time like this. Much of what we say depends on how well we know the person who has had the unfortunate experience. But in every case we support the person; offer words of consolation, comfort, and encouragement; and try to show that we understand what the person is feeling.

Some of the simplest and most common ways of expressing sympathy are as follows. Try to think of several more ways.

✦ I am/was $\begin{Bmatrix} \text{deeply} \\ \text{really} \\ \text{truly} \end{Bmatrix}$ sorry to hear about . . . (your father's death).

✦ I'm sorry that . . . (you lost your job).

♣ I want to tell you how sorry I am that . . . (your grandmother is ill).

✦ I was $\begin{Bmatrix} \text{shocked} \\ \text{sorry} \\ \text{upset} \end{Bmatrix}$ to learn that . . . (you'll be leaving the company).

♣ What a shame that . . . (you didn't win the photography contest)!

✦ How $\begin{Bmatrix} \text{shocking} \\ \text{sad} \\ \text{awful} \\ \text{terrible} \\ \text{horrible} \end{Bmatrix}$ to hear about . . . (Joe's accident)!

♣ That's too bad about . . . (Harry's dog). (*Informal*)

✦ Too bad that . . . (you didn't make an A on the quiz). (*Informal*)

✦ _____

✦ _____

PRACTICE 1

Respond to each of these unfortunate situations by offering some sympathy.

EXAMPLE: *Your friend didn't win the student government election.*

You: *It's such a shame you didn't win the election, Mary. I was hoping you would!*

1. Your roommate lost his or her job.
   You:

2. Your friend's cat died.
   You:

3. Your sister lost in a national gymnastics competition.
   You:

4. Your friend had a skiing accident and broke an arm and a leg.
    You:

5. A co-worker's apartment was robbed.
    You:

Many times we want to show people that we understand what they are going through (experiencing) or how they must feel. We empathize with their sadness or disappointment. Here are some typical ways of expressing this shared sorrow:

* ✦ I know how you must feel.
* ✦ I understand what you're going through right now.
* ✦ I know your feelings.

* ✦ _____
* ✦ _____

Finally, we often show further concern by offering our assistance in some way:

* ✦ Please let me know if there's anything I can do.
* ✦ I'll be here if you need me.
* ✦ If you need me, please call.
* ✦ Is there anything I can do for you?
* ✦ Please don't hesitate to ask if there's something I can do.
* ✦ _____
* ✦ _____

How much sympathy we show naturally depends on the seriousness of the situation. Situations may vary from bad luck to problems (financial, social, business, etc.) to failures to illnesses to death. A certain amount of tact (knowing not only what but also how much to say in delicate situations) is necessary.

PRACTICE 2

Using the same offers of sympathy you made in Practice 1, add a sentence or two to show that you understand the people's feelings, and then offer your help if it is needed. Remember, however, that these additional expressions of concern may not be necessary or appropriate in all situations. Your teacher can give you more guidelines.

EXAMPLE (from Practice 1): *I know how disappointed you must be because I've lost a few elections, too.*

1. _____

_____

2. _____

_____

3. _____

_____

4. _____

_____

5. _____

_____

Responding to Sympathy Offered   Responding to or accepting sympathy can be done simply, without a lot of unnecessary words:

+ I'm deeply { moved. / touched. / grateful. } Thank you very much. (*Formal*)
+ I appreciate your kindness.
+ Thank you.
+ It's very { nice / kind / sweet } of you to offer to help.
+ Thank you for { your sympathy. / your kindness. / all your help. / showing you care. / being here when I needed you. / your concern. / your great support. }

♣ Yes, I'll call you if I need you. Thanks.

♣ _____

♣ _____

PRACTICE 3

Respond to each of the following expressions of sympathy, using some of the words or phrases you have just learned—and others that you think would be appropriate.

EXAMPLE: **Henry:** *I was shocked and upset to hear about your brother's bad experience, Ali. Being robbed at gunpoint must be an awful experience!*

Ali: *It was pretty bad for him, but I think he's okay. Thanks for your concern, Henry.*

1. **Barbara:** I'm truly sorry about your grandmother, Irene. I know you were very close to her. Is there anything I can do for you?

    Irene:

2. **James:** I was really shocked to hear you didn't get the college loan, Aziz. I know how disappointed you must feel because I didn't win that baseball scholarship I was hoping for.

    Aziz:

3. **Mrs. Gray:** It's really a shame that your garden was hurt so badly by the storm last night, Patty. You had worked so hard on it! But I'll be glad to help you try to save some of the plants if I can.

    Patty:

4. **Brian:** I feel just awful about your tie, Pedro. You let me borrow it, and I almost ruined it! I'm sorry, and I'll take it to the cleaners tomorrow morning.

    Pedro:

5. **Glenda:** How awful about your car, Mike! I'm just glad you weren't hurt! If you need a ride or want to borrow mine, just call.

    Mike:

Bereavement

Bereavement (the loss of a loved one through death) is one of the most difficult situations to know how to handle. When someone dies, we often avoid using the words *death, dead,* or *died.* We can speak of death without using those words directly. One way of doing so is to use a *euphemism,* a less offensive expression that is substituted for an offensive or disagreeable word or phrase. A euphemism for the verb *die* is *pass away* or *pass on.* People often refer to someone's *death* as a *passing.* For instance, when sympathizing with a friend whose father has died, you might say, "I was so sorry to hear about your father's passing away." At other times we just say, "I was sorry to hear about your father" and stop there. Everyone knows he died. It's not necessary to use the words *death* or *passing away,* and it sometimes makes the tragedy a little easier to accept or handle.

There are many traditions and social and religious customs surrounding death. This chapter will not attempt to explain all these details, but it will describe briefly a few of them. When a person dies, the family of the deceased usually puts an announcement of the death and all the details of the religious services, remaining family, and other information about the deceased in a special section of the newspaper called the *obituaries.*

Friends and relatives usually "pay their respects" (offer sympathy and condolences) to the deceased and his or her family by visiting the funeral home where the deceased is often displayed in a **casket**° or **coffin.**° They drop by to look at the deceased one last time and offer sympathy to the family members who are there.

A funeral service usually follows at a church or synagogue and/or at graveside (where the burial takes place). At the funeral service, people listen to a minister or rabbi (and sometimes to others who knew the deceased well) praise the deceased and offer sympathy and encouragement to the family and friends. Songs or hymns are sometimes sung, and prayers are said.

Afterward, close friends and relatives drop by the home of the closest family member of the deceased and once more pay their respects and offer sympathy. As additional ways of showing sympathy, people send sympathy cards and flowers or make contributions of money to charitable organizations (such as the Cancer Society) selected by the family.

Americans also have the custom of preparing some type of food and taking it to the bereaved family on, before, or after the day of the funeral. It is a polite, kind way of helping the family out while they attend to other, more important matters. Visitors who drop by the home after the funeral to pay their respects to the family are usually offered something to eat and drink.

A **casket** or **coffin** is a box in which a dead person is buried.

This has been a *very* brief explanation of some of the etiquette and customs surrounding bereavement. Many religions have their own customs and procedures. Your teacher and your American friends may be able to provide further explanation and answer some of your questions.

SITUATIONAL DIALOGS

It's impossible to give examples of every kind of sad or tragic experience for which you might have to offer sympathy and consolation, but the following dialogs illustrate some typical unfortunate incidents and how sympathy might be offered and accepted. Choose partners, take roles, read the dialogs, and then answer the questions that follow.

A. **Claude:** Phil, I was really sorry to hear about your car being stolen. Do the police have any **leads?**°
Phil: Only a few, I'm afraid.
Claude: Well, if you need to borrow my car, just ask.
Phil: Thanks a lot, Claude. I will.

What Do You Think?

1. *What other ways could Claude have offered Phil sympathy?*

Leads are clues or evidence that help solve a puzzle or crime.

2. *How is Phil using the expression* I'm afraid? *What other words or phrases could he also have used?*
3. *Change the dialog slightly. Claude shares Phil's feelings because Claude's motorcycle was stolen a few months ago, and the police never recovered it.*

B. **Keiko:** I heard about your accident, Carla. Are you okay?
   Carla: Yes, I'm fine, but my car's going to be in the shop for several days.
   Keiko: I'll be glad to give you a ride to work until it's fixed.
   Carla: Thanks. That's sweet of you.

What Do You Think?

1. *Add a stronger expression of sympathy to Keiko's first remark.*
2. *How does Keiko offer her help? In what other ways could she have done so?*
3. That's sweet of you *is an expression used more often by women than men. Do you know of other words and expressions that women tend to use more than men? If Keiko had been talking to a man, what might he have said?*

C. **Mike:** Hi, honey. How did it go at work today?
   Yoko: I'm so upset, Mike! I found out I didn't get the promotion I was hoping for!
   Mike: I can't believe it! I'm really sorry, honey. I know how much you were counting on it. And if anyone deserved it, you did!
   Yoko: Thanks, Mike. I really *did* think I was going to get it. That's what makes the disappointment so much worse!
   Mike: Don't let it get you down. There'll be other promotions.

What Do You Think?

1. *What is Mike and Yoko's relationship? What clues help support your opinion?*
2. *How understanding and sympathetic is Mike? How does he try to make Yoko feel better?*
3. *Mike tells Yoko, "Don't let it get you down." What does that expression mean? In what other ways could he have expressed the same idea?*

D. **Jean:** Celina, I was shocked to hear about José's skiing accident! I'm so sorry!
   Celina: Thank you, Jean. We're just thankful that it wasn't any worse than it was.

Sorry to hear about your accident!!

Hope you're back on your feet . . . in a hurry!

Our best wishes,
Patty and Asim

Jean: Please let me know if there's anything I can do. I'll be glad to look after the kids while you go to the hospital.

Celina: Thanks a lot. I might **take you up on it**° tomorrow if you don't mind.

Jean: Not at all. And please tell José we're all thinking about him and wishing him a fast recovery. I'll send him a **card**° tomorrow.

Celina: I will. See you tomorrow.

What Do You Think?

1. *In what other ways could Jean have expressed her opening remarks about José's skiing accident?*
2. *How does she offer her help?*
3. *In what other situations might you use* take you up on it? *Give several examples.*

Take (someone) **up on** (something) means "accept an offer."
We often send sick people "get-well" **cards** to show we are thinking about them and hope that they recover fast.

 E. **Brenda:** Elena, I'm deeply sorry to hear about your grand-
     mother. She was a wonderful person, and I loved her
     like my own grandmother.
  Elena: Thank you for your sympathy; I'm deeply touched.
     She loved you, too.
  Brenda: Please let me know if there's anything I can do. I
     brought over a baked chicken. I know you have
     enough things to worry about without having to think
     about cooking.
  Elena: That was really thoughtful, Brenda. And thanks for
     the flowers, too. They're beautiful.
  Brenda: Well, I'll let you go now. There are a lot of other peo-
     ple waiting to talk to you. I'll see you tomorrow at the
     services. In the meantime, if there's anything at all I
     can do, just ask.
  Elena: Thanks, Brenda. I will.

What Do You Think?

 1. Why doesn't Brenda use the word death *in her expression of sympathy?*
 2. What does Elena mean by I'm deeply touched? *At what other times
   might we use this expression?*
 *3. What kind of funeral services do you have in your native country?
   Compare and contrast customs and etiquette for American funerals
   with those in your culture.*

DIALOG COMPLETIONS Choose partners and complete the following di-
alogs, either by offering or responding to sympathy in each situation.

  1. **Ralph:** Hey, Carl! Barry told me about your team losing
     the Midwest Championship. **That's a tough
     break!**°
   Carl:
   Ralph: Yeah, maybe you'll win next year. You guys are
     good.
   Carl:

  2. **Anna:** Joe, I heard you father-in-law passed away. I want
     to offer you my deepest sympathy.
   Joe:

That's a tough break is an informal expression of condolence. It means "That's too
bad. I'm sorry."

Anna: Don't mention it. It was the least I could do. Please tell your wife how sorry I am. And call me if there's anything I can do.

Joe:

3. **Hiroko:** That's a real shame your brother can't come for a visit this summer, Kim. I know you really miss him.

    Kim:

    Hiroko: Why don't you come over and visit my family sometime? I know we can't take the place of the real thing, but we can try.

    Kim:

    Hiroko:

4. **Frank:** Hello, Don. How did the city tennis tournament go?

    Don:

    Frank: Really? That's too bad. I thought you played a lot better than Roberts.

    Don:

    Frank: Well, don't feel too bad. I lost the surfing championship to a guy that I *know* I could beat now. You'll do better next year, I'm sure!

    Don:

5. **Barbara:**

    Vince: Yeah. I came in third place. I was really hoping to win.

    Barbara:

    Vince: Thanks for your support, Barb. I'll see you later.

6. **Abdulla:**

    Juan: I'm deeply moved, Abdulla. You've been a good friend, and I appreciate all you've done.

    Abdulla:

    Juan: Thanks. I'll see you tomorrow at the funeral.

    Abdulla:

    Juan: I will, but you've already done more than enough.

7. **Thomas:**

    Gina: It's very nice of you to be so concerned, Thomas, but, really, I feel a lot better now.

    Thomas:

    Gina: Thanks, Thomas. I'll call you if I need you.

8.   **Eri:**   I want to tell you how bad I feel about your not getting the raise, Lynn.

   Lynn:

   Eri: Yes, but you—of all the people in your division—deserved one. I understand how disappointed you must feel.

   Lynn:

   Eri:

9. **Roberto:**

   June: I appreciate your sympathy, Roberto. I hope he'll be all right, but this is his second heart attack in five years. He's not a very strong man.

   Roberto:

   June: You're very nice. Thank you, Roberto.

10. **Jacques:**

   Carol: No! Really, Jacques? That's terrible! Did you call the police?

   Jacques:

   Carol: Oh, no! What a shame! What else did they take?

   Jacques:

   Carol:

   Jacques:

ROLE PLAYS   Write a short dialog for each situation described, expressing sympathy and responding to the sympathy shown. With a partner, act out the role plays in front of a small group of classmates and let them judge how well you chose and used the language.

1. Sam's best friend fell down a flight of stairs and broke his leg.

2. Olive's daughter's cat was run over and killed. Her daughter is very upset.

3. Jason's girlfriend's mink jacket was stolen at a restaurant.

4. Sara's mother broke her favorite crystal bowl, which she received for a wedding gift 35 years ago. She is unhappy.

5. Martin's uncle lost a city election in a very close race.

6. Tom's roommate just learned that his cousin was killed in a boating accident.

7. Patty tried out for a community theater play but didn't get the part. Her roommate knows she wanted the part very much.

8. Jennifer scorched and ruined her favorite blouse. Her mother is sympathetic.

9. Steve's soccer team lost the state championship. His friend Mike sees him afterward.

10.   David just learned that his father has cancer. His roommate Greg offers sympathy.

REAL **PEOPLE,** REAL **SITUATIONS,** REAL **LANGUAGE**

A.   We send sympathy cards to people who have lost a loved one in death and get-well cards to people who have had operations or are sick. Go into a card store and look through the card selection. Find about five different cards that offer some kind of sympathy, record the messages as best you can, and tell for what reason you would send each card.

B.   Even though television is not *real* life, the characters in comedies and dramas are usually portraying real-life people. This exercise requires you to watch TV movies, situational comedies, or dramas and try to watch for and listen to people offering sympathy for various reasons. In journal entry form, record at least five different examples.

> **EXAMPLE:**   *Wednesday, 9 P.M.—"Dynasty." Crystal offers sympathy to Blake, her husband, for losing a big business deal to a competitor.*
>
> **Crystal:**   *Blake, darling, I'm terribly sorry about the South China Sea oil leases. I know they meant a lot to you.*
>
> **Blake:**   *I'm very disappointed, darling. I worked so hard on that project....*
>
> **Crystal:**   *Other deals will come along, Blake. They always do.*

CHAPTER 18

_____

_____

_____

HIDING FEELINGS

We've already talked a lot about hiding feelings in the earlier chapters on giving excuses, complimenting, and making requests. But it might be good to discuss why we sometimes want or need to hide our real feelings. One of the most obvious reasons is to avoid hurting a person's feelings. If a friend is searching for a compliment and asks, "How do you like my new shoes?" and you think they are awful, you can't (or don't want to) tell your friend your true feelings, so you hide them. Sometimes you use vague or neutral responses, like "I don't think I've ever seen any quite like that" or "Oh, they're nice." The word _nice_ has been overused and abused in English, but it comes in handy sometimes when we need to hide our true feelings. Just to review, we might use some of these expressions to avoid hurting people's feelings:

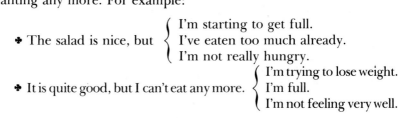

As mentioned in Chapter 12, "Complimenting and Responding," it is often good to try to find *one* aspect of the item being asked about to compliment, even if, in general, you dislike the entire item. If you hate your friend's shoes, but the color is not too bad, you could at least say, "Oh, I like the color." That way, you're hiding your true feelings (the general dislike), but you're at least expressing one truth that may serve as the compliment your friend is looking for.

What do you do if someone very directly asks you how you like another person? For example, suppose Hannah asks, "Hey, Patsy. How do you like your new roommate?" If Patsy likes the roommate, there's no problem, but if she doesn't (and if she doesn't want to criticize her new roommate or possibly offend someone who *does* like her), she could say,

+ Well, she seems nice, but I've only known her a few days.
+ It's still a little early to tell, but I'm sure I will when I get to know her a little better.
+ Well, she seems interesting, but I don't know her very well yet.
+ She has a good sense of humor. (Find *one* positive aspect to compliment.)

When someone offers us something more to eat or drink and we don't like it very much, we often hide our true feelings by giving some excuse for not wanting any more. For example:

+ The salad is nice, but { I'm starting to get full. / I've eaten too much already. / I'm not really hungry.

+ It is quite good, but I can't eat any more. { I'm trying to lose weight. / I'm full. / I'm not feeling very well.

PRACTICE 1

An acquaintance or friend asks you your opinion on the following items. You don't like them, but you don't want to hurt anyone's feelings. Choose a partner to ask the question, and then make your responses. When you finish, change roles and have your partner respond a little differently.

EXAMPLE: *José—his new shirt*

José: *I got this shirt at Ellman's yesterday. What do you think about it?*
You: *It's quite unusual, and the pattern's very interesting, too.*

1. Julie—new shade of nail polish
   Julie:
     You:

2. Ameed—song he wrote
   Ameed:
     You:

3. Frank—mustache he's growing
   Frank:
     You:

4. Nora—her new boyfriend
   Nora:
     You:

5. Lauren—chicken dish she made
   Lauren:
     You:

Often, it helps the situation if we politely choose an alternative if we don't really like what is being asked about or suggested. For example,

+ That's a pretty blouse, but I think the green one suits you better.
+ A movie would be fine, but what about going bowling for a change?
+ Yes, the beans are delicious, but I'd really prefer some more corn, please.

When we can offer an alternative to what the person wants or suggests, we often soften the feeling of disappointment that would have occurred if we had expressed our real feelings.

PRACTICE 2

Respond to these questions by suggesting an alternative.

John: *I really want to do something tonight. What about dinner at the new Chinese restaurant on Freedom Drive?*

> **You:** *That's an idea, but what would you say to having Italian food instead?*

1. **Peggy:** Do you like my new hairstyle? I parted it on the other side and curled it.
   You:

2. **Wilma:** Would you like some more fish?
   You:

3. **Ali:** How about playing tennis after work today?
   You:

4. **Anna:** I'm thinking about buying a Buick Skylark. What do you think?
   You:

5. **Hans:** I want to buy my teacher a present. What about a watch?
   You:

When we don't want to sound as if we're complaining, we often hide our feelings and tell a *white lie*; that is, we don't tell the truth, but the lie won't hurt anyone. For example,

> **Carl:** How do you feel, Ali?
> **Ali:** Oh, pretty well. I could be worse.

"I could be worse" is a tactful way of saying, "I don't feel very well, but I don't want to complain too much." Other responses used to hide feelings are as follows:

+ All right, I guess.
+ Okay.
+ I can't/shouldn't complain.
+ I'm starting to feel better.
+ I've felt better/worse.
+ _____
+ _____

PRACTICE 3

You don't feel well, or something you're being asked about is not going very well, but you don't want to complain. Hide your feelings appropriately in your response.

        EXAMPLE: **Harvey:** *How's your term paper going?*

                         You: *Oh, it's okay, but I've had better days.*

1. **Abdulla:** How're you doing? I heard you had a bad cold.
   You:

2. **Karen:** How's your job hunting going?
   You:

3. **Anne:** How's your garden doing this summer?
   You:

4. **Betina:** How're you feeling today?
   You:

5. **Harvey:** How's your new job?
   You:

One of the hardest feelings to hide is disappointment. If you are expecting a car for your graduation present from your parents and you get an exercise bicycle, you can't help feeling disappointed; but you usually don't want to show that disappointment, so you compliment the gift, smile, and say something positive:

- ✤ Oh, what a nice gift. I was hoping I'd get one.
- ✤ Thanks a lot. It's really nice.
- ✤ What a thoughtful gift! I really appreciate it.

If the disappointment is in something abstract (not concrete), like not getting a promotion you were hoping for or not winning a Ping-Pong tournament, we often use expressions like the following to hide our feelings:

- ✤ Oh, it's okay/all right.
- ✤ I hope I'll have better luck next time.
- ✤ Well, that's life!
- ✤ **It's no big deal!**° (*Informal*)
- ✤ _____
- ✤ _____

It's no big deal (or *thing*) means "It's not that important."

PRACTICE 4

You're disappointed in something that happened (or didn't happen), but you don't want to show it. Respond when the person tells you he or she is sorry.

> **EXAMPLE:**   **Arlene:**   *I'm really sorry you didn't get* **a raise.°**
> *I thought you deserved one if anyone did!*
>
> **You:**   *Thanks, Arlene, but it's not that important.*

1.   **Greg:**   I'm sorry you didn't get the college loan. I know you were hoping for it.

   You:

2.   **David:**   I'm sorry you didn't win the tennis match. I thought you were the stronger player.

   You:

3.   **Anne:**   I heard your parents had to cancel their visit to see you. I'm really sorry.

   You:

4.   **Theresa:**   I'm sorry to hear you won't be able to make it to the beach next weekend.

   You:

5.   **Saeed:**   I feel bad that you didn't make the soccer team. You were really good.

   You:

There are many other feelings we often try to hide besides disappointment—anger, fear, sadness, annoyance, and others—and we sometimes do this by keeping silent or by not letting our facial expression or body language give us away (reveal our true feelings). But if someone asks, "Are you afraid?" or "Aren't you nervous?" and we don't want them to know we are, we often do not tell the truth. Instead, we might say:

✦ No, I'm $\left\{ \begin{array}{l} \text{fine.} \\ \text{all right.} \\ \text{okay.} \end{array} \right.$

✦ Not $\left\{ \begin{array}{l} \text{at all.} \\ \text{much.} \\ \text{really.} \end{array} \right.$

A raise is an increase in salary.

Hiding feelings, however, is often more nonverbal than verbal. It involves controlling our facial expressions, hand and body movements, eye contact, and more. We can say, "I'm not nervous at all," but if our hands are shaking, our voice is quivering, our palms are sweating, and we can't look the person in the eye, these nonverbal signals will surely give us away—no matter what our words say.

SITUATIONAL DIALOGS   Choose partners, take roles, and read the following dialogs that illustrate hiding feelings. When you have finished, discuss the questions.

A.   *Larry was hoping he'd be promoted to manager, but another employee was.*

Yasser: I'm really sorry you didn't get the promotion, Larry.
Larry: Oh, that's okay. I wasn't really expecting it anyway.
Yasser: Yeah, well I thought you deserved it instead of Ned Jackson!
Larry: Thanks, Yasser, but I guess that's just the way it goes.

What Do You Think?

1.   *What does* That's the way it goes *mean? Do you have a similar expression in your native language? In what other situations might you use it?*
2.   *What kind of body language might Larry use when he says it?*
3.   *If Larry had wanted his true feelings (deep disappointment) to show, how might he have responded?*

B.   *Laura had her **heart set on**° a stereo for her birthday, but her father gave her a sports watch instead. However, she doesn't want to appear ungrateful or hurt his feelings.*

Father: Happy birthday, Laura!
Laura: Oh—a watch!
Father: You don't have one, do you?
Laura: No, I sure don't.
Father: Good. I know how much you enjoy jogging and swimming, so I thought it would come in handy. Do you really like it?
Laura: Yes, it's very nice. Thank you.
Father: You're welcome.

When you have your **heart set on** something, you are really hoping that something will happen or that you will receive that something, and almost anything else will be disappointing.

What Do You Think?

1. *What kinds of body language and nonverbal signals might give
    Laura's feelings away? If Laura had wanted to show her disappoint-
    ment, what might she have said?*
2. *What does Laura say (and what might she do) to try not to let her real
    feelings show?*
3. *Can you tell what* come in handy *means from the way it is used in the
    sentence? How might we use this expression in other situations?*

C. *Saleh has to give a speech in front of his conversation class, and he's
    very nervous, but he doesn't want to admit it.*

George: Well, Saleh, it's your turn next. How do you feel?
Saleh: Oh, fine. Fine.
George: Really? You don't look so fine. Are you nervous?
Saleh: No, not at all. I'm as ready as I'll ever be.
George: Okay. Good luck.

What Do You Think?

1. *What nonverbal cues might make George question Saleh's response of
    "Fine"?*
2. *What does* I'm as ready as I'll ever be *mean? At what other times
    would we use this phrase?*
3. *What are some nonverbal signals that might indicate fear? Happiness?
    Sadness? Loneliness? Anger?*

D. *Maria is a little upset that Don didn't call her last night, as he said he
    would. But when she sees him, she doesn't want him to know her disap-
    pointment and real feelings.*

Don: Hi, Maria. How are you?
Maria: Oh, fine. How about you?
Don: Just great. Listen, I'm really sorry about last night.
Maria: Last night?
Don: Yeah. Don't you remember? I said I would call you, and I
    didn't. I'm really sorry.
Maria: Oh, no problem. I went out anyway.
Don: You did?
Maria: Yeah. To a friend's house. And I didn't get in till late.
Don: Oh.

What Do You Think?

1. *How well do you think Maria hides her true feelings? How does she do
    this?*

2. *What do you think her plan is? Why is she acting so nonchalant and almost indifferent (as if she doesn't care)?*

3. *Does her plan succeed? Can you tell anything by Don's reaction?*

DIALOG COMPLETIONS   Choose a partner and complete the following dialogs appropriately, hiding your feelings so that you don't hurt anyone's feelings, appear to complain, or show great disappointment. Then, alternate roles and try the dialogs again, using different words and phrases.

1. *Walid and his roommate Greg are back from a party. Walid questions Greg about his (Walid's) date, whom Greg did not particularly care for.*

Walid: So, Greg, what did you think about Doris?
Greg:
Walid: Didn't she have a great personality?
Greg:
Walid: Well, wait till you get to know her a little better. I know you'll really like her.
Greg:

2. *Florence was hoping for some earrings from her boyfriend Paul, but he gives her a cookbook. She's very disappointed but doesn't want to show it.*

Paul: Happy birthday, Florence. (She opens the gift.) Surprised?
Florence:
Paul: Well, I know how much you love to cook, and my mother said this cookbook was the *best*, so I thought you might like it.
Florence:
Paul: You're very welcome.

3. *Bassim didn't go to the party last night because he had to study, and he was quite disappointed.*

Carl: You missed a great party last night, Bassim. Where were you?
Bassim:
Carl: Oh, that's too bad. I wish you had been there. It was a lot of fun.

Bassim:
   Carl: Well, I hope you're planning to go to the lake party next Saturday.
Bassim:

4.   *Neal and Yoko have been to see a movie. Neal knows that Yoko loved it, but he hated it. However, he doesn't want to hurt her feelings.*

Yoko: That was a fantastic movie, wasn't it, Neal?
Neal:
Yoko: What did you think about the guy who played Ben? Wasn't he terrific?
Neal:
Yoko: I think I could see it again and like it just as much!
Neal:

5.   *Joyce is having dinner with Ali, and she doesn't really like the food, but she doesn't want Ali to know because he has gone to a lot of trouble to fix it.*

   Ali: How do you like the tuna I fixed, Joyce?
Joyce:
   Ali: Well, you haven't eaten very much.
Joyce:
   Ali: Would you care for some more salad?
Joyce:
   Ali: I didn't know you were on a diet.
Joyce:

6.   *Ron was almost sure he would be accepted by Duke University, but he receives a rejection. He doesn't want to show his disappointment to his roommate.*

Arthur: Hey, Ron, I saw the letter from Duke on your desk. What did they say?
   Ron:
Arthur: Oh, I'm really sorry.
   Ron:

7.   *Nora has spent a lot of money on a dress to wear to a friend's wedding. Betty doesn't like it at all, but she doesn't want to hurt Nora's feelings.*

Nora: After two weeks, I finally found the dress I've been looking for. See?

Betty:
Nora: No, the color is "ice blue." Isn't it beautiful?
Betty:
Nora: Do you think it's appropriate for Ellen and Mark's wedding?
Betty:

8. *Enrique is starting to feel a little better after his illness, but he doesn't want anyone to know he still feels somewhat sick.*

   Iris: Hi, Enrique. I heard you were sick.
Enrique:
   Iris: Are you feeling better now?
Enrique:
   Iris: You look a little pale. Are you sure you're okay?
Enrique:

9. *Aziz has bought a brown and white striped jacket that his roommate thinks is **tacky.**°*

Aziz: How do you like my new jacket, Lex? I got it on sale at Ivey's Men's Shop.
  Lex:
Aziz: Should I wear it to the party tonight?
  Lex:
Aziz: Maybe you're right. I probably don't need to dress so formally.
  Lex:

10. *Jack has started wearing his hair a different way, and his girlfriend Naomi doesn't really like it.*

 Jack: Well, you haven't said anything about my hair, Naomi. Don't you like it?
Naomi:
 Jack: Don't you think it makes me look older—and better?
Naomi:

ROLE PLAYS   Here are ten situations in which hiding feelings—for one reason or another—is an essential part. Choose partners, take roles, and create a

---

Tacky means "not in style," "in bad taste," or "poorly made."

dialog for each. When you finish, change roles and re-create new role plays by using different words and expressions.

1. Phyllis is disappointed in the gift her roommate gives her for her birthday, but she doesn't want her to know because Sally has gone to a lot of trouble to buy it.

2. David wants to wear a tacky tie and shirt to his graduation. His girlfriend Pam tries to hide her feelings when he asks her opinion, but it's difficult.

3. Bob is extremely disappointed he was not chosen as the graduation speaker. Margaret, a good friend, thinks Bob should have been chosen instead of Scott Nelson.

4. Carolyn is in love with Max, whom Anna does not like at all. Carolyn asks Anna's opinion of Max.

5. Vicki is wearing heavy makeup and flashy, showy clothes, and she has spent a lot of time getting ready. Carl doesn't like what she has chosen to wear to dinner with his boss and her husband, but he doesn't want to hurt Vicki's feelings.

6. Pedro wants to buy his teacher an expensive goodbye gift, but Brad, his American roommate, feels it would be inappropriate. He tries to suggest some alternatives, without hurting Pedro's feelings.

7. Mark has been excitedly waiting for his date with Brenda. Now, however, he feels as if he might be getting sick, and Brenda notices something is wrong. Mark wants to hide his real feelings because he doesn't want to spoil the evening.

8. Tom is very disappointed that he wasn't invited to Ahmed's party, but he doesn't want anyone to know how he feels. Not knowing that he wasn't invited, Norma asks Tom why he wasn't at Ahmed's party last night.

9. Theresa has gone to a lot of trouble and expense to make dinner for Luis, but he doesn't like her cooking. She tries to offer him more of almost everything, and Luis doesn't want to offend her.

10. Joan has started wearing her hair a different way, and her roommate Helen thinks it looks terrible. She wants to say something, but she doesn't want to hurt Joan's feelings.

REAL **PEOPLE,** REAL **SITUATIONS,** REAL **LANGUAGE**

In this communication task, we will stretch the definition of *real* a little and use television for gathering language samples. If you can find samples of people hiding their feelings in your work, school, or social community, *do* record these examples, but it will probably be very difficult because it's often impossible to tell. So for this exercise, watch several TV programs (soap operas, situation comedies, dramas), and in your journal write down the name of the show and the character(s) involved and briefly describe the situation, showing the feelings being hidden. If you can include some of the actual dialog, do so. Pay special attention to nonverbal signals that might indicate that the people are not showing their real feelings.

EXAMPLE: *Thursday, June 7—"Cheers"*

In this episode Diane and Sam are not dating anymore, but Diane still likes Sam a lot, but she doesn't want him to know it. Sam teases her and Diane tries to ignore him. He asks her to go with him to a baseball game, and she lies and says she's busy. But her voice shakes, and she spills a drink she is carrying because she's so nervous around him. When Sam asks, "You still like me, don't you?" she replies (without smiling), "You're a nice person, Sam, but I have as much romantic interest in you as I have in that coatrack over there!" She blushes and walks out of the room.

When you have gathered your five samples, your teacher may ask you to bring them to class to discuss and compare with those of your classmates.

INDEX OF VOCABULARY
TERMS AND IDIOMS*

* These terms and idioms appear in boldface in text and are glossed and defined at the bottom of the pages on which they first appear.